U·X·L Encyclopedia of
Drugs & Addictive Substances

U·X·L Encyclopedia of
Drugs & Addictive Substances

Volume 2:
Caffeine to Diuretics

Barbara C. Bigelow, MAT

Kathleen J. Edgar, Project Editor

U·X·L

An imprint of Thomson Gale, a part of The Thomson Corporation

THOMSON
━━━━★━━━━
GALE

Detroit • New York • San Francisco • San Diego • New Haven, Conn. • Waterville, Maine • London • Munich

U·X·L Encyclopedia of Drugs & Addictive Substances

Barbara C. Bigelow, MAT

Project Editor
Kathleen J. Edgar

Editorial
Stephanie Cook, Madeline Harris, Melissa Hill, Kristine Krapp, Paul Lewon, Elizabeth Manar, Heather Price

Rights and Acquisitions
Ron Montgomery, Shalice Shaw-Caldwell

Imaging and Multimedia
Leitha Etheridge-Sims, Lezlie Light, Dan Newell, Christine O'Bryan

Product Design
Pamela A. E. Galbreath, Tracy Rowens

Composition
Evi Seoud, Mary Beth Trimper

Manufacturing
Rita Wimberely

LIBRARY OF CONGRESS CATALOGING-IN-PUBLICATION DATA

Bigelow, Barbara C.
   UXL encyclopedia of drugs & addictive substances / Barbara C. Bigelow, Kathleen J. Edgar.
      p. cm.
   Includes bibliographical references and index.
   ISBN 1-4144-0444-1 (set hardcover : alk. paper) – ISBN 1-4144-0445-X (volume 1) – ISBN 1-4144-0446-8 (volume 2) – ISBN 1-4144-0447-6 (volume 3) – ISBN 1-4144-0448-4 (volume 4) – ISBN 1-4144-0449-2 (volume 5)
   1. Drugs–Encyclopedias, Juvenile. 2. Drugs of abuse–Encyclopedias, Juvenile. 3. Substance abuse–Encyclopedias, Juvenile. I. Title: Encyclopedia of drugs & addictive substances. II. Title: UXL encyclopedia of drugs and addictive substances. III. Edgar, Kathleen J. IV. Title.
      RM301.17.B54 2006
      615'.1'03–dc22
                                                        2005017640p

This title is also available as an e-book.
ISBN: 1414406193 (set).
Contact your Gale sales representative for ordering information.

Printed in the United States of America
10 9 8 7 6 5 4 3 2 1

Table of Contents

Volume 3

Volume 4

Volume 5

Alternative Drug Names

45-minute psychosis *see* **Dimethyltryptamine (DMT)**
714s *see* **Methaqualone**

A

A-bomb *see* **Marijuana**
A2 *see* **Benzylpiperazine/Trifluoromethyl-phenylpiperazine**
Abyssinian tea *see* ***Catha Edulis***
Acapulco gold *see* **Marijuana**
Ace *see* **Marijuana**
Acid *see* **LSD (Lysergic Acid Diethylamide)**
ADAM *see* **Designer Drugs** and **Ecstasy (MDMA)**
African black *see* **Marijuana**
African salad *see* ***Catha Edulis***
Afro *see* **2C-B (Nexus)** and **Designer Drugs**
Ah-pen-yen *see* **Opium**
AIP *see* **Heroin**
Air blast *see* **Inhalants**
Allium sativum see **Herbal Drugs**
Amp *see* **Amphetamines**
Amys *see* **Amyl Nitrite, Inhalants,** and **Tranquilizers**
Andro *see* **Steroids**
Angel dust *see* **Designer Drugs** and **PCP (Phencyclidine)**
Antifreeze *see* **Heroin**
Antipsychotics *see* **Tranquilizers**
Anxiolytics *see* **Tranquilizers**
Apache *see* **Fentanyl**
Aries *see* **Heroin**
Aunt Hazel *see* **Heroin**
Aunt Mary *see* **Marijuana**
Aunti *see* **Opium**
Aunti Emma *see* **Opium**

B

Backbreaker *see* **LSD (Lysergic Acid Diethylamide)**
Balloons *see* **Inhalants** and **Nitrous Oxide**
Bang *see* **Inhalants**

Barbs *see* **Barbiturates** and **Tranquilizers**

Barr *see* **Codeine**

Battery acid *see* **LSD (Lysergic Acid Diethylamide)**

Batu *see* **Methamphetamine**

Bees *see* **2C-B (Nexus)** and **Designer Drugs**

Bennies *see* **Amphetamines**

Benzos *see* **Benzodiazepines** and **Tranquilizers**

Bhang *see* **Marijuana**

Bidis *see* **Nicotine**

Big chief *see* **Mescaline**

Big d *see* **Hydromorphone**

Big H *see* **Heroin**

Big Harry *see* **Heroin**

Big O *see* **Opium**

Black *see* **Opium**

Black hash *see* **Opium**

Black pearl *see* **Heroin**

Black pill *see* **Opium**

Black Russian *see* **Opium**

Black stuff *see* **Opium**

Black tar *see* **Heroin**

Blanche *see* **Marijuana**

Blind squid *see* **Ketamine**

Block *see* **Opium**

Blotter *see* **LSD (Lysergic Acid Diethylamide)**

Blow *see* **Cocaine**

Blue cap *see* **Mescaline**

Blue dolls *see* **Barbiturates**

Blue Nitro *see* **GBL**

Blues *see* **Barbiturates** and **Tranquilizers**

Blunt *see* **Marijuana**

Boat *see* **PCP (Phencyclidine)**

Bonita *see* **Heroin**

Boo *see* **Marijuana**

Boom *see* **Marijuana**

Boomers *see* **LSD (Lysergic Acid Diethylamide)** and **Psilocybin**

Booty juice *see* **Ecstasy (MDMA)**

Booze *see* **Alcohol**

Bozo *see* **Heroin**

Brain damage *see* **Heroin**

Brew *see* **Alcohol**

Brick gum *see* **Heroin**

Bromo *see* **2C-B (Nexus)** and **Designer Drugs**

Brown acid *see* **LSD (Lysergic Acid Diethylamide)**

Brown sugar *see* **Heroin**

Buddha *see* **Opium**
Bull dog *see* **Heroin**
Bundle *see* **Heroin**
Bush *see* **Marijuana**
Bushman's tea *see* ***Catha Edulis*** and **Dimethyltryptamine (DMT)**
Butterbur *see* **Herbal Drugs**
Buttons *see* **Mescaline** and **Methaqualone**
Buzz bombs *see* **Inhalants** and **Nitrous Oxide**
BZDs *see* **Tranquilizers**
BZP *see* **Benzylpiperazine/Trifluoromethyl-phenylpiperazine**

C

C *see* **Cocaine**
Cactus buttons *see* **Mescaline**
Cactus head *see* **Mescaline**
Cadillac *see* **Designer Drugs**
Camellia sinensis see **Herbal Drugs**
Caps *see* **Psilocybin**
Cartridges *see* **Nitrous Oxide**
Cat valium *see* **Designer Drugs** and **Ketamine**
Chalk *see* **Designer Drugs** and **Methamphetamine**
Chamaemelum nobile see **Herbal Drugs**
Chamomile *see* **Herbal Drugs**
Chandoo/Chandu *see* **Opium**
Charas *see* **Marijuana**
Charley *see* **Heroin**
Chat *see* ***Catha Edulis***
Cherry meth *see* **Designer Drugs** and **GHB**
Chew *see* **Nicotine**
Chewing tobacco *see* **Nicotine**
Chicken powder *see* **PMA and PMMA**
Chicken yellow *see* **PMA and PMMA**
Chief *see* **Mescaline**
China girl *see* **Fentanyl**
China town *see* **Fentanyl**
China white *see* **Fentanyl** and **Heroin**
Chinese molasses *see* **Opium**
Chinese tobacco *see* **Opium**
Chronic *see* **Marijuana**
Cid *see* **LSD (Lysergic Acid Diethylamide)**
Cigarettes *see* **Nicotine**
Cigars *see* **Nicotine**
Circles *see* **Rohypnol**
Cloud-9 *see* **2C-B (Nexus)** and **Designer Drugs**

Coffin nails *see* **Nicotine**
Coke *see* **Cocaine**
Comfrey *see* **Herbal Drugs**
Contact lenses *see* **LSD (Lysergic Acid Diethylamide)**
Copilots *see* **Dextroamphetamine**
Coties *see* **Codeine**
Crack cocaine *see* **Cocaine**
Crank *see* **Designer Drugs** and **Methamphetamine**
Crystal *see* **Designer Drugs** and **Methamphetamine**
Crystal meth *see* **Designer Drugs** and **Methamphetamine**
Cubes *see* **Psilocybin**

D

D-ball *see* **Steroids**
D-bol *see* **Steroids**
D's *see* **Hydromorphone**
Dagga *see* **Marijuana**
Dance fever *see* **Fentanyl**
Death *see* **PMA and PMMA**
Deca *see* **Steroids**
Deca-D *see* **Steroids**
Delantz *see* **Hydromorphone**
Delaud *see* **Hydromorphone**
Delida *see* **Hydromorphone**
Demmies *see* **Meperidine**
Depo-T *see* **Steroids**
DET *see* **Dimethyltryptamine (DMT)**
Dex *see* **Dextromethorphan**
Dexies *see* **Dextroamphetamines**
Diesel *see* **Heroin**
Dietary supplements *see* **Creatine**
Dillies *see* **Hydromorphone**
Disco biscuit *see* **Designer Drugs**
Disco biscuits *see* **Ecstasy** and **Methaqualone**
Discorama *see* **Inhalants**
Diviner's sage *see* ***Salvia Divinorum***
DM *see* **Dextromethorphan**
Dollies *see* **Methadone**
Dolls *see* **Barbiturates** and **Methadone**
Dope *see* **Marijuana**
Dopium *see* **Opium**
Dors and fours *see* **Codeine**
Doses *see* **LSD (Lysergic Acid Diethylamide)**
Dots *see* **LSD (Lysergic Acid Diethylamide)**

Double-stacked *see* **PMA and PMMA**

Dover's deck *see* **Opium**

Down *see* **Codeine**

Downers *see* **Barbiturates, Benzodiazepines, Over-the-Counter Drugs,** and **Tranquilizers**

Drank *see* **Codeine**

Dream gun *see* **Opium**

Dream stick *see* **Opium**

Dreams *see* **Opium**

Drex *see* **Dextromethorphan**

Drug store heroin *see* **Hydromorphone**

Dust *see* **Designer Drugs, Hydromorphone,** and **PCP (Phencyclidine)**

DXM *see* **Dextromethorphan**

E

E *see* **Designer Drugs** and **Ecstasy (MDMA)**

Easing powder *see* **Opium**

Easy lay *see* **GHB**

Echinacea *see* **Herbal Drugs**

Echinacea purpurea see **Herbal Drugs**

Elderberry *see* **Herbal Drugs**

Electric kool-aid *see* **LSD (Lysergic Acid Diethylamide)**

Elephant *see* **PCP (Phencyclidine)**

Embalming fluid *see* **Designer Drugs**

Empathy *see* **Ecstasy (MDMA)**

Ephedra *see* **Herbal Drugs**

Ephedra sinica see **Herbal Drugs**

Essence *see* **Ecstasy (MDMA)**

Eve *see* **2C-B (Nexus)** and **Designer Drugs**

F

Fags *see* **Nicotine**

Fantasia *see* **Dimethyltryptamine (DMT)**

Fi-do-nie *see* **Opium**

Firewater *see* **GBL**

Fizzies *see* **Methadone**

Footballs *see* **Hydromorphone**

Forget-me pill *see* **Rohypnol**

Foxy *see* **Dimethyltryptamine (DMT)**

Foxy methoxy *see* **Dimethyltryptamine (DMT)**

Friend *see* **Fentanyl**

Fry *see* **Designer Drugs** and **Marijuana**

Fry sticks *see* **Marijuana**
Fungus *see* **Psilocybin**

G

G *see* **GHB**
G-riffick *see* **GHB**
G3 *see* **GBL**
Gamma G *see* **GBL**
Gamma X *see* **GBL**
Gangster *see* **Marijuana**
Ganja *see* **Marijuana**
Garlic *see* **Herbal Drugs**
Gas *see* **Inhalants**
Gat *see* ***Catha Edulis***
Gear *see* **Steroids**
Gee *see* **Opium**
Georgia home boy *see* **Designer Drugs** and **GHB**
GH Revitalizer *see* **GBL**
Ginkgo *see* **Herbal Drugs**
Ginkgo biloba *see* **Herbal Drugs**
Ginseng *see* **Herbal Drugs**
Glass *see* **Designer Drugs** and **Methamphetamine**
Glue *see* **Inhalants**
Go-pills *see* **Dextroamphetamine**
God's medicine *see* **Opium**
Gondola *see* **Opium**
Goodfellas *see* **Fentanyl**
Goofballs *see* **Tranquilizers**
Goop *see* **Designer Drugs**
Goric *see* **Opium**
Grass *see* **Marijuana**
Great bear *see* **Fentanyl**
Great tobacco *see* **Opium**
Green tea *see* **Herbal Drugs**
Grievous bodily harm *see* **Designer Drugs** and **GHB**
Gum *see* **Opium**
Guma *see* **Opium**

H

H *see* **Heroin**
Happy pills *see* **Antidepressants** and **Tranquilizers**
Harry *see* **Heroin**
Hash *see* **Marijuana**

Hash oil *see* **Marijuana**

He-man *see* **Fentanyl**

Herb *see* **Marijuana**

Herbal ecstasy *see* ***Salvia Divinorum*** and **Benzylpiperazine/
  Trifluoromethyl-phenylpiperazine**

Herbal speed *see* **Benzylpiperazine/Trifluoromethyl-phenylpiperazine**

Hierba Maria *see* ***Salvia Divinorum***

Hillbilly heroin *see* **Oxycodone**

Hippie crack *see* **Inhalants** and **Nitrous Oxide**

Hippy flip *see* **Psilocybin**

Hog *see* **PCP (Phencyclidine)**

Honey oil *see* **Inhalants** and **Ketamine**

Hooch *see* **Alcohol**

Hop/Hops *see* **Opium**

Huff *see* **Inhalants**

Hug drug *see* **Designer Drugs** and **Ecstasy (MDMA)**

Hypericum perforatum see **Herbal Drugs**

I

Ice *see* **Designer Drugs** and **Methamphetamine**

Indian snakeroot *see* **Tranquilizers**

Invigorate *see* **GBL**

J

Jackpot *see* **Fentanyl**

Jet *see* **Designer Drugs** and **Ketamine**

Joint *see* **Marijuana**

Jolt *see* **GBL**

Joy plant *see* **Opium**

Juice *see* **Hydromorphone** and **Steroids**

Junk *see* **Steroids**

K

K *see* **Designer Drugs** and **Ketamine**

Karo *see* **Codeine**

Kat *see* ***Catha Edulis***

Kava *see* **Herbal Drugs**

Kef *see* **Marijuana**

Ket *see* **Designer Drugs** and **Ketamine**

Khat *see* ***Catha Edulis***

Kick *see* **Inhalants**

Kief *see* **Marijuana**
Kif *see* **Marijuana**
Killer *see* **PMA and PMMA**
Killer joints *see* **PCP (Phencyclidine)**
Killer weed *see* **PCP (Phencyclidine)**
Killers *see* **Oxycodone**
King ivory *see* **Fentanyl**
Kit kat *see* **Ketamine**
Kreteks *see* **Nicotine**

L

La rocha *see* **Rohypnol**
Laughing gas *see* **Inhalants** and **Nitrous Oxide**
Lean *see* **Codeine**
Leaves of Mary *see* ***Salvia Divinorum***
Legal E *see* **Benzylpiperazine/Trifluoromethyl-phenylpiperazine**
Legal X *see* **Benzylpiperazine/Trifluoromethyl-phenylpiperazine**
Liberty caps *see* **Psilocybin**
Liquid E *see* **GHB**
Liquid ecstasy *see* **GHB**
Liquid gold *see* **Amyl Nitrite**
Liquid X *see* **GHB**
Little d *see* **Hydromorphone**
Locker room *see* **Amyl Nitrite** and **Inhalants**
Looney tunes *see* **LSD (Lysergic Acid Diethylamide)**
Lords *see* **Hydromorphone**
Love drug *see* **Methaqualone**
Lovelies *see* **PCP (Phencyclidine)**
Lucy in the sky with diamonds *see* **LSD (Lysergic Acid Diethylamide)**
Ludes *see* **Methaqualone** and **Tranquilizers**
Lunch money *see* **Rohypnol**

M

M *see* **Morphine**
Ma huang see **Ephedra**
Magic mushrooms *see* **Psilocybin**
Mahuang see **Ephedra**
Mandies *see* **Methaqualone**
Mandrakes *see* **Methaqualone**
Mandrax *see* **Methaqualone**
Manteca *see* **Heroin**
Mary Jane *see* **Marijuana**
Matricaria recutita see **Herbal Drugs**

Max *see* **Designer Drugs**
Medusa *see* **Inhalants**
Mel *see* **Melatonin**
Melliquid *see* **Melatonin**
Mellow tonin *see* **Melatonin**
Mentha pulegium *see* **Herbal Drugs**
Mesc *see* **Mescaline**
Mescal *see* **Mescaline**
Meth *see* **Designer Drugs** and **Methamphetamine**
Mexican brown *see* **Fentanyl**
Mexican mint *see* ***Salvia Divinorum***
Mexican mud *see* **Heroin**
Mexican mushrooms *see* **Psilocybin**
Mexican Valium *see* **Rohypnol**
Microdots *see* **LSD (Lysergic Acid Diethylamide)**
Midnight oil *see* **Opium**
Mind erasers *see* **Rohypnol**
Miraa *see* ***Catha Edulis***
Miss Emma *see* **Morphine**
Mitsubishi *see* **PMA and PMMA**
Mitsubishi double-stack *see* **PMA and PMMA**
MLT *see* **Melatonin**
Monkey *see* **Morphine**
Moon *see* **Mescaline**
Moon gas *see* **Inhalants**
Moonshine *see* **Alcohol**
Mormon tea *see* **Ephedra**
Morph *see* **Morphine**
Mud *see* **Heroin**
Murder 8 *see* **Fentanyl**
Mushies *see* **Psilocybin**
Mushrooms *see* **Psilocybin**
MX missile *see* **Psilocybin**

N

Neuroleptics *see* **Tranquilizers**
Nexus *see* **2C-B (Nexus)** and **Designer Drugs**
Nice and easy *see* **Heroin**
Nickel *see* **Marijuana**
Nitrous *see* **Nitrous Oxide**
Nods *see* **Codeine**
Noise *see* **Heroin**
Nose candy *see* **Cocaine**
Number 4 *see* **Heroin**

Number 8 *see* **Heroin**
Nurse *see* **Heroin**

O

O *see* **Opium**
O.P. *see* **Opium**
Oat *see* *Catha Edulis*
OCs *see* **Oxycodone**
Oil *see* **Marijuana**
Old man *see* **Marijuana**
Ope *see* **Opium**
Oxies *see* **Oxycodone**
Oxycons *see* **Oxycodone**
Oz *see* **Inhalants**
Ozone *see* **PCP (Phencyclidine)**

P

P-dope *see* **Fentanyl**
P-funk *see* **Fentanyl**
Panax ginseng *see* **Herbal Drugs**
Panes *see* **LSD (Lysergic Acid Diethylamide)**
Party pill *see* **Benzylpiperazine/Trifluoromethyl-phenylpiperazine**
Pastora *see* *Salvia Divinorum*
PCE *see* **PCP (Phencyclidine)**
Pearls *see* **Amyl Nitrite** and **Inhalants**
Peg *see* **Heroin**
Pen yan *see* **Opium**
Pennyroyal *see* **Herbal Drugs**
Pep pills *see* **Amphetamines** and **Dextroamphetamine**
Perc-o-pop *see* **Fentanyl**
Percs *see* **Oxycodone**
Perks *see* **Oxycodone**
Persian white *see* **Fentanyl**
Petasites hybridus *see* **Herbal Drugs**
Pin gon *see* **Opium**
Pin yen *see* **Opium**
Pink spoons *see* **Oxycodone**
Piper methysticum *see* **Herbal Drugs**
Piperazine *see* **Benzylpiperazine/Trifluoromethyl-phenylpiperazine**
Poison *see* **Fentanyl**
Poor man's cocaine *see* **Methamphetamine**
Poor man's heroin *see* **Oxycodone**
Poor man's pot *see* **Inhalants**

Poppers *see* **Amyl Nitrite** and **Inhalants**

Pot *see* **Marijuana**

Powder *see* **Cocaine**

Pox *see* **Opium**

Psilcydes *see* **Psilocybin**

Psychedelic mushrooms *see* **Psilocybin**

Purple haze *see* **LSD (Lysergic Acid Diethylamide)**

Purple hearts *see* **Barbiturates**

Purple passion *see* **Psilocybin**

Q

Qaadka *see* ***Catha Edulis***

Qat *see* ***Catha Edulis***

Quaalude *see* **Methaqualone**

Quads *see* **Methaqualone**

Quat *see* ***Catha Edulis***

Quay *see* **Methaqualone**

R

R-2 *see* **Rohypnol**

R-ball *see* **Ritalin and Other Methylphenidates**

Ragers *see* **Steroids**

Rainbows *see* **Barbiturates** and **Tranquilizers**

Rauwolfia see **Tranquilizers**

Rave *see* **Ecstasy (MDMA)**

ReActive *see* **GBL**

Red birds *see* **Barbiturates**

Red death *see* **PMA and PMMA**

Red devils *see* **Barbiturates, Dextromethorphan, Over-the-Counter Drugs,** and **Tranquilizers**

Red mitsubishi *see* **PMA and PMMA**

Reds *see* **Barbiturates**

Reefer *see* **Marijuana**

REMForce *see* **GBL**

RenewTrient *see* **GBL**

Rest-eze *see* **GBL**

Revivarant *see* **GBL**

Rib *see* **Rohypnol**

Ro *see* **Rohypnol**

Roach *see* **Marijuana**

Roaches *see* **Rohypnol**

Roachies *see* **Rohypnol**

Roapies *see* **Rohypnol**

Robo *see* **Dextromethorphan**
Robo-tripping *see* **Dextromethorphan**
Roche *see* **Rohypnol**
Rock *see* **Cocaine**
Rocket fuel *see* **PCP (Phencyclidine)**
Roids *see* **Steroids**
Roll *see* **Ecstasy (MDMA)**
Roofies *see* **Rohypnol**
Rope *see* **Rohypnol**
Rophies *see* **Rohypnol**
Rophy *see* **Rohypnol**
Ruffies *see* **Rohypnol**
Ruffles *see* **Rohypnol**
Rush *see* **Amyl Nitrite** and **Inhalants**

S

Salty dog *see* **GHB**
Salty water *see* **GHB**
Salvia *see* ***Salvia Divinorum***
Sambucus nigra see **Herbal Drugs**
Sauce *see* **Alcohol**
Saw palmetto *see* **Herbal Drugs**
Schoolboy *see* **Codeine**
Scooby snacks *see* **Ecstasy (MDMA)**
Scoop *see* **GHB**
Sedative-hypnotics *see* **Tranquilizers**
Semilla de la Virgen *see* ***Salvia Divinorum***
Sensi *see* **Marijuana**
Serenoa repens see **Herbal Drugs**
Shabu *see* **Methamphetamine**
Shays *see* **Rohypnol**
Shepherdess *see* ***Salvia Divinorum***
Sherm *see* **PCP (Phencyclidine)**
Shermans *see* **PCP (Phencyclidine)**
Sh#t *see* **Heroin**
Shoot the breeze *see* **Inhalants**
Shrooms *see* **Psilocybin**
Sillies *see* **Psilocybin**
Silly putty *see* **Psilocybin**
Simple Simon *see* **Psilocybin**
Sinsemilla *see* **Marijuana**
Ska Maria Pastora *see* ***Salvia Divinorum***
Skag *see* **Heroin**
Skee *see* **Opium**

Skittles *see* **Dextromethorphan** and **Over-the-Counter Drugs**

Skunk *see* **Marijuana**

Sleeping pills *see* **Barbiturates**

Smack *see* **Heroin** and **Hydromorphone**

Smoke *see* **Marijuana**

Smokes *see* **Nicotine**

Snappers *see* **Amyl Nitrite** and **Inhalants**

Sniff *see* **Inhalants**

Snow *see* **Cocaine**

Snuff *see* **Nicotine**

Soap *see* **Designer Drugs** and **GHB**

Somniset *see* **Melatonin**

Sopors *see* **Tranquilizers**

Special K *see* **Designer Drugs** and **Ketamine**

Speed *see* **Adderall, Amphetamines, Designer Drugs, Dextroamphetamine,** and **Methamphetamine**

Spirits *see* **Alcohol**

Spit *see* **Nicotine**

Splif *see* **Marijuana**

St. John's wort *see* **Herbal Drugs**

Stacy *see* **Designer Drugs**

Stuff *see* **Heroin** and **Steroids**

Stupefi *see* **Rohypnol**

Suds *see* **Alcohol**

Sunshine *see* **LSD (Lysergic Acid Diethylamide)**

Supergrass *see* **PCP (Phencyclidine)**

Superweed *see* **PCP (Phencyclidine)**

Supps *see* **Creatine**

Symphytum officinale see **Herbal Drugs**

Synthetic heroin *see* **Fentanyl**

Syrup *see* **Codeine**

T

T-threes *see* **Codeine**

Tango & Cash *see* **Fentanyl**

Tar *see* **Marijuana**

Texas shoeshine *see* **Inhalants**

TFMPP *see* **Benzylpiperazine/Trifluoromethyl-phenylpiperazine**

Thai sticks *see* **Marijuana**

Thrust *see* **Amyl Nitrite** and **Inhalants**

Tic tac *see* **PCP (Phencyclidine)**

Tina *see* **Methamphetamine**

TNT *see* **Fentanyl**

Toilet water *see* **Inhalants**

Tombstone *see* **Fentanyl**
Toonies *see* **2C-B (Nexus)** and **Designer Drugs**
Tootsie roll *see* **Heroin**
Topi *see* **Mescaline**
Toxy *see* **Opium**
Toys *see* **Opium**
Tranks *see* **Benzodiazepines** and **Tranquilizers**
Tranx *see* **Tranquilizers**
Trash *see* **Methamphetamine**
Triple-C *see* **Dextromethorphan** and **Over-the-Counter Drugs**
Tschat *see* ***Catha Edulis***
Tussin *see* **Dextromethorphan**

U

Uppers *see* **Adderall, Amphetamines, Dextroamphetamine,** and **Over-the-Counter Drugs**
Utopia *see* **2C-B (Nexus)** and **Designer Drugs**

V

V35 *see* **GBL**
Valerian *see* **Herbal Drugs** and **Tranquilizers**
Valeriana officinalis see **Herbal Drugs**
Velvet *see* **Dextromethorphan**
Venus *see* **2C-B (Nexus)** and **Designer Drugs**
Verve *see* **GBL**
Vino *see* **Alcohol**
Virgin Mary's herb *see* ***Salvia Divinorum***
Virgin's seed *see* ***Salvia Divinorum***
Vitamin D *see* **Dextromethorphan**
Vitamin K *see* **Designer Drugs** and **Ketamine**
Vitamin R *see* **Ritalin and Other Methylphenidates**

W

Wack *see* **PCP (Phencyclidine)**
Water pills *see* **Diuretics**
Weed *see* **Marijuana**
West Coast *see* **Ritalin and Other Methylphenidates**
Wets *see* **PCP (Phencyclidine)**
When-shee *see* **Opium**
Whip-its *see* **Nitrous Oxide**
Whippets *see* **Inhalants** and **Nitrous Oxide**

Whippits *see* **Nitrous Oxide**
White mitsubishi *see* **PMA and PMMA**
White stuff *see* **Heroin** and **Morphine**
Whiteout *see* **Inhalants**
Windowpanes *see* **LSD (Lysergic Acid Diethylamide)**
Wolfies *see* **Rohypnol**

X

X *see* **Designer Drugs** and **Ecstasy (MDMA)**
XTC *see* **Designer Drugs** and **Ecstasy (MDMA)**

Y

Ya ba see **Methamphetamine**
Yellow jackets *see* **Barbiturates** and **Tranquilizers**
Yellow sunshine *see* **LSD (Lysergic Acid Diethylamide)**
Yellows *see* **Barbiturates**

Z

Ze *see* **Opium**
Zen *see* **LSD (Lysergic Acid Diethylamide)**
Zero *see* **Opium**
Zip *see* **Methamphetamine**
Zonked *see* **GHB**

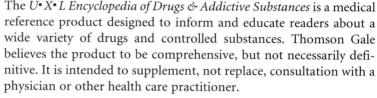

The *U•X•L Encyclopedia of Drugs & Addictive Substances* is a medical reference product designed to inform and educate readers about a wide variety of drugs and controlled substances. Thomson Gale believes the product to be comprehensive, but not necessarily definitive. It is intended to supplement, not replace, consultation with a physician or other health care practitioner.

Although Thomson Gale has made substantial efforts to provide information that is accurate, comprehensive, and up-to-date, Thomson Gale makes no representations or warranties of any kind, including without limitation, warranties of merchantability or fitness for a particular purpose, nor does it guarantee the accuracy, comprehensiveness, or timeliness of the information contained in this product. Readers should be aware that the universe of medical knowledge is constantly growing and changing, and that differences of medical opinion exist among authorities. Readers are also advised to seek professional diagnosis and treatment of any possible substance abuse problem, and to discuss information obtained from this book with their health care provider.

Preface

Education is the most powerful tool an individual can have when facing decisions about drug use. The *U•X•L Encyclopedia of Drugs & Addictive Substances* puts clear, comprehensive, and current information on fifty-two drugs at readers' fingertips. The set was designed with middle-school students in mind but can serve as a useful resource for readers of all ages. Each of the entries in this five-volume encyclopedia offers insights into the history, usage trends, and effects of a specific drug or addictive substance.

What Does "Addiction" Mean?

According to the National Institute on Drug Abuse's *NIDA InfoFacts: Understanding Drug Abuse and Addiction,* dated March 2005, drug addiction is more than just "a lot of drug use." The term "addiction" is described as:

- an overpowering desire, craving, or need to take a certain drug
- a willingness to obtain the drug by any means
- a tendency to keep increasing the dose that is consumed
- a psychological and/or physical dependence on the effects of the drug
- an inability to stop using the drug without treatment
- an illness that has harmful effects on the individual and on society.

What Can Readers Expect to Find in This Encyclopedia?

Every entry in the *U•X•L Encyclopedia of Drugs & Addictive Substances* has been painstakingly researched and is based on data from the latest government and university studies on the use and abuse of drugs and other addictive substances. In fact, the results of certain studies were first released to the public while this project was being researched. We are pleased to be able to pass along to readers some of the most up-to-date information on drug use available as this project went to press.

Please note that every effort has been made to secure the most recent information available. Readers should bear in mind that many major studies take years to conduct. Also, several additional years may pass before the data from these studies are made available to the public. As such, in some cases, the most recent information available in 2005 dated from 2001 or 2002. We've presented older statistics as well if they are of particular interest and no more recent data exist.

Some of the substances profiled in the *U•X•L Encyclopedia of Drugs & Addictive Substances* are legal. Examples of legal—but nevertheless addictive—substances are caffeine, nicotine, and certain over-the-counter medications. Many other substances described in this set are illicit, or illegal. Drugs that fall into this category include cocaine, ecstasy (MDMA), and heroin, among many others.

One of the leading concerns of the late 1990s and early 2000s was the spike in methamphetamine abuse. Methamphetamine, or "meth," is a highly addictive drug that can kill. It is interesting to note that methamphetamine is available by prescription for a limited number of medical uses. However, the bulk of the illicit meth that is sold on the streets is smuggled in from Mexico or manufactured by so-called "bathtub chemists" in the United States. This nickname is given to amateur drug makers working in illegal, makeshift labs. These drug makers are out to make a quick buck. They produce their drugs as cheaply as possible, often adding other dangerous substances or filler ingredients to their homemade concoctions. The risks involved in making and taking laboratory-produced mind-altering substances are discussed at length in this encyclopedia.

The Coining of a Brand-New Term: "Generation Rx"

Among the most notable trends in drug use during the first five years of the twenty-first century was the growing abuse of two types of substances: 1) inhalants, including glue, nitrous oxide, and spray paint, and 2) prescription drugs, especially painkillers and stimulants. Drugs such as oxycodone (OxyContin), Adderall, and methylphenidate (Ritalin) have been approved by the U.S. Food and Drug Administration (FDA) for legitimate uses when prescribed by a physician. Increasingly, however, these drugs have made their way from home medicine cabinets to schools and dance clubs. Because of the sizable increase in prescription drug abuse among young people, the term "Generation Rx" is frequently used to describe the teens of the early 2000s.

The magnitude of inhalant and prescription drug abuse problems first became apparent with the release of the 2004 Monitoring the Future (MTF) study results. MTF is a survey of drug use and attitudes conducted by the University of Michigan with funds from the National Institute on Drug Abuse (NIDA). In late April of 2005, the Partnership for a Drug-Free America released its 2004 Partnership Attitude Tracking Study (PATS). At that time, the extent of

Vicodin abuse, in particular, became apparent. Vicodin is the brand name of the prescription painkiller hydrocodone. To ensure that information on this growing Vicodin trend was available to readers of this encyclopedia, we have included an informative sidebar and other information on the drug within the Meperidine entry. Please consult the master index for a complete list of pages that address the topic of Vicodin.

Format

The *U•X•L Encyclopedia of Drugs & Addictive Substances* is arranged alphabetically by drug name over five volumes. Each entry follows a standard format and includes the following sections:

- What Kind of Drug Is It?
- Overview
- What Is It Made Of?
- How Is It Taken?
- Are There Any Medical Reasons for Taking This Substance?
- Usage Trends
- Effects on the Body
- Reactions with Other Drugs or Substances
- Treatment for Habitual Users
- Consequences
- The Law
- For More Information

Each entry also includes the official drug name, a list of street or alternative names for the drug, and the drug's classification according to the U.S. government's Controlled Substances Act (1970). Important glossary terms are highlighted in the text in small caps with the definitions of the words appearing in the margin.

Features

All entries contain informative sidebars on historical, social, legal, and/or statistical aspects of the drugs. This encyclopedia contains nearly 200 sidebars. In addition, the encyclopedia features more than 300 graphics, including black and white photos, maps, tables, and other illustrations.

The *U•X•L Encyclopedia of Drugs & Addictive Substances* also includes:

- Alternative Drug Names guide. As most students recognize drugs by their common rather than official names, this guide to street and other alternative names points students to the correct entry name.

- Chronology. This section presents important historical moments in the history of drugs, from the discovery of dried peyote buttons in c. 5000 BCE to the withdrawal of the prescription drug Palladone in 2005.
- Words to Know. This master glossary defines difficult terms to help students with words that are unfamiliar to them.
- Color insert. Included in each volume, the insert visually informs readers about various drug topics discussed in the set, such as natural sources of drugs, herbal and dietary supplements, older illicit drugs, prescription drugs, public service announcement posters, and the rave culture.
- Highlights of the U.S. Controlled Substances Act (CSA) of 1970. This section discusses the various drug schedules created by the U.S. government and what they mean.
- Where to Learn More. This bibliography presents important sources (books, periodicals, Web sites, and organizations) where more information on drugs and addictive substances can be obtained.
- Cumulative Index. The master index points readers to topics covered in all five volumes of the encyclopedia.

Special Thanks

Various individuals are to be thanked for aiding in the creation of the *U•X•L Encyclopedia of Drugs & Addictive Substances*. These include the following writers and editors: Pamela Willwerth Aue, Denise Evans, Joan Goldsworthy, Margaret Haerens, Anne Johnson, Jane Kelly Kosek, Mya Nelson, Diane Sawinski, and Les Stone.

In addition, special thanks go out to the project's advisory board members. Thomson Gale would like to express its appreciation to the following board members for their time and valuable contributions:

- Carol M. Keeler, Media Specialist, Detroit Country Day Upper School, Beverly Hills, Michigan
- Nina Levine, Library Media Specialist, Blue Mountain Middle School, Cortlandt Manor, New York
- Toni Thole, Health Educator, Vicksburg Middle School, Vicksburg, Michigan
- Susan Vanneman, NBPTS, Robin Mickle Middle School, Lincoln Public Schools, Lincoln, Nebraska

Comments and Suggestions

We welcome your comments on the *U•X•L Encyclopedia of Drugs & Addictive Substances* and suggestions for other topics to

consider. Please write: Editors, *U•X•L Encyclopedia of Drugs &
Addictive Substances,* Thomson Gale, 27500 Drake Rd., Farmington
Hills, MI 48331-3535; call toll free: 1-800-877-4253; fax to 248-699-
8097; or send e-mail via http://www.gale.com.

c. 5000 BCE Dried peyote buttons dating from this era are later found in Shumla Cave, Texas.

c. 4000 BCE Opium poppies are cultivated in the Fertile Crescent (now Iran and Iraq) by the ancient cultures of Mesopotamia.

1552 BCE An ancient Egyptian papyrus text from the city of Thebes lists 700 uses for opium.

c. 1300 BCE A Peruvian carving depicting a San Pedro cactus, a source of mescaline, is made on stone tablets.

c. 700 BCE Archaeological tablets record that Persians and Assyrians used cannabis as a drug.

c. 199 Galen (129–c. 199), a medical authority during late Antiquity and the Middle Ages, creates a philosophy of medicine, anatomy, and physiology that remains virtually unchallenged until the sixteenth and seventeenth centuries.

c. 200 Chinese surgeons boil hemp in wine to produce an anesthetic called *ma fei san.*

c. 400 Hemp is cultivated in Europe and in England.

600-900 Arabic traders introduce opium to China.

1000 In Coahuila, Mexico, corpses are buried with beaded necklaces of dried peyote buttons.

c. 1200 Peoples of pre-Hispanic America throughout the Inca Empire (1200–1553) chew coca leaves for their stimulating effects and view the plant as a divine gift of the Sun God.

c. 1300 Arabs develop the technique of roasting coffee beans (native to the Kaffa region of Ethiopia), and cultivation for medicinal purposes begins.

c. 1350 Germany bans the sale of alcohol on Sundays and other religious holidays.

c. 1500 Following the Spanish conquest of the Aztecs, unsuccessful attempts are made to prohibit the use of the "magic mushroom" (*Psilocybe* mushrooms) in Central America.

c. 1500 With the rise of national navies during the sixteenth century, hemp farming is encouraged in England and continental Europe to meet the demand for rope and naval rigging.

1524 Paracelsus (1493–1541), Swiss physician and alchemist, mixes opium with alcohol and names the resulting product laudanum.

1556 Andre Thevet brings tobacco seeds to France from Brazil, thus introducing tobacco to Western Europe. Jean Nico suggests that tobacco has medicinal properties in 1559 at the French court, and the plant is renamed nicotina in his honor. By 1565, tobacco seeds are brought to England, where smoking is later made popular by Sir Walter Raleigh.

1612 Tobacco cultivation begins in America and soon becomes a major New World crop. Exports to England begin in 1613, with the first shipment by John Rolfe.

1640 First distillery is established in the United States.

1772 Nitrous oxide is discovered by British scientist, theologian, and philosopher Joseph Priestly (1733–1804).

1775 William Withering, a British physician with a strong interest in botany, introduces the drug digitalis (Foxglove *Digitalis purpurea*) into common medical practice for the treatment of dropsy. Dropsy is a now-obsolete term for edema (fluid retention or swelling) due to heart failure.

1798 Government legislation is passed to establish hospitals in the United States devoted to the care of ill sailors. This initiative leads to the establishment of a Hygenic Laboratory that eventually grows to become the National Institutes of Health.

1799 Chinese emperor Kia King's ban on opium fails to stop the profitable British monopoly over the opium trade.

1799 British scientist Humphry Davy (1778–1829) suggests nitrous oxide can be used to reduce pain during surgery.

c. 1800 Records show that chloral hydrate is used in the "Mickey Finn" cocktail—a drink used to knock people out. The Mickey Finn was used by people wanting to abduct or lure sailors to serve on ships bound for sea.

1803 German scientist Friedrich Sertürner isolates morphine as the most active ingredient in the opium poppy.

1824 Performances in London of "M. Henry's Mechanical and Chemical Demonstrations" show the effects of nitrous oxide on audience volunteers.

1827 Caffeine from tea, originally named "theine," is isolated.

1828 Nicotine ($C_{10} H_{14} N_2$, beta-pyridyl-alpha-N methylpyrrolidine), a highly poisonous alkaloid, is first isolated from tobacco.

1829 Salicin, the precursor of aspirin, is purified from the bark of the willow tree.

1832 French chemist Michel-Eugène Chevreul (1786–1889) isolates creatine from muscle tissue.

1832 Pierre-Jean Robiquet (1780–1840) discovers codeine. Codeine is an alkaloid found in opium that is now used in prescription pain relievers and cough medicines.

1837 Edinburgh chemist and physician William Gregory discovers a more efficient method to isolate and purify morphine.

1839 The First Opium War begins between Britain and China. The conflict lasts until 1842. Imperial Chinese commissioner Lin Tse-Hsu seizes or destroys vast amounts of opium, including stocks owned by British traders. The Chinese pay compensation of more than 21 million silver dollars, and Hong Kong is ceded to Britain under the Treaty of Nanking.

1841 The anesthetic properties of ether are first used by Dr. Crawford W. Long as he surgically removes two tumors from the neck of an anesthetized patient.

1844 The first recorded use of nitrous oxide in U.S. dentistry occurs and involves Quincy Colton, a former medical student, and dentist Horace Wells.

1848 The hypodermic needle is invented, allowing for quicker delivery of morphine to the brain.

1856 The Second Opium War begins between Britain and China. The conflict lasts until 1860. Also known as the Arrow War, or the Anglo-French War in China, the war breaks out after a British-flagged ship, the *Arrow*, is impounded by China. France joins Britain in the war after the murder of a French missionary. China is again defeated and made to pay another large compensation. Under the Treaty of Tientsin, opium is again legalized.

1860 German chemist, Albert Niemann, separates cocaine from the coca leaf.

1861–1865 Morphine gains wide medical use during the American Civil War. Many injured soldiers return from the war as morphine addicts. Morphine addiction becomes known as the "soldiers' disease."

1862 The Department of Agriculture establishes the Bureau of Chemistry, the forerunner of the U.S. Food and Drug Administration (FDA).

1863 German chemist Adolf von Baeyer (1835–1917) discovers barbituric acid.

1864 Amyl nitrite is first synthesized. During the last decades of the twentieth century, amyl nitrite and similar compounds (e.g., butyl, isobutyl, isoamyl, isopropyl, and cyclohexyl nitrates and nitrites) become the chemical basis of "poppers."

1864 German scientists Joseph von Mering (1849-1908) and Nobel prizewinner Emil Hermann Fischer (1852-1919) synthesize the first barbiturate.

1867 Thomas Lauder Brunton (1844–1916), a medical student in Scotland, discovers that amyl nitrite relieves angina by increasing blood flow to the heart. A few years later, nitroglycerine is discovered to have a similar dilating effect. Although both can still be prescribed for angina, nitroglycerine became more commonly prescribed because it is more easily administered and has fewer side effects.

1871 Companies in both the United States and the United Kingdom succeed in producing compressed and liquid nitrous oxide in cylinders.

1874 British chemist Alder Wright uses morphine to create diacetylmorphine (heroin), in an effort to produce a less addictive painkiller.

1879 The Memphis, Tennessee, public health agency targets opium dens by making it illegal to sell, own, or borrow "opium or any deleterious drug." Critics point out that it is unfair to deny opium to Chinese immigrants while allowing white citizens to freely purchase morphine. In fact, people could legally inhale, drink, or inject morphine at that time. It wasn't until 1909 that federal law outlawed smoking or possessing opium.

1882 Production of the drug barbital begins, and doctors start using the barbiturate in various treatments.

1887 Amphetamines are first synthesized.

1889 French-born scientist Charles Edouard Brown-Sequard (1817–1894) reports that he has injected himself with a compound taken from the testicles of dogs. He says the compound made him feel stronger and more energetic.

1891 *The British Medical Journal* reports that Indian hemp was frequently prescribed for "a form of insanity peculiar to women."

1893 The first diet pills (e.g., thyroid extracts) are marketed in United States.

1895 Heinrich Dreser, working for the Bayer Company in Germany, produces a drug he thinks is as effective as morphine in reducing pain, but without its harmful side effects. Bayer began mass production of diacetylmorphine, and in 1898 begins marketing the new drug under the brand name "Heroin" as a cough sedative.

1896 More than 300 opium "dens" are in operation in New York City alone.

1897 German chemist Arthur Heffter identifies mescaline as the chemical responsible for peyote's hallucinogenic effects.

1898 German chemical company Bayer aggressively markets heroin as a cough cure for the rampant disease of the time, tuberculosis.

1901 Jokichi Takamine (1854–1922), Japanese American chemist, and T. B. Aldrich first isolate epinephrine from the adrenal gland. Later known by the trade name Adrenalin, it is eventually identified as a neurotransmitter.

1903 Barbiturate-containing Veronal is marketed as a sleeping pill.

1903 Barbiturates (a class of drugs with more effective sedative-hypnotic effects) replace the use of most sedative bromides.

1903 To determine the safety of additives and preservatives in foods and medicines, the U.S. government establishes a "poison squad," a group of young men who volunteer to eat foods treated with chemicals such as borax, formaldehyde, and benzoic acid. The poison squad was established by Dr. Harvey W. Wiley (1844–1930), head of the U.S. Bureau of Chemistry, the precursor to the FDA.

1906 The U.S. Congress passes the Pure Food and Drug Act.

1909 Congressional legislation stops U.S. imports of smokable opium or opium derivatives except for medicinal purposes.

1910 Britain signs an agreement with China to dismantle the opium trade. However, the profits made from its cultivation, manufacture, and sale are so enormous that no serious interruption occurs until World War II (1939–1945) closes supply routes throughout Asia.

1912 Casimir Funk (1884–1967), Polish American biochemist, coins the term "vitamine." Because the dietary substances he discovers are in the amine group, he calls all of them "life-amines" (using the Latin word *vita* for "life").

1912 Ecstasy, 3,4-Methylenedioxymethamphetamine (MDMA), is developed in Germany.

1912 Phenobarbital is introduced under the trade name Luminal.

1912 The U.S. Public Health Service is established.

1912 The U.S. Congress enacts the Shirley Amendment that prohibits false therapeutic claims in advertising or labeling medicines.

1913 The U.S. Congress passes the Gould Amendment requiring accurate and clear labeling of weights, measures, and numbers on food packages.

1914 The Harrison Narcotic Act bans opiates and cocaine in the United States. Their use as local anesthetics remains legal, however.

1916 Oxycodone is first developed in Germany and marketed under the brand name Eukodal.

1918 The Native American Church (NAC) is founded and combines Christian practices with the use of peyote rituals. Ultimately, the U.S. government exempts the NAC from its ban on peyote if the drug is used as part of a bona fide religious ceremony. This point remains a center of legal controversy in states that want to limit peyote use or outlaw it completely.

1919 The Eighteenth Amendment to the U.S. Constitution (ratified on January 29, 1919) begins the era of Prohibition in the United States. It prohibits the sale and consumption of alcohol in the nation.

1919 Methamphetamine is first manufactured in Japan.

1925 The League of Nations adopts strict rules governing the international heroin trade.

1926 Phencyclidine (PCP) is first synthesized.

1927 Albert Szent-Györgyi (1893–1986), Hungarian American physicist, discovers ascorbic acid, or vitamin C, while studying oxidation in plants.

1929 Scottish biochemist Alexander Fleming (1881–1955) discovers penicillin. He observes that the mold *Penicillium notatum* inhibits the growth of some bacteria. This is the first antibiotic, and it opens a new era of "wonder drugs" to combat infection and disease.

1930 The U.S. Food, Drug, and Insecticide Administration is renamed the U.S. Food and Drug Administration (FDA).

1932 Pharmaceutical manufacturer Smith, Kline and French introduces Benzedrine, an over-the-counter amphetamine-based inhaler for relieving nasal congestion.

1933 The Twenty-first Amendment to the U.S. Constitution repeals the Eighteenth Amendment and makes it legal to sell and consume alcohol in United States again.

1935 The Federal Bureau of Narcotics, forerunner of the modern Drug Enforcement Administration (DEA), begins a campaign that portrays marijuana as a drug that leads users to addiction, violence, and insanity. The government produces films such as *Marihuana* (1935), *Reefer Madness* (1936), and *Assassin of Youth* (1937).

1935 The first Alcoholics Anonymous (AA) group is formed in Akron, Ohio.

1935 Testosterone is first isolated in the laboratory.

1936 The U.S. government begins to open a series of facilities to help deal with the rising number of opiate addicts in the nation.

1937 Amphetamine is used to treat a condition known as minimal brain dysfunction, a disorder later renamed attention-deficit/hyperactivity disorder (ADHD).

1937 Diethylene glycol, an elixir of sulfanilamide, kills 107 people, including many children. The mass poisoning highlights the need for additional legislation regarding drug safety.

1937 The Marijuana Tax Act effectively makes it a crime to use or possess the drug, even for medical reasons.

1938 The Federal Food, Drug, and Cosmetics Act gives regulatory powers to the FDA. It also requires that new drugs be clinically tested and proven safe.

1938 Meperidine is synthesized. Other synthetic opioids soon follow.

1938 Swiss chemist Albert Hofmann (1906–) at Sandoz Laboratories synthesizes LSD. After initially testing it on animals, Hofmann accidentally ingests some of the drug in 1943, revealing LSD's hallucinogenic properties.

1938 The Wheeler-Lea Act empowers the U.S. Federal Trade Commission to oversee non-prescription drug advertising otherwise regulated by the FDA.

1939 Ernest Chain (1906–1979) and H. W. Florey (1898–1968) refine the purification of penicillin, allowing the mass production of the antibiotic.

1939 Methadone, a synthetic opioid narcotic, is created in Germany. Originally named Amidon, early methadone was used mainly as a pain reliever.

1942 The Opium Poppy Control Act outlaws possession of opium poppies in United States.

1944 To combat battle fatigue during World War II, nearly 200 million amphetamine tablets are issued to American soldiers stationed in Great Britain during the war.

1944 The U.S. Public Health Service Act is passed.

1945 After World War II, anabolic-androgenic steroids (AASs) are given to many starving concentration camp survivors to help them add skeletal muscle and build up body weight.

1948 A U.S. Supreme Court ruling allows the FDA to investigate drug sales at the pharmacy level.

1948 The World Health Organization (WHO) is formed. The WHO subsequently becomes the principal international organization managing public health related issues on a global scale. Headquartered in Geneva, Switzerland, the WHO becomes, by 2002, an organization of more than 190 member countries. The organization contributes to international public health in areas including disease prevention and control, promotion of good health, addressing disease outbreaks, initiatives to eliminate diseases (e.g., vaccination programs), and development of treatment and prevention standards.

1949 The FDA publishes a "black book" guide about the toxicity of chemicals in food.

1950 A U.S. Court of Appeals rules that drug labels must include intended regular uses of the drug.

1951 The U.S. Durham-Humphrey Amendment defines conditions under which drugs require medical supervision and further requires that prescriptions be written only by a licensed practitioner.

1952 The tranquilizer Reserpine rapidly begins replacing induced insulin shock therapy (injecting patients with insulin until their blood sugar levels fall so low that they become comatose), electroconvulsive (ECT) therapy (inducing seizures by passing an electric current through the brain), and lobotomy (making an incision in the lobe of the brain) as treatments for certain types of mental illness.

1953 British novelist Aldous Huxley (1894–1963) publishes *The Doors of Perception*, a book in which he recounts his experiences with peyote.

1953 Jonas Salk (1915–1995) begins testing a polio vaccine comprised of a mixture of killed viruses.

1953 Narcotics Anonymous (NA) is founded.

1953 The U.S. Federal Security Agency becomes the Department of Health, Education, and Welfare (HEW).

1954 Veterinarians begin using piperazines, which are designed to rid the lower intestinal tract of parasitic worms.

1955 Scientists in India first synthesize methaqualone.

1956 The American Medical Association defines alcoholism as a disease.

1956 Dimethyltriptamine (DMT) is recognized as being hallucinogenic.

1957 Researchers John Baer, Karl Beyer, James Sprague, and Frederick Novello formulate the drug chlorothiazide, the first of the thiazide diuretics. This groundbreaking discovery marks a new era in medicine as the first safe and effective long-term treatment for chronic hypertension and heart failure.

1958 Aaron B. Lerner isolates melatonin from the pineal gland.

1958 The FDA publishes a list of substances generally recognized as safe.

1958 The Parke-Davis pharmaceutical company synthesizes and patents PCP. After testing, Parke-Davis sells the drug as a general anesthetic called Sernyl.

1958 The U.S. government passes food additives amendments that require manufacturers to establish safety and to eliminate additives demonstrated to cause cancer.

1959 Fentanyl, first synthesized in Belgium by Janssen Parmaceutica, is used as a pain management drug.

1960 The FDA requires warnings on labels of potentially hazardous household chemicals.

1960 Gamma butyrolactone (GBL) is first synthesized.

1960 GBH, a fast-acting central nervous system depressant, is developed as an alternative anesthetic (painkiller) for use in surgery because of its ability to induce sleep and reversible coma.

1961 Commencing a two-year study, Harvard professor Timothy Leary attempts to reform criminals at the Massachusetts Correctional Institute. The inmates are given doses of psilocybin and psychological therapy. Ultimately, the psilocybin-subjected inmates have the same rate of return to prison as the inmates who were not part of the study. In addition to this, they have more parole violations than the general parolees.

1961 Ketamine (originally CI581) is discovered by Calvin Stevens of Wayne State University in Detroit, Michigan.

1962 The American Medical Association publishes a public warning in its journal *JAMA* regarding the increasingly widespread use of LSD for recreational purposes.

1962 Thalidomide, a sleeping pill also used to combat morning sickness in pregnant women, is discovered to be the cause of widespread and similar birth defects in babies born in Great

Britain and western Europe. Earlier, Dr. Frances Kelsey of the FDA had refused to approve the drug for use in the United States pending further research. Due to her steadfast refusal, countless birth defects are prevented in the United States.

1962 The U.S. Congress passes the Kefauver-Harris Drug Amendments that shift the burden of proof of clinical safety to drug manufacturers. For the first time, drug manufacturers have to prove their products are safe and effective before they can be sold.

1964 The first Surgeon General's Report on Smoking and Health is released. The U.S. government first acknowledges and publicizes that cigarette smoking is a leading cause of cancer, bronchitis, and emphysema.

1965 At the height of tobacco use in the United States, surveys show 52 percent of adult men and 32 percent of adult women use tobacco products.

1965 Because of disturbing side effects including horrible nightmares, delusions, hallucinations, agitation, delirium, disorientation, and difficulty speaking, PCP use on humans is stopped in the United States. PCP continued to be sold as a veterinary anesthetic under the brand name Sernylan.

1965 The manufacture of LSD becomes illegal in the United States. A year later it is made illegal in the United Kingdom. The FDA subsequently classifies LSD as a Schedule I drug in 1970.

1965 The U.S. Congress passes the Drug Abuse Control Amendments—legislation that forms the FDA Bureau of Drug Abuse Control and gives the FDA tighter regulatory control over amphetamines, barbiturates, and other prescription drugs with high abuse potential.

1966 The FDA and the National Academy of Sciences begin investigation of the effectiveness of drugs previously approved because they were thought to be safe.

1966 The U.S. Narcotic Addiction Rehabilitation Act gives federal financial assistance to states and local authorities to develop a local system of drug treatment programs. Methadone clinic treatment programs begin to rise dramatically.

1967 A "Love-In" in honor of LSD is staged at Golden Gate Park in San Francisco, California. Before LSD was made illegal, more than 40,000 patients were treated with LSD as part of psychiatric therapy.

1967 News accounts depict illicit use of PCP, then sometimes known as the "Peace Pill," in the Haight-Ashbury district of San Francisco during the "Summer of Love." PCP reemerges in the early 1970s as a liquid, crystalline powder, and tablet.

1968 Psilocybin and *Psilocybe* mushrooms are made illegal in United States.

1970 The U.S. Congress passes the Controlled Substance Act (CSA). It puts strict controls on the production, import, and prescription of amphetamines. Many amphetamine forms, particularly diet pills, are removed from the over-the-counter market.

1970 Ketamine is used as a battlefield anesthetic agent during the Vietnam war (1954–1975).

1970 The U.S. Comprehensive Drug Abuse Prevention and Control Act classifies drugs in five categories based on the effect of the drug, its medical use, and potential for abuse.

1970 Widespread use of peyote is halted by the Comprehensive Drug Abuse Prevention and Control Act of 1970. During the 1950s and 1960s, peyote was legal throughout most of the United States. During the peak of the psychedelic era, dried peyote cactus buttons were readily available through mail-order catalogs.

1971 Cigarette advertising is banned from television and radio. The nonsmokers' rights movement begins.

1971 The United Kingdom passes the Misuse of Drugs Act.

1974 2C-B is first produced by American chemist and pharmacologist Alexander Shulgin.

1974 The first hospice facility opens in the United States.

1975 Anabolic-androgenic steroids (AASs) are added to the International Olympic Committee's list of banned substances.

1975 Rohypnol, developed by the pharmaceutical firm of Hoffmann-La Roche, is first sold in Switzerland as a sleeping aid for the treatment of insomnia. Reports begin surfacing that Rohypnol is abused as a recreational or "party" drug, often in combination with alcohol and/or other drugs. It also becomes known as a date rape drug.

1976 The FBI warns that "crack" cocaine use and cocaine addiction are on the rise in the United States.

1976 Oxycodone is approved by the FDA. Various formulations follow, including drugs that combine oxycodone with either aspirin or acetaminophen.

1976 The U.S. Congress passes the Proxmire Amendments to stop the FDA from regulating vitamin and mineral supplements as drugs based on their potency or strength. This legislation also prohibits the FDA from regulating the potency of vitamin and mineral supplements.

1978 The American Indian Religious Freedom Act is passed and protects the religious traditions of Native Americans, including the use of peyote.

1978 Because of escalating reports of abuse, PCP is withdrawn completely from the U.S. market. Since 1978, no legal therapeutic use of PCP exists.

1980 The FDA proposes removing caffeine from its Generally Recognized as Safe list. Subsequently, the FDA concludes in 1992 that, after reviewing the scientific literature, no harm is posed by a person's intake of up to 100 milligrams (mg) of caffeine per day.

1980 World Health Organization (WHO) classifies khat as a drug of abuse that may produce mild to moderate psychological dependency.

1981 Alprazolam (Xanax) is introduced and subsequently becomes the most widely prescribed benzodiazepine.

1982 The FDA issues regulations for tamper-resistant packaging after seven people die in Chicago from ingesting Tylenol capsules laced with cyanide. The following year, the federal Anti-Tampering Act is passed, making it a crime to tamper with packaged consumer products.

1983 The U.S. Congress passes the Orphan Drug Act, which allows the FDA to research and market drugs necessary for treating rare diseases.

1984 Methaqualone (Quaalude, Sopor), a nonbarbiturate hypnotic that is said to give a heroin-like high without drowsiness, is banned in the United States.

1984 Nicotine gum is introduced.

1985 The FDA approves synthetic THC, or dronabinol (Marinol), to help cancer patients undergoing chemotherapy.

1985 Ecstasy (MDMA) becomes illegal in the United States.

1985 The United Kingdom passes the Intoxicating Substances (Supply) Act, making it an offense to supply a product that will be abused. Subsequent legislation, the Cigarette Lighter Refill (safety) Regulations, passed in 1999, regulates the sale of purified liquefied petroleum gas, mainly butane. Butane is the substance most often involved in inhalant deaths in the United Kingdom.

1986 The United Kingdom passes the Medicines Act.

1986 The U.S. Congress passes the Anti-Drug Abuse Act. This federal law includes mandatory minimum sentences for first-time offenders with harsher penalties for possession of crack cocaine than powder cocaine.

1986 The U.S. Surgeon General's report focuses on the hazards of environmental tobacco smoke to nonsmokers.

1987 The legal drinking age is raised to 21 years in United States.

1988 Canadian sprinter Ben Johnson (1961–) tests positive for anabolic-androgenic steroids (AASs) at the Seoul Olympic games and forfeits his gold medal to the second-place finisher, American Carl Lewis (1961–).

1990 The FDA bans the use of GHB, a drug related to GBL, a central nervous system depressant with sedative-hypnotic and hallucinogenic properties.

1990 The U.S. Supreme Court decision in *Employment Division v. Smith* says that the religious use of peyote by Native Americans is not protected by the First Amendment.

1991 Anabolic-androgenic steroids (AASs) are listed as Schedule III drugs in accord with the U.S. Controlled Substances Act (CSA).

1991 Nicotine skin patches are introduced.

1992 The Karolinska Institute publishes a study that finds subjects who take creatine supplements can experience a significant increase in total muscle creatine content. Creatine is thrust onto the global athletic scene as British sprinters Linford Christie and Sally Gunnel win Olympic gold in Barcelona after reportedly training with the aid of creatine supplementation. Subsequently, a lack of well-designed clinical studies of creatine's long-term effects combined with loose regulatory standards for creatine supplement products causes some athletic associations, including the U.S. Olympic Committee (USOC), to caution against its use without banning it outright.

1993 2C-B becomes widely known as a "rave" drug in United States.

1993 The first news accounts that cite the use of Rohypnol as a "date rape" drug are published. Rohypnol becomes one of more than 20 drugs that law enforcement officials assert are used in committing sexual assaults.

1993 The U.S. Religious Freedom Restoration Act and the American Indian Religious Freedom Act Amendments (AIRFA) restore the rights of Native Americans to use peyote in religious ceremonies.

1994 Cigarette industry secrets are revealed causing a storm of controversy. The list of some 700 potential additives shows 13 additives that are not allowed to be used in food.

1994 The U.S. Congress passes the Dietary Supplement Health and Education Act (DSHEA) in an effort to standardize the manufacture, labeling, composition, and safety of botanicals, herbs, and nutritional supplements. It expressly defines a dietary supplement as a vitamin, a mineral, an herb or other botanical, an amino acid, or any other "dietary substance." The law prohibits claims that herbs can treat diseases or disorders, but it allows more general health claims about the effect of herbs on the "structure or function" of the body or about the "well-being" they induce. Under the Act, supplement manufacturers are allowed to market and sell products without federal regulation. As a result, the FDA bears the burden of having to prove an herbal is unsafe before it can restrict its use.

1995 2C-B is classified as a Schedule I drug under the U.S. Controlled Substances Act (CSA).

1995 A study published by the *British Journal of Urology* asserts that khat (*Catha edulis*) chewing inhibits urine flow, constricts blood vessels, and promotes erectile dysfunction.

1995 A study by the Rand Corporation finds that every dollar spent in drug treatment saves society seven dollars in crime, policing, incarceration, and health services.

1995 The National Household Survey on Drug Abuse finds inhalants to be the second most commonly abused illicit drug by American youth ages 12–17 years, after marijuana.

1996 Anabolic-androgenic steroids (AASs) and other performance-enhancing drugs are added to the United Kingdom Misuse of Drugs Act.

1996 Nicotine nasal spray is introduced.

1996 The U.S. Drug-Induced Rape Prevention and Punishment Act makes it a felony to give an unsuspecting person a drug with the intent of committing violence, including rape. The law also imposes penalties of large fines and prison sentences of up to 20 years for importing or distributing more than one gram of date-rape drugs.

1997 2C-B is banned in Great Britain.

1997 The FDA proposes new rules regarding some ephedra dietary supplements and seeks to regulate certain products containing the drug. The FDA claims that certain ephedrine alkaloids resemble amphetamine, which stimulates the heart and nervous system. Congress rejects the FDA's attempt to subject ephedra products to regulation. In 2000, an ephedra study published in the *New England Journal of Medicine* shows a link between heart attacks, strokes, seizures, and mental side effects (including anxiety, tremulousness, and personality changes) with ephedra intake. Other possible mental side effects associated with ephedra are depression and paranoid psychosis.

1997 The FDA investigates the link between heart valve disease in patients using the Fen-Phen drug combination for weight loss. The FDA notes that the Fen-Phen treatment had not received FDA approval.

1997 The Institute of Medicine (IOM), a branch of the National Academy of Sciences, publishes the report *Marijuana: Assessing the Science Base*, which concludes that cannabinoids show significant promise as analgesics, appetite stimulants, and antiemetics. It states that further research into producing such medicines was warranted.

1997 Oregon voters approve the Death with Dignity Act, allowing terminally ill people to receive prescriptions for lethal doses of drugs to end their lives.

1997 Rohypnol is banned in the United States.

1997 The *Journal of the American Medical Association (JAMA)* publishes a study indicating that ginkgo dietary supplements might be useful in treating Alzheimer's disease, sparking additional research interest.

1997 The National Institutes of Health (NIH) estimate that approximately 600,000 people in the United States are opiate-dependent, meaning they use an opiate drug daily or on a frequent basis.

1998 A study at the Psychiatric University Hospital in Zurich, Switzerland, demonstrates that psilocybin produces a psychosis-like syndrome in healthy humans that is similar to early schizophrenia.

1998 Amendments made to the U.S. Higher Education Act make anyone convicted of a drug offense ineligible for federal student loans for one year up to an indefinite period of time. Such convictions may also render students ineligible for state aid.

1998 The nicotine inhaler (Nicotrol Inhaler) is introduced.

1998 The tobacco industry settles lengthy lawsuits by making a historic agreement with the States' Attorneys General called the Master Settlement Agreement (MSA). In exchange for protection from further lawsuits, the industry agrees to additional advertising restrictions and to reimburse the states billions of dollars over 25 years to pay for smoking-related illnesses.

1998 The U.S. Drug Free Communities Act offers federal money to communities to help educate citizens on the dangers on methamphetamine use and production.

1998 The U.S. Speed Trafficking Life in Prison Act increases penalties for the production, distribution, and use of methamphetamine.

1999 The Drug Enforcement Administration (DEA) lists GBL as a scheduled (controlled) substance.

1999 The FDA lists ketamine as a Schedule III drug.

1999 National Household Survey on Drug Abuse (NHSDA) estimates that a third of the American population (then an estimated 72 million people) had tried marijuana at least once.

1999 DEA agents seize 30 gallons (113.5 liters) of a dimethyltriptamine (DMT) tea called "hoasca" from the office of the O Centro Espirita Beneficiente Uniao do Vegetal (UDV), a New Mexico-based religious organization with approximately 500 members. The organization subsequently sued the U.S. Government, alleging a violation of their constitutional right of freedom of religion.

2000 The *Journal of Pharmacy and Pharmacology* concludes that khat (*Catha edulis*), like amphetamines and ibuprofen, can relieve pain.

2000 The National Cancer Institute (NCI) estimates that 3,000 lung cancer deaths, and as many as 40,000 cardiac deaths per year among adult nonsmokers in the United States can be attributed to passive smoke or environmental tobacco smoke (ETS).

2000 The U.S. Congress considers but does not pass the Pain Relief Promotion Act, which would have amended the Controlled Substances Act to say that relieving pain or discomfort—within the context of professional medicine—is a legitimate use of controlled substances. The bill died in the Senate.

2000 The U.S. Congress Ecstasy Anti-proliferation Act increases federal sentencing guidelines for trafficking and possessing with intent to sell ecstasy (MDMA). It drastically increases jail terms for fewer numbers of pills in personal possession.

2000 The U.S. Congress passes a transportation spending bill that includes creating a national standard for drunk driving for adults at a 0.08 percent blood alcohol concentration (BAC) level. States are required to adopt this stricter standard by 2004 or face penalties. By 2001, more than half the states adopt this stricter standard.

2000 U.S. President William J. Clinton (1946–) signs the Hillory J. Farias and Samantha Reid Date-Rape Drug Prohibition Act into law.

2001 The *American Journal of Psychiatry* publishes studies providing evidence that methamphetamine can cause brain damage that results in slower motor and cognitive functioning—even in users who take the drug for less than a year.

2001 *International Journal of Cancer* researchers assert that khat (*Catha edulis*) chewing, especially when accompanied by alcohol and tobacco consumption, may cause cancer.

2001 National Football League (NFL) joins the National Collegiate Athletic Association (NCAA) and the International Olympic Committee (IOC) in issuing a ban on ephedrine use. The NFL ban on ephedrine prohibits NFL players and teams from endorsing products containing ephedrine or companies that sell or distribute those products.

2001 National Institute of Drug Abuse (NIDA) research reveals that children exposed to cocaine prior to birth sustained long-lasting brain changes. Eight years after birth, children exposed to cocaine prior to birth had detectable brain chemistry differences.

2001 A thoroughbred race horse wins a race at Suffolk Downs in Massachusetts but then tests positive for BZP (also known as Equine Ecstasy).

2001 The U.S. Supreme Court rules (unanimously) in *United States vs. Oakland Cannabis Buyers' Cooperative* that the cooperatives permitted under California law to sell medical marijuana to patients who had a physician's approval to use the drug were unconstitutional under federal law.

2002 Companies begin developing drink coasters and other detection kits that allow consumers to test whether drinks have been drugged. If date-rape drugs are present, a strip on the testing kit changes color when a drop of the tampered drink is placed on it.

2002 A Florida physician is convicted of manslaughter for prescribing OxyContin to four patients who died after overdosing on the powerful opiate. News reports allege that he is the first doctor ever convicted in the death of patients whose deaths were related to OxyContin use.

2002 Health Canada, the Canadian health regulatory agency, requests a voluntary recall of products containing both natural and chemical ephedra.

2002 The U.S. military's use of go-pills (dextroamphetamine) comes under fire after two U.S. Air Force pilots are involved in a friendly fire incident in Afghanistan. Four Canadian soldiers are killed and eight wounded when one of the American pilots bombs them from his F-16 after mistaking them for the enemy.

2002 In the aftermath of the September 11, 2001, terrorist attacks on the United States, the U.S. government dramatically increases funding to stockpile drugs and other agents that can be used to counter a bioterror attack.

2002 Several states, including Connecticut and Minnesota, pass laws that ban teachers from recommending psychotropic drugs, especially Ritalin, to parents.

2002 A U.S. federal district court judge rejects a U.S. Justice Department attempt to overturn Oregon's physician-assisted suicide law. The Justice Department had claimed that the state law violated the federal Controlled Substances Act.

2002-2003 During the severe acute respiratory syndrome (SARS) scare, many people visit Chinese herbalists to purchase a mixture of herbs to help protect them from the disease.

2003 More than 2,200 pounds (998 kilograms) of khat are seized at the Dublin Airport in Ireland. The bundles were being sent to New York from London.

2003 The FDA approves the use of Prozac in depressed children as young as seven years old.

2003 The U.S. government implements the Reducing Americans' Vulnerability to Ecstasy Act.

2003 Steve Bechler, a pitcher with the Baltimore Orioles, collapses during a preseason workout in Florida and dies the next day. His death is linked to the use of ephedra.

2003 More than 3,500 children in the United States are involved in meth lab incidents during the year.

2004 Australian police begin stopping motorists randomly to conduct saliva tests to check for various illegal drugs, including marijuana and amphetamines.

2004 Adderall XR is approved by the FDA for use by adults with ADHD.

2004 The FDA announces that "black box" labeling of antidepressants will become mandatory.

2004 The federal court case regarding the O Centro Espirita Beneficiente Uniao do Vegetal religious sect concludes with the group winning the right to use an hallucinogenic tea in its religious services.

2004 The FDA bans the use of ephedra in the United States following reports of more than 150 deaths linked to the supplement.

2004 The Warner Bros. movie *Scooby-Doo 2: Monsters Unleashed* contains a scene showing Shaggy taking a hit of nitrous oxide off a whipped cream can. The scene angers many parents who have lost children due to inhalant abuse.

2004-2005 BZP is still being sold over-the-counter in New Zealand as an herbal party pill. In 2005, the DEA officially classifies BZP as a Schedule I drug in the United States.

2004-2005 After the fall of the Taliban government in Afghanistan in late 2001, opium poppy production begins to soar by 2004. Street heroin becomes purer and available in larger quantities. Prices reach a twenty-year low.

2005 Baseball players and managers are called to testify before Congress about steroid use in the Major Leagues.

2005 The Partnership for a Drug-Free America releases a study showing that prescription drug abuse among teens is growing rapidly. Teens are dubbed "Generation Rx."

2005 The U.S. Supreme Court agrees to hear a case involving Oregon's physician-assisted suicide law.

2005 Utah-based Nutraceutical International successfully challenges the FDA ban on ephedra in federal court. U.S. judge Tena Campbell rules that the FDA has failed to prove that the company's ephedra-based product is unsafe.

2005 The FDA launches a pilot program using high-tech radio frequency identification (RFID) tags to track the movement of bottles of the most addictive prescription painkillers.

2005 The Canadian government joins several European nations (most notably the Netherlands) in a pilot program to give free heroin to heroin addicts to help them stabilize their lives, eventually overcome addiction, and prevent them from contracting diseases by sharing dirty needles.

2005 The U.S. Supreme Court rules against the use of medical marijuana. At the time of the ruling, ten states allow medical marijuana to be used by cancer, AIDS, and other patients suffering severe pain when prescribed by a physician.

2005 The FDA issues a public health advisory about the use of fentanyl skin patches after receiving reports that people have died or experienced serious side effects after overdosing on the drug.

2005 The new opiate drug Palladone is pulled off the market for further research by its maker, Purdue Pharma.

2005 Oregon lawmakers vote to make over-the-counter cold and allergy remedies containing pseudoephedrine available by prescription only beginning in mid-2006. The move is taken to make it harder for illegal methamphetamine "cooks" to obtain the ingredient. A dozen other states move the product "behind the counter."

A

acetaminophen: Pronounced uh-SEE-tuh-MINN-uh fenn; a non-aspirin pain reliever, such as Tylenol.

acetylcholine: Pronounced uh-settle-KOH-leen; a neurotransmitter that forms from a substance called choline, which is released by the liver.

acquired immunodeficiency syndrome (AIDS): An infectious disease that destroys the body's immune system, leading to illness and death.

active ingredient: The chemical or substance in a compound known or believed to have a therapeutic, or healing, effect.

adenosine triphosphate (ATP): An important energy-carrying chemical, created with the assistance of creatine.

adrenaline: Pronounced uh-DREN-uh-linn; a natural stimulant produced by the human body; also known as epinephrine (epp-ih-NEFF-run).

adverse reactions: Side effects, or negative health consequences, reported after taking a certain substance.

aerobic exercises: Exercises performed to increase heart health and stamina, such as jogging, biking, and swimming, usually lasting between twenty minutes and an hour.

aerosol: Gas used to propel, or shoot out, liquid substances from a pressurized can.

alchemists: Those who study or practice medieval chemical science aimed at discovering a cure for all illnesses.

alcoholism: A disease that results in habitual, uncontrolled alcohol abuse; alcoholism can shorten a person's life by damaging the brain, liver, and heart.

alkaloid: A nitrogen-containing substance found in plants.

Alzheimer's disease: A brain disease that usually strikes older individuals and results in memory loss, impaired thinking, and personality changes; symptoms worsen over time.

amines: Organic (or carbon-containing) chemical substances made from ammonia.

amino acids: Any of a group of chemical compounds that form the basis for proteins.

ammonia: A strong-smelling colorless gas made of nitrogen and hydrogen; often used as a cleaning agent in its liquid form.

amnesia: The loss of memory.

amphetamines: Pronounced am-FETT-uh-meens; stimulant drugs that increase mental alertness, reduce appetite, and help keep users awake.

anabolic agents: Substances that promote muscle growth.

anaerobic exercise: Short, strenuous exercises that require sudden bursts of strength, such as weight lifting and batting a baseball.

analgesics: Pain relievers or the qualities of pain relief.

analogs: Drugs created in a laboratory, having a slightly different chemical composition than a pharmaceutical, yet having the same effects on the brain as the pharmaceutical.

anemia: A blood condition that results in the decreased ability of the blood to transport enough oxygen throughout the body.

anesthesiologists: Medical doctors trained to use medications to sedate a surgery patient.

anesthetic: A substance used to deaden pain.

angina pectoris: Pronounced an-JINE-uh peck-TOR-ess; a feeling of suffocation and pain around the heart that occurs when the blood supply to the heart is not adequate.

anhedonia: Pronounced ann-heh-DOE-nee-uh; the inability to experience pleasure from normally enjoyable life events.

anorectics: Pronounced ah-nuh-RECK-ticks; diet pills that cause a loss of appetite; they were developed to replace amphetamines.

anorexia: Pronounced ah-nuh-REK-see-uh; a severe eating disorder characterized by an intense fear of gaining weight, a refusal to eat, a distorted sense of self-image, and excessive weight loss.

antagonist: Pronounced ann-TAG-uh-nist; a drug that opposes the action of another drug.

anthelmintic: Pronounced ant-hel-MINN-tick; a substance that helps destroy and expel parasitic worms, especially worms located in the intestines.

antidote: A remedy to reverse the effects of a poison.

antihistamines: Drugs that block *histamine,* a chemical that causes nasal congestion related to allergies.

antioxidant: A chemical that neutralizes free radicals (chemicals with an unpaired electron) that can damage other cells.

antitussants: Pronounced an-ty-TUH-sihvs; medicines that quiet coughs.

anxiety: A feeling of being extremely overwhelmed, restless, fearful, and worried.

anxiety disorders: A group of mental disorders or conditions characterized in part by extreme restlessness, uncontrollable feelings of fear, excessive worrying, and panic attacks.

aphrodisiac: Pronounced aff-roh-DEE-zee-ack; a drug or other substance that excites or increases sexual desire.

arthritis: Painful swelling of joints caused by abnormal bone growth or wear and tear on the joint.

asphyxiation: Death or unconsciousness caused by one of three things: 1) a lack of adequate oxygen, 2) the inhalation of physically harmful substances, or 3) the obstruction of normal breathing.

asthma: Pronounced AZ-muh; a lung disorder that interferes with normal breathing.

ataxia: Pronounced uh-TAKS-ee-uh; loss of control of muscle coordination.

attention-deficit/hyperactivity disorder (ADHD): A disorder characterized by impulsive behavior, difficulty concentrating, and hyperactivity that interferes with social and academic functioning.

autism: Pronounced AW-tizm; a psychological disorder, usually diagnosed in children, that affects emotional development, social interactions, and the ability to communicate effectively.

ayahuasca: One of several teas of South American origin used in religious ceremonies, known to contain dimethyltryptamine (DMT); also a plant.

B

barbiturates: Pronounced bar-BIH-chuh-rits; drugs that act as depressants and are used as sedatives or sleeping pills; also referred to as "downers."

bathtub chemists: Inexperienced and illegal drug makers who concoct homemade drugs; also referred to as "kitchen chemists" or "underground chemists."

behavior modification: A type of therapy that changes behavior by substituting desired responses for undesired ones.

benzodiazepines: A type of drug used to treat anxiety.

binge drinking: Consuming a lot of alcohol in a short period of time.

bipolar disorder: A psychological disorder that causes alternating periods of depression and extreme elevation of mood.

black market: The illegal sale or trade of goods; drug dealers are said to carry out their business on the "black market."

boils: Large pimples that are inflamed and filled with pus.

bone marrow: Soft tissue in the center of bones where blood cell formation occurs.

bronchitis: An illness that affects the bronchial tubes in the lungs, leading to shortness of breath and coughing.

bronchodilator: A drug that relaxes breathing muscles, allowing air to flow more easily through the tubes that lead to the lungs.

bufotenine: The component of venom from the toad genus *Bufo* that contains dimethyltryptamine (DMT).

bulimia: Pronounced bull-EEM-eeh-yuh; an eating disorder that involves long periods of bingeing on food, followed by self-induced vomiting and abuse of laxatives.

C

cancer: Out-of-control cell growth leading to tumors in the body's organs or tissues.

cannabinoids: Chemical compounds found in cannabis plants and in small amounts in the brains of humans and animals.

carbon monoxide: A poisonous gas with no odor; carbon monoxide is released when cigarettes burn.

carcinogens: Chemicals that can cause cancer in the body.

cardiovascular illnesses: Illnesses involving the heart and blood vessels.

carries: Doses of methadone given to users to take home for another day.

chemotherapy: A medically supervised regimen of drugs used to kill cancer cells in the body. The drugs have potential side effects including nausea, vomiting, and other reactions.

cholesterol: Pronounced kuh-LESS-tuhr-ol; an essential substance made of carbon, hydrogen, and oxygen that is found in animal cells and body fluids; in high amounts, it may be deposited in blood vessels, resulting in dangerous blockages of blood flow.

cirrhosis: Pronounced sir-OH-sis; destruction of the liver, possibly leading to death.

clinical trials: Scientific experiments that test the effect of a drug in humans.

club drugs: Mostly synthetic, illegal substances found at raves and nightclubs, including the drugs ecstasy, GHB, ketamine, LSD, methamphetamines, PCP, and Rohypnol.

coca paste: An impure freebase made from coca leaves and used mainly in South America; coca paste is smoked and is highly addictive.

cocaethylene: A substance formed by the body when cocaine and alcohol are consumed together; it increases the chances of serious adverse reactions or sudden death from cocaine.

cognitive behavioral therapy (CBT): A type of therapy that helps people recognize and change negative patterns of thinking and behavior.

coma: A state of unconsciousness from which a person cannot be aroused by noise or other stimuli.

congestive heart failure (CHF): Inability of the heart to circulate, or pump, the blood throughout the body with sufficient force.

constipation: An inability to have a bowel movement.

control group: In a drug test, the group that does *not* receive the drug being tested.

controlled substance analog: Any chemical compound that acts on the body the same way a controlled substance does.

coroner: An official who investigates unexplained deaths.

corticosteroids: Pronounced kor-tih-koh-STEH-roydz; medications widely prescribed to treat inflammation.

crack cocaine: A highly addictive, smokable freebase cocaine made by combining powder cocaine with water and sodium bicarbonate.

cravings: Overwhelming urges to do something, such as take an illegal drug.

Crohn's disease: A serious disease of the intestines that causes inflammation, along with severe pain, diarrhea, nausea, and sometimes extreme weight loss.

cutting: Adding other ingredients to a powdered drug to stretch the drug for more sales.

cyanide: A poisonous chemical compound that shuts down the respiratory system, quickly killing people who have been exposed to it.

cyanosis: Bluish or purplish skin caused by a lack of oxygen in the blood.

D

decongestant: A drug that relieves nasal congestion.

dehydration: An abnormally low amount of fluid in the body.

delirium: A mental disturbance marked by confusion, hallucinations, and difficulty focusing attention and communicating.

delusions: False, unshakable beliefs indicating severe mental difficulties; "delusional" refers to the inability to distinguish between what is real and what seems to be real.

dementia: Pronounced dih-MENN-shuh; a brain disorder that causes a reduction in a person's intellectual functioning, most often affecting memory, concentration, and decision-making skills.

dependent: When a user has a physical or psychological need to take a certain substance in order to function.

depressants: Substances that slow down the activity of an organism or one of its parts.

depression: A mood disorder that causes people to have feelings of hopelessness, loss of pleasure, self-blame, and sometimes suicidal thoughts.

designer drugs: Harmful and addictive substances that are manufactured illegally in homemade labs.

detoxification: Often abbreviated as detox; a difficult process by which substance abusers stop taking those substances and rid their bodies of the toxins that accumulated during the time they consumed such substances.

diabetes: A serious disorder that causes problems with the normal breakdown of sugars in the body.

dietary supplements: Products including vitamins, herbal extractions, and synthetic amino acids sold for specific uses such as weight loss, muscle building, or prevention of disease.

dilate: Expand or open up.

dissociation: A psychological syndrome in which the mind seems detached from the body; sometimes referred to as an "out of body" experience.

dissociative anesthetics: Pronounced dih-SOH-shee-uh-tiv ANN-ess-THET-iks; drugs that cause users to feel as if their minds are separated from their bodies.

diuretic: Pronounced die-er-EH-tik; substances that reduce bodily fluids by increasing the production of urine.

divination: The mystical experience of seeing into the future, witnessing a hidden truth, or gaining a deep insight.

doctor shopping: A practice in which an individual continually switches physicians so that he or she can get enough of a prescription drug to feed an addiction; this makes it difficult for physicians to track whether the patient has already been prescribed the same drug by another physician.

dopamine: Pronounced DOPE-uh-meen; a combination of carbon, hydrogen, nitrogen, and oxygen that acts as a neurotransmitter in the brain.

dysphoria: Pronounced diss-FOR-ee-yuh; an abnormal feeling of anxiety, discontent, or discomfort; the opposite of euphoria.

E

edema: Pronounced ih-DEEM-uh; water buildup in the body's tissues that causes swelling.

electrolytes: Charged atoms such as sodium, potassium, chloride, calcium, and magnesium that conduct electrical impulses in the body, and therefore are essential in nerve, muscle, and heart function.

elixirs: Pronounced ih-LIK-suhrs; medicines made of drugs in a sweetened alcohol solution.

emaciated: Pronounced ee-MASE-ee-ate-ed; very thin and sickly looking.

endocrine system: The bodily system made of glands that secrete hormones into the bloodstream to control certain bodily functions.

endogenous: Pronounced en-DAH-juh-nuss; produced within the body.

endorphins: A group of naturally occurring substances in the body that relieve pain and promote a sense of well-being.

enkephalins: Pronounced en-KEFF-uh-linz; naturally occurring brain chemicals that produce drowsiness and dull pain.

enzymes: Substances that speed up chemical reactions in the body.

ephedrine: Pronounced ih-FEH-drinn; a chemical substance that eases breathing problems.

epilepsy: A disorder involving the misfiring of electrical impulses in the brain, sometimes resulting in seizures and loss of consciousness.

epinephrine: Pronounced epp-ih-NEFF-run; a hormone that increases heart rate and breathing; also called adrenaline.

ergot: Pronounced URH-got; a fungus that grows on grains, particularly rye, and contains lysergic acid, a chemical used to make LSD.

esophagus: The muscular tube connecting the mouth to the stomach.

essential amino acid: An amino acid that is only found in food; amino acids make up proteins.

estrogen: A hormone responsible for female reproductive traits.

ethanol: The colorless flammable liquid in alcoholic drinks; ethanol is the substance that gets people drunk.

ether: A flammable liquid used as an anesthetic.

euphoria: Pronounced yu-FOR-ee-yuh; a state of extreme happiness and enhanced well-being; the opposite of dysphoria.

expectorant: A cough remedy used to bring up mucus from the throat or bronchial tubes; expectorants cause users to spit up thick secretions from their clogged breathing passages.

F

fetal alcohol effects (FAE): The presence of some—but not all—of the symptoms of fetal alcohol syndrome (FAS).

fetal alcohol syndrome (FAS): A pattern of birth defects, learning deficits, and behavioral problems affecting the children of mothers who drank heavily while pregnant.

fix: A slang term referring to a dose of a drug that the user highly craves or desires.

forensics: The scientific analysis of physical evidence.

freebase: Term referring to the three highly addictive forms of cocaine that can be smoked: 1) coca paste, which is made from processed coca leaves, 2) freebase, which is made with powder cocaine, ammonia, and ether, and 3) crack, which is made with powder cocaine and sodium bicarbonate.

fry sticks: Marijuana cigarettes laced with formaldehyde, a chemical used to keep dead tissues from decaying.

G

general anesthetic: Anesthetics that cause a loss of sensation in the entire body, rather than just a specific body part, and bring on a loss of consciousness.

glaucoma: An eye disease that causes increased pressure within the eyeball and can lead to blindness.

glycerin: A syrupy form of alcohol.

Golden Triangle: The highlands of Southeast Asia, including parts of Burma, Laos, Vietnam, and Thailand, where opium poppies are grown illegally.

gynecomastia: Pronounced GY-nuh-koh-MASS-tee-uh; the formation of female-type breasts on a male body.

H

hallucinations: Visions or other perceptions of things that are not really present.

hallucinogen: A substance that brings on hallucinations, which alter the user's perception of reality.

hangover: An uncomfortable set of physical symptoms caused by drinking too much alcohol; symptoms include headache, upset stomach, and trembling feelings and are caused by an expansion of blood vessels in the brain.

hashish: Concentrated, solidified cannabis resin.

heat exhaustion: A condition that results from physical exertion in extreme heat; symptoms range from clammy and cool skin, tiredness, nausea, weakness, confusion, and vision problems to a possible loss of consciousness.

heat stroke: A condition resulting from longtime exposure to high temperatures; symptoms include an inability to sweat, a very high body temperature, and, eventually, passing out.

hemp: Cannabis plant matter used to make fibers.

hepatitis: A group of viruses that infect the liver and cause damage to that organ.

herniated disk: A rupture of a spinal disk that puts painful pressure on nerves in the spinal column.

high: Drug-induced feelings ranging from excitement and joy to extreme grogginess.

hippocampus: A part of the brain that is involved in learning and memory.

histamines: Pronounced HISS-tuh-meenz: chemicals released by the body during an allergic reaction; they cause: 1) an increase in gastric secretions, 2) the dilation, or opening up of capillaries, 3) constriction of the muscles around the airway, and 4) a decrease in blood pressure.

hormone: (from the Greek word *hormo,* meaning "to set in motion") a chemical messenger that is formed in the body and transported by the blood to a certain target area, where it affects the activity of cells.

hospice: A special clinic for dying patients where emphasis is placed on comfort and emotional support.

huffing: Inhaling through the mouth, often from an inhalant-soaked cloth.

hydrocarbon: A compound containing only two elements: carbon and hydrogen; hydrocarbons are found in petroleum and natural gas.

hydrochloride: A chemical compound composed of the elements hydrogen and chlorine, often in the form of a crystallized salt.

hyperkalemia: A dangerous build-up of excess potassium in the body.

hypertension: Long-term elevation of blood pressure.

hyperthermia: A dangerous rise in body temperature.

hypogonadism: Pronounced high-poh-GO-nad-izm; a lack of activity in the male testicles, which can be caused by low testosterone levels.

hypokalemia: A loss of potassium in the body.

hyponatremia: Pronounced HY-poh-nuh-TREE-mee-uh; a potentially fatal condition brought on by drinking too much water; can cause swelling of the brain or sodium imbalance in the blood and kidneys.

hypothalamus: A region of the brain that secretes hormones.

hypoxia: A dangerous condition brought on by an inadequate amount of oxygen circulating throughout the body.

I

illicit: Unlawful.

impulsive behavior: (sometimes called impulsivity) Acting quickly, often without thinking about the consequences of one's actions.

incontinence: The loss of bladder and/or bowel control.

infertility: The inability to have children.

inflammation: A physical reaction to injury, infection, or exposure to an allergen characterized by redness, pain or swelling.

ingest: To take in for digestion.

inhalant: A chemical that gives off fumes or vapors that are sniffed, or breathed in.

inhibitions: Inner thoughts that keep people from engaging in certain activities.

insomnia: Difficulty falling asleep or an inability to sleep.

intermediaries: Chemical compounds that are intended for use in the manufacture of more complex substances.

intoxicating: Causing drunkenness, but not necessarily from alcohol; the loss of physical or mental control due to the use of any drug is termed "intoxication."

intramuscular: Injected into a muscle.

intravenous: Injected into a vein.

intubation: Putting a plastic tube into the lungs through the nose and throat, thus opening the airway of a person unable to breathe independently.

K

kidney: The body's urine-producing organ.

L

laxatives: Drugs that help produce bowel movements.

levomethorphan: A synthetic substance that mimics the behavior of opiates such as heroin, morphine, or codeine; levomethorphan is the parent drug of dextromethorphan.

lipase: A substance that speeds up the breakdown of fats in the body.

local anesthetic: A painkiller applied directly to the skin or mucus membranes.

loop of Henle: The U-shaped part of the nephron (tiny filtering unit of the kidney) where reabsorption processes take place.

M

mania: A mental disorder characterized by intense anxiety, aggression, and delusions.

menopause: A hormonal process associated with aging in females that results in an inability to become pregnant; also known as the "change of life."

menstrual cycle: Commonly referred to as a woman's "period"; the monthly discharge of blood and other secretions from the uterus of nonpregnant females.

metabolism: The process by which food is converted to energy that the body uses to function.

methylation: Pronounced meh-thuh-LAY-shun; the process of synthesizing or transforming codeine from morphine.

microgram: A millionth of a gram; there are 28 grams in 1 ounce.

miscarry: When a pregnancy ends abruptly because a woman is physically unable to carry the fetus (unborn baby) until it is able to survive on its own.

morphine: An addictive opiate that is used to kill pain and bring on relaxation and sleep.

mucus: A secretion released by the body to prevent germs and allergens from entering the bloodstream.

multiple sclerosis: A progressive illness that affects muscle tissue, leading to pain and inability to control body movements.

muscle dysmorphia: Pronounced muh-SUL diss-MORE-fee-uh; a mental disorder leading to a desire for larger and larger muscles.

mycologist: A person who studies mushrooms.

N

narcolepsy: A sleep disorder characterized by daytime tiredness and sudden attacks of sleep.

narcotic: A painkiller that may become habit-forming; in a broader sense, any illegally purchased drug.

nausea: Upset stomach, sometimes with vomiting.

nephrons: Tiny working units of the kidney; each kidney has more than a million nephrons.

neurological: Related to the body's nervous system.

neuron: A cell in the central nervous system that carries nerve impulses.

neurotransmitter: A substance that helps spread nerve impulses from one nerve cell to another.

nitrite: A negatively charged molecule of nitrogen and oxygen.

nitroglycerin: A heavy, oily, highly explosive liquid that—when used in very small doctor-prescribed amounts—relieves the pain of angina pectoris in heart patients.

nitrous oxide: A gas given to surgical patients to induce sleep.

norepinephrine: Pronounced nor-epp-ih-NEFF-run; a natural stimulant produced by the human body.

noxious: Physically harmful.

nurse anesthetist: (full title is certified registered nurse anesthetist, or CRNA) Nurses who receive special training in the administration of anesthesia.

O

obsessive-compulsive disorder (OCD): An anxiety disorder that causes people to dwell on unwanted thoughts, act on unusual urges, and perform repetitive rituals such as frequent hand washing.

obstetrician: A physician specializing in the birthing process.

opiate: Any drug derived from the opium poppy or synthetically produced to mimic the effects of the opium poppy; opiates tend to decrease restlessness, bring on sleep, and relieve pain.

opioid: A substance created in a laboratory to mimic the effects of naturally occurring opiates such as heroin and morphine.

opium dens: Darkly lit establishments, often in the Chinatown section of big cities, where people went to smoke opium; many dens had beds, boards, or sofas upon which people could recline while experiencing the effects of the drug.

organic: A term used to describe chemical compounds that contain carbon.

osteoporosis: A loss in bone density resulting in thinned and fragile bones.

ovulation: The release of an egg from an ovary.

P

panic attacks: Unexpected episodes of severe anxiety that can cause physical symptoms such as shortness of breath, dizziness, sweating, and shaking.

paranoia: Abnormal feelings of suspicion and fear.

parasitic infections: Infection with parasites, which are organisms that must live with, in, or on other organisms to survive.

Parkinson's disease: An incurable nervous disorder that worsens with time and occurs most often after the age of fifty; it is generally caused by a loss of dopamine-producing brain cells; symptoms include overall weakness, partial paralysis of the face, trembling hands, and a slowed, shuffling walk.

passive smoking: Inhaling smoke from someone else's burning cigarette.

pesticide: A chemical agent designed to kill insects, plants, or animals that threaten gardens, crops, or farm animals.

phenethylamine: A type of alkaloid, or nitrogen-containing molecule.

phenylketonuria: Pronounced fenn-uhl-keet-uh-NORR-ee-yuh; an inherited disorder that interferes with the breakdown of a certain protein called phenylalanine (fenn-uhl-AL-uh-neen). Phenylalanine is found in milk, eggs, and other foods. Without treatment, this protein builds up in the bloodstream and causes brain damage.

phlegm: Pronounced FLEM; thick, germ-filled mucus secreted by the respiratory system.

phobias: Extreme and often unexplainable fears of certain objects or situations.

piperazines: Pronounced pih-PAIR-uh-zeens; chemical compounds made of carbon, hydrogen, and nitrogen that are used medically to destroy worms and other parasites in humans and animals.

placebo: Pronounced pluh-SEE-boh; a "sugar pill" or "dummy pill" that contains no medicine.

placebo effect: A psychological effect noted by researchers in which patients' conditions improve if they *believe* they are taking a medication that will relieve their symptoms.

pneumonia: A disease of the lung, usually brought on by infection, that causes inflammation of the lung tissue, fluid buildup inside the lungs, lowered oxygen levels in the blood, and difficulty breathing.

postmortem examinations: Examining the body after death; also called an autopsy.

postpartum depression: A form of depression that affects more than one in ten new mothers; symptoms include sadness, anxiety, irritability, tiredness, interrupted sleep, a loss of enjoyment or desire to do anything, and guilt over not being able to care properly for their babies.

post-traumatic stress disorder (PTSD): An illness that can occur after experiencing or witnessing life-threatening events, such as serious accidents, violent assaults, or terrorist attacks; symptoms include reliving the experience through nightmares and flash-backs, having problems sleeping, and feeling detached from reality.

potent: Powerful.

powder cocaine: (cocaine hydrochloride) an addictive psychoactive substance derived from coca leaves; it is either snorted into the nose or mixed with water and injected into the veins.

premenstrual syndrome: Symptoms that occur in some women about a week before the start of their monthly period and may include irritability, fatigue, depression, and abdominal bloating.

propellant: A gas that pushes out the contents of a bottle, can, or cylinder.

prostate: A male reproductive gland.

pseudoephedrine: Pronounced SUE-doh-ih-FEH-drinn; a chemical similar to ephedrine that is used to relieve nasal congestion.

psychedelic: The ability to produce hallucinations or other altered mental states.

psychoactive: Mind-altering; a psychoactive substance alters the user's mental state or changes one's behavior.

psychological addiction or psychological dependence: The belief that a person needs to take a certain substance in order to function, whether that person really does or not.

psychosis: Pronounced sy-KOH-sis; a severe mental disorder that often causes hallucinations and makes it difficult for people to distinguish what is real from what is imagined.

psychostimulant: Pronounced SY-koh-STIM-yew-lent; a stimulant that acts on the brain.

psychotherapy: The treatment of emotional problems by a trained therapist using a variety of techniques to improve a patient's outlook on life.

psychotic behavior: A dangerous loss of contact with reality, sometimes leading to violence against self or others.

psychotropic: Having an effect on the mind.

pulmonary hypertension: A life-threatening condition of continuous high blood pressure in the blood vessels that supply the lungs.

Q

quarantined: Isolated in order to prevent the spread of disease.

R

raves: Overnight dance parties that typically involve huge crowds of people, loud techno music, and illegal drug use.

receptors: Group of cells that receive stimuli.

recreational drug use: Using a drug solely to achieve a high, not to treat a medical condition.

respiratory depression: A slowed breathing rate; severe cases can cause a person to slip into a coma or even stop breathing entirely.

retina: A sensory membrane in the eye.

rhabdomyolysis: Pronounced rabb-doh-my-OLL-uh-sis; destruction of muscle tissue leading to paralysis.

rush: A feeling of euphoria or extreme happiness and well-being.

S

schizophrenia: A mental disease characterized by a withdrawal from reality and other intellectual and emotional disturbances.

screw music: An engineered music inspired by codeine use that uses existing songs but slows them down and makes certain segments repetitive.

secondhand smoke: The smoke from a cigarette user and breathed in by someone nearby.

sedation: Drowsiness or lowered levels of activity brought on by a drug.

sedative: A drug used to treat anxiety and calm people down.

sedative-hypnotic agents: Drugs that depress or slow down the body.

self-mutilation: Deliberately cutting or injuring oneself in some way.

senility: Pronounced suh-NILL-ih-tee; a condition associated with old age; symptoms include a decrease in the ability to think clearly and make decisions.

serotonin: A combination of carbon, hydrogen, nitrogen, and oxygen; it is found in the brain, blood, and stomach lining and acts as a neurotransmitter and blood vessel regulator.

shaman: Spiritual leader who cures the sick and uncovers hidden truths.

sinsemilla: Literally, "without seeds"; buds from female marijuana plants carrying the highest concentration of THC.

sodium bicarbonate: A fizzy, liquid, over-the-counter antacid taken by mouth to relieve upset stomachs.

sodium pentathol: A drug given to surgical patients to induce sleep, usually administered by injection.

solvent: A substance, usually liquid, that dissolves another substance.

speed: The street name for amphetamines.

speedball: A combination of cocaine (a stimulant) and heroin (a depressant); this combination increases the chances of serious adverse reactions and can be more toxic than either drug alone.

steroids: Drugs that mimic the actions of testosterone, a hormone found in greater quantities in males than in females, and help build muscle mass and strength.

stimulant: A substance that increases the activity of a living organism or one of its parts.

stroke: A loss of feeling, consciousness, or movement caused by the breaking or blocking of a blood vessel in the brain.

sudden sniffing death (SSD) syndrome: Death that occurs very quickly after inhaled fumes take the place of oxygen in the lungs; SSD is most often caused by butane, propane, and aerosol abuse.

suffocate: Unable to breathe; death caused by a blockage of air to the lungs.

sulfuric acid: A strong and oily compound made of hydrogen, sulfur, and oxygen; it is capable of eating away at other substances.

suppository: Medicine that is delivered through the anus.

sympathomimetics: Pronounced SIMM-path-oh-muh-MEH-ticks; medications similar to amphetamines but less powerful and with less potential for addiction.

synapses: Junctions between two nerve cells where signals pass.

synthetic: Made in a laboratory.

T

tactile: Pronounced TAK-tuhl; relating to the sense of touch.

testicular atrophy: Pronounced tess-TIK-you-lar AH-truh-fee; the shrinking of the male testicles, which sometimes results from overdoses of testosterone or anabolic-androgenic steroids.

testosterone: Pronounced tess-TOS-tuhr-own; a hormone—found in greater quantities in males than in females—that is responsible for male traits and the male sex drive.

THC: The main active ingredient in cannabis.

thebaine: pronounced thee-BAIN; one of the active alkaloids in opium, used to create synthetic painkillers.

theobromine: Pronounced THEE-uh-BROH-meen; a xanthine found in cacao (kah-KOW) beans (the source of chocolate).

theophylline: Pronounced thee-AFF-uh-lun; a xanthine found in tea leaves.

thyroid: An important gland, or group of cells, in the body that secretes chemical messengers called hormones; these hormones control metabolism, the process by which food is converted to energy that the body uses to function.

tics: Repetitive, involuntary jerky movements, eye blinking, or vocal sounds that patients cannot suppress on their own.

tinctures: Combinations of an active drug and a liquid alcohol.

tolerance: A condition in which higher and higher doses of a drug are needed to produce the original effect or high experienced.

toluene: Pronounced TOL-yuh-ween; a household and industrial solvent common in many inhaled substances, including model airplane glue, spray paint, correction fluid, paint thinners, and paint removers.

Tourette's syndrome: A severe tic disorder that causes distress and significant impairment to those affected by it.

toxic: Harmful, poisonous, or capable of causing death.

trafficking: Making, selling, or distributing a controlled drug.

trance: A sleep-like state in which important body functions slow down.

tranquilizers: Drugs such as Valium and Librium that treat anxiety; also called benzodiazepines (pronounced ben-zoh-die-AZ-uh-peens).

traumatic: Dangerous, life-threatening, and difficult to forget.

trip: An intense and usually very visual experience produced by an hallucinogenic drug.

tuberculosis: Pronounced tuh-burk-yuh-LOH-siss; a highly contagious disease of the lungs.

tryptamine compound: A crystalline compound of carbon, hydrogen, and nitrogen that is made in plant and animal tissues.

U

ulcers: The breakdown of mucus membranes, usually in the stomach.

V

vapors: Gas or fumes that can be irritating or physically harmful when inhaled.

venom: A liquid poison created by an animal for defense against predators or for killing prey.

W

withdrawal: The process of gradually cutting back on the amount of a drug being taken until it is discontinued entirely; also the accompanying physiological effects of terminating use of an addictive drug.

X

xanthine: Pronounced ZAN-thene; a compound found in animal and plant tissue.

Caffeine

Official Drug Name: Caffeine
Also Known As: None
Drug Classifications: Not scheduled; stimulant

What Kind of Drug Is It?

Caffeine is a natural stimulant. A stimulant is a substance that increases the activity of a living organism or one of its parts. Caffeine was named after the shrubby coffee plant, which is native to the eastern African nation of Ethiopia. Although coffee is an ancient drink, it was not until 1821 that German chemist Friedlieb Ferdinand Runge finally isolated caffeine from the coffee bean.

Chemically speaking, caffeine is a bitter white ALKALOID. Its chemical formula is $C_8H_{10}N_4O_2$, and it is found especially in coffee and tea. Caffeine is considered both a drug and a psychoactive substance. Such substances alter the user's mental state or change behavior.

As a mild stimulant, it is often used medicinally to treat certain kinds of headache pain. Caffeine consumption speeds up the rate at which chemical reactions occur in the body. By increasing the heart and breathing rates, it helps more oxygen get to the brain. It also acts as a diuretic (pronounced die-er-EH-tik), a substance that reduces bodily fluids by increasing the production of urine.

Overview

Caffeine is said to be consumed on a regular basis by up to 90 percent of the world's people. Humankind's fascination with caffeine dates back to prehistoric times. Andrew Weil and Winifred Rosen retold the story of coffee's accidental discovery in *From Chocolate to Morphine.* "Legend has it that coffee was first discovered long ago by Ethiopian nomads [or wanderers] who noticed that their domestic animals became frisky" after eating the red fruit of a certain shrub. "When people tried eating the seeds," continued the authors, "they got frisky, too, and eventually they learned to make a flavorful drink from the roasted seeds." By the fifteenth century, just as the Middle Ages (c. 500–c. 1500) were coming to a close, coffee had become a popular drink in the Arab world.

Thousands of years earlier, the Chinese were already steeping and drinking tea as a beverage believed to lengthen life.

alkaloid: a nitrogen-containing substance found in plants

135

A plantation worker in Indonesia looks for mature coffee beans.
© Dean Conger/Corbis.

A Chinese myth about the discovery of tea dates back more than 4,000 years. According to the tale, a Chinese emperor brewed the first cup of tea after a mysterious leaf fell into the water his servant had boiled for him. The leaf, so the story goes, was from a wild tea tree.

The Road from Picking to Profits

Centuries of war, land-grabbing, oceanic explorations, and trading led to the arrival of coffee and tea in Europe by the 1500s. Coffee use spread throughout the continent and then to America. In the eighteenth century, coffee plantations were actively producing the bean in Indonesia and the West Indies.

Since then, caffeine has been credited with transforming the United States and countries in Europe from agricultural nations to industrial nations. This change has made "the modern world

The Boston Tea Party of 1773 shows the importance that American colonists placed on tea. Upset about British taxes on tea, colonists disguised themselves as Mohawk Indians and boarded several British East India Company ships. They dumped 342 crates of tea into Boston Harbor in protest of the taxes. © Bettmann/Corbis.

possible," wrote T. R. Reid in *National Geographic* in 2005. "Boiling water to make coffee or tea helped decrease the incidence of disease among workers in crowded cities. And the caffeine in their systems kept them from falling asleep over the machinery."

Coffee farming in the South American nation of Colombia is done the old-fashioned way, noted Ruth Morris in *Life* in 2005. The process "still relies on strained back muscles, wooden tools, and traditional methods" such as mule power "that haven't changed much since coffee was first produced here in the early 1800s." After observing coffee farmers firsthand, Morris explained: "It's a long way from these Colombian hills to 'Skim latte, no foam, please.'"

Crazy for Coffee

How much do you know about coffee? Ruth Morris' article "America's Bottomless Cup" in *Life* magazine and the Web site www.coffeekids.org offer many interesting facts about growing, producing, and drinking coffee. For example, did you know that:

- It takes 4,000 coffee beans to produce one pound of coffee; that is more beans than the average coffee tree yields in a year.
- Americans consume 3 billion pounds of coffee each year.
- Worldwide coffee consumption is estimated at 11 billion pounds per year.
- The average coffee farm in the poverty-stricken nation of Colombia makes about $1,900 each year.
- The female Colombian farm workers who pick out flawed coffee beans—by hand—from enormous troughs of beans make only $5 per day.
- In the coffee-growing regions of Mexico, Guatemala, Nicaragua, and Costa Rica, most coffee farmers earn just a few pennies per pound for their harvest.

xanthine: pronounced ZAN-thene; a compound found in animal and plant tissue

theophylline: pronounced thee-AFF-uh-lun; a xanthine found in tea leaves

theobromine: pronounced THEE-uh-BROH-meen; a xanthine found in cacao (kah-KOW) beans (the source of chocolate)

What Is It Made Of?

Caffeine, the active substance responsible for the stimulant effect of the coffee plant's berry, is a XANTHINE. Xanthines are compounds made of the elements carbon, hydrogen, nitrogen, and oxygen. Some xanthines occur in the blood, urine, and muscle tissue of animals; others are found in certain plants.

The caffeine xanthine is one of the family of stimulants present in more than sixty different species of plants. The pure chemical is a yellowish-white, bitter crystal. Other xanthines related to caffeine include THEOPHYLLINE and THEOBROMINE. The pods of cacao beans (better known in the United States as cocoa beans) are ground to make chocolate.

How Is It Taken?

The vast majority of caffeine is ingested in a beverage such as coffee, tea, or soft drinks. Beyond beverages, caffeine is also consumed in snacks such as chocolate candy bars. Pain relievers, including aspirin, acetaminophen, and ibuprofen, may contain some caffeine. The stimulant effects of the caffeine allow the pain relievers to act more quickly.

Caffeine is also found in nonprescription aids and herbal preparations for alertness and dieting. Pure caffeine in tablet form is available over-the-counter in substances such as No-Doz and Vivarin. The caffeine in these tablets has the same effect as the caffeine found in coffee or tea—it is just more concentrated. Many abused illegal drugs contain caffeine, either for added effect or as a "filler," used in powder form to cut the strength of street drugs.

CNN medical correspondent Dr. Sanjay Gupta told interviewer Daryn Kagan that people need to be more informed about the "hidden" caffeine content in the foods they eat. "Half a cup of ... coffee ice cream from Häagen-Dazs has actually more caffeine than a Coke," remarked Gupta. "Most people are surprised by that." Another example cited by Gupta involved carbonated soft drinks. Ounce for ounce, Sunkist orange soda—a beverage not often thought of as a high source of caffeine—has nearly the same caffeine content as a Coke.

This Coca-Cola ad from the nineteenth century promotes the beverage, which contained caffeine, as being able to help the tired brain and relieve exhaustion. Early Coca-Cola products were also said to contain small amounts of cocaine. © *Bettmann/Corbis.*

Many people think that dark-colored soft drinks contain caffeine and the light-colored ones do not. However, many popular root beers contain no caffeine while the light-colored Mountain Dew contains more caffeine than a regular Coke. Some manufacturers

How Much Caffeine Is in That?

Ever wonder how much caffeine is in a certain product? Various Web sites list the caffeine content of many of the most popular products containing caffeine. Among those Web sites are: American Beverage Association <http://www.ameribev.org/health/caffeinecontent.asp> and Center for Science in the Public Interest <http://cspinet.org/new/cafchart.htm>. Here are some examples of popular products and their caffeine content:

Soft Drinks

- 12 oz. A&W Root Beer: 0 mg
- 12 oz. Coca-Cola: 34 mg
- 12 oz. Diet Coke: 45 mg
- 12 oz. Mountain Dew: 55 mg
- 12 oz. Sunkist Orange: 42 mg

Energy Drinks

- 12 oz. Red Bull: 115 mg

Coffee, Tea, Hot Chocolate

- 8 oz. coffee (brewed): 80-135 mg
- 8 oz. decaffeinated coffee (brewed): 3-5 mg
- 8 oz. tea (brewed): 40-60 mg
- 8 oz. iced tea: 15-40 mg (depending on brand)
- 8 oz. hot chocolate: 5-14 mg

Candy Bars

- 1.5 oz. milk chocolate bar: 10 mg
- 1.5 oz. dark chocolate bar: 31 mg

Over-the-Counter Pills

- 1 tablet No-Doz: 100 mg
- 1 tablet Excedrin: 65 mg
- 1 tablet Midol: 32.4 mg

now offer their popular products in caffeine-free versions as well. If in doubt, check the ingredients on the can or bottle. It will note if the beverage contains caffeine or not.

MSNBC.com reported in 2004 that "in North America, 80 percent to 90 percent of adults drink caffeine regularly." Each day in the United States, the average person consumes about 280 milligrams of caffeine, which equals roughly a mug or two of coffee or three to five cans of soft drinks.

Are There Any Medical Reasons for Taking This Substance?

Many headache medications contain caffeine, which helps speed up the action of ANALGESICS. Because caffeine cuts blood flow in the brain, it should not be used by people at risk for or recovering from a STROKE. By slowing blood flow through the brain, caffeine could starve already struggling nerve cells. Rumors of caffeine's effectiveness and safety as a weight loss agent have persisted for years, but they have never been medically proven.

analgesics: pain relievers or the qualities of pain relief

stroke: a loss of feeling, consciousness, or movement caused by the breaking or blocking of a blood vessel in the brain

Breathing rates increase in response to caffeine. Theophylline has an especially strong effect on respiration, affecting the smooth muscle of the bronchial tree in the lungs. This is why theophylline is sometimes used as a treatment for ASTHMA. Doctors may recommend weak tea for their asthmatic patients with colds, as the tea will aid in clearing mucus from the respiratory tract.

Usage Trends

Ninety-five percent of all caffeine is consumed in the form of tea and coffee. In the United States and Scandinavian countries, coffee is the main source of total caffeine consumption. In the United Kingdom, tea accounts for about three-quarters of the total caffeine intake. Following water, tea is the most popular beverage in the world.

"People generally take caffeine in forms so diluted as to make it highly unlikely that excessive doses—more than 300 or 400 milligrams at a sitting—will be ingested," noted Edward M. Brecher in *The Consumers Union Report on Licit and Illicit Drugs.* "People have also developed the custom of drinking coffee and tea after a meal," he added, offering "further protection for the stomach lining."

From Beans and Leaves to Power Drinks

Both health claims and controversies have followed caffeine through the centuries. Studies warning of the harmful effects of caffeine began surfacing in the 1960s. By the early 2000s, though, most follow-ups to those studies failed to duplicate the initial findings. Around the same time, youth culture began to thrive on the excessive use of caffeine. New drinks such as Red Bull, Jolt, and Adrenaline Rush purposely contained large amounts of the stimulant.

Although moderate use of caffeine has been deemed safe by medical researchers, the "power drinks" of the twenty-first century increased the risk of possible negative effects on users. While doing

Caffeinated water hit store shelves in the 1990s. It was offered as an alternative for people who wanted the caffeine but did not want to drink coffee, tea, or soft drinks. *AP/Wide World Photos.*

asthma: pronounced AZ-muh; a lung disorder that interferes with normal breathing

Caffeine Consumption

Many people throughout the world consume caffeine every day. Caffeine is found in coffee, tea, soft drinks, chocolate, and even over-the-counter drugs, among other products. Here are more facts about this popular natural stimulant.

- Medical experts recommend that the caffeine intake for children be limited to 100 milligrams daily.
- The average daily consumption of caffeine for adults in the United States is about 280 milligrams.
- Approximately 600 milligrams of caffeine have the same stimulating effect as 20 milligrams of amphetamines (am-FETT-uh-meens). (Prescription-only stimulant drugs, amphetamines increase mental alertness, reduce appetite, and help keep users awake.)
- About 1.5 billion cups of coffee are consumed every day throughout the world.
- Most of the caffeine in soft drinks is added by the manufacturers. The kola nut, the source of some of the flavoring of cola drinks, has only a bit of caffeine, providing about 5 percent of the total amount in a standard serving.

research in London, Reid interviewed several young users of Red Bull. "I've had eight. . . . I'm flying," reported one. Another compared drinking two tins of the energy drink to "drinking a pint of SPEED."

Critics of popular beverages such as Red Bull and Adrenaline Rush suggest that the caffeine content, along with the massive doses of sugar in each can, pose a significant health risk. These drinks do provide users with an energy boost. But some researchers think they also increase the chance of dehydration among athletes and all-night dancers. The high sugar content of the drinks impairs the body's ability to replenish fluids lost through sweat.

Energy drinks are also used as mixers for alcoholic drinks. The combination of the two can cause heart damage. In addition, "people who ingest a lot of caffeine, a stimulant, along with a lot of alcohol . . . won't realize how drunk they really are," warned Elizabeth Cohen on the *CNN.com/HEALTH* Web site. This could lead people to believe they are capable of driving when they really are not.

Effects on the Body

"The reasons for the attraction" to caffeine, wrote Jennie Kim in *The Hoya*, "lie in the short-term effects . . . often referred to as a caffeine 'lift.'" Within about fifteen minutes of consumption, a caffeinated beverage will cause the drinker to feel more alert. But, according to Reid, "the instant surge is mostly placebo"—the belief that the substance will produce a desired effect in the user, even if the substance itself is not capable of producing that effect. Reid added: "[C]affeine's effects don't peak for up to an hour after it hits the bloodstream."

Whether it takes fifteen minutes or sixty minutes after consumption for a "caffeine buzz" to kick in, the stimulant effects of this substance are very real. Simple intellectual tasks are performed more readily, as are physical jobs that require endurance. However, fine motor movements may become more difficult to carry out, perhaps due to the slight hand tremors

speed: the street name for amphetamines

It takes 4,000 coffee beans to produce one pound of coffee. That is more beans than the average coffee tree yields in a year. © Renée Comet/ PictureArts/Corbis.

that become more pronounced with higher doses of caffeine. Larger doses of caffeine, especially in people who do not use it regularly, typically cause headache and nervousness.

The effects of caffeine last for about five hours after it is ingested. Taken near bedtime, caffeine will delay the time it takes for the user to fall asleep. It will also reduce the depth and quality of sleep. These effects are evident with the amount of caffeine present in a cup or two of coffee, approximately 80 to 250 milligrams. People who have consumed caffeine shortly before trying to sleep tend to move around in bed more and wake up more easily than sleepers who have not consumed caffeine prior to bedtime.

More Harmful Side Effects

After being taken by mouth, caffeine dissolves easily in body fats. It does not encounter any barrier as it spreads throughout the body, so it rapidly crosses the mucosa (the mucus membrane) of the stomach and soaks through the blood-brain barrier. Caffeine affects the brain, the digestive system, heart and breathing rates, and the kidneys. When consumed in very large amounts, it can cause users to experience an increase in muscle activity, a rise in body temperature, a decrease in appetite, and problems sleeping.

In addition to increased heartbeat and rate of respiration, stomach acid production rises, sometimes causing indigestion. Urination is also stimulated. Caffeine directly affects the kidneys, cutting their ability to reabsorb ELECTROLYTES and water. For every single cup of coffee or two to three cans of caffeinated soft drink consumed, about five milligrams of calcium, an important electrolyte, are lost in the urine.

Caffeine temporarily increases blood pressure. In healthy users, the body is able to compensate for this increase and adjust back to its normal blood pressure rate. However, people with HYPERTENSION or who are at high risk for heart attacks may have a more sensitive response to the drug and are advised to minimize their caffeine intake. Even in people without heart disease, the effects of caffeine on the heart can be considerable. Rapid or irregular heartbeats can result from ingesting the substance in very large amounts.

For migraine headache sufferers, the effect of caffeine on the blood vessels around the brain is beneficial. It constricts both the inner and outer vessels, relieving pain. Also, because caffeine-containing drinks such as coffee increase the acidity in the stomach, they speed the absorption of pain medications. Some people, however, find that caffeine irritates their stomachs and intestinal tracts. It is still unclear if the effect is from the caffeine itself, or from another as-yet-undetermined substance that could be in coffee. Large amounts of caffeine may also contribute to OSTEOPOROSIS, particularly in elderly women.

Caffeine Can Be Toxic

Toxic or poisonous effects, such as persistent insomnia and anxiety, only become evident when people drink more than eight

electrolytes: charged atoms such as sodium, potassium, chloride, calcium, and magnesium that conduct electrical impulses in the body, and therefore are essential in nerve, muscle, and heart function

hypertension: long-term elevation of blood pressure

osteoporosis: a loss in bone density resulting in thinned and fragile bones

Women and Caffeine, 1969

In 1969, Dr. Avram Goldstein and Dr. Sophia Kaizer, both of the Stanford University School of Medicine, decided to examine why so many people drink coffee. They focused their study on the coffee-drinking habits of 239 young women.

The women were asked a series of questions. A full 60 percent of them claimed that they drank their first cup of coffee in the morning "because they needed it." Heavier users reported symptoms of withdrawal when they skipped their morning coffee. These symptoms ranged from "headache" and "irritability" to an "inability to work effectively."

The next phase of the experiment produced interesting results. Some of the women agreed to brew and drink nine unmarked vials of coffee—one each morning over the course of nine days. Three of the vials contained no caffeine, three contained 150 milligrams of caffeine, and three contained 300 milligrams of caffeine. Each day, the group was asked to record their moods every half hour for two hours after drinking whatever vial they brewed that day. None of them knew who was drinking what each morning.

The Goldstein–Kaizer study is credited with proving that caffeine is indeed a mind-affecting drug. Heavy coffee drinkers reported feeling nervous, sluggish, and irritable on the mornings they drank the caffeine-free coffee. Among light coffee drinkers, jittery feelings and stomach problems plagued them on mornings when they drank the highly caffeinated coffee.

The results of the Goldstein–Kaizer study were first published in the July 8, 1969, issue of *Clinical Pharmacology and Therapeutics*. The information was adapted by Edward M. Brecher for use in *The Consumers Union Report on Licit and Illicit Drugs*, 1972.

or nine cups of coffee or tea a day. Insomnia is when someone has difficulty falling asleep or an inability to sleep. Anxiety is a feeling of being extremely overwhelmed, restless, fearful, and worried.

Convulsions and delirium can follow enormous doses. Morris noted that the amount of caffeine in forty-nine eight-ounce cups of coffee can actually be fatal to a human being if consumed by mouth in a short period of time. That works out to about 4,000 to 6,600 milligrams of caffeine in a sitting.

Dangers can occur when caffeine-containing beverages are mixed with caffeine tablets such as No-Doz or Vivarin, both of which are sold without a prescription at drugstores. These tablets have high concentrations of caffeine in them. Taking them at higher than recommended doses, especially along with coffee, tea, or other caffeinated drinks, can cause toxic results.

Babies born to women who consume *extremely large amounts* of caffeine during pregnancy have demonstrated delayed growth and problems with mental or physical development. As of 2005, doctors were advising pregnant women to keep their caffeine consumption within the bounds of a cup or two of coffee per day to ensure the good health of their babies. Pregnant women who have MISCARRIED in the past are advised to avoid caffeine totally.

Reactions with Other Drugs or Substances

Caffeine cannot sober up someone who is drunk or save someone who is overdosing on a SEDATIVE. It *can,* however, alter the rate of absorption in the digestive system. Consuming caffeine in combination with drugs such as oral contraceptives and alcohol can delay the body's ability to rid itself of the caffeine.

Treatment for Habitual Users

Legally, caffeine is not regulated as a dangerously addictive substance. Yet, WITHDRAWAL from caffeine is documented in medical literature as a recognized set of symptoms. Physical and PSYCHOLOGICAL DEPENDENCE on coffee, for instance, tends to occur at rates of five or more cups per day. Many people who regularly consume caffeine and then suddenly stop will experience headaches, irritability, muscle aches, extreme tiredness, and impaired concentration.

A major symptom of quitting caffeine abruptly is a moderate to severe headache that generally begins within eighteen hours of the last dose. The feeling has been described as a fullness in the head that turns into a throbbing pain and is worsened by physical activity. Sadness and mild nausea are also reported by a quarter of those individuals who get the withdrawal headache. Those who chronically consume 500 to 600 mg of caffeine per day are more likely to experience withdrawal if they suddenly cease their habit. *MSNBC.com* reported that 13 percent of coffee addicts "were sick enough to lose time at work" when the source of their caffeine was taken away. Withdrawal symptoms can last as long as nine days.

In "Decreasing Your Caffeine Intake," registered dietician Karen Schroeder advises users who want to cut back on their caffeine intake to do so gradually. "Decreasing over a period of time" rather than going "cold turkey" may help minimize the symptoms of withdrawal. For starters, Schroeder suggests "mixing half regular and half decaffeinated coffee" or brewing tea "for a shorter time," since "a one-minute brew contains about half of the caffeine that a three-minute brew contains."

miscarried: having lost a baby before it is born

sedative: a drug used to treat anxiety and calm people down

withdrawal: the process of gradually cutting back on the amount of a drug being taken until it is discontinued entirely; also the accompanying physiological effects of terminating use of an addictive drug

psychological dependence: the belief that a person needs to take a certain substance in order to function

Caffeine is found in chocolate. However, the amount of caffeine in candy is usually far less than what is found in a typical cup of coffee.
© C/B Productions/Corbis.

Consequences

As of 2005, there was no evidence that caffeine use alone was linked to the socially damaging behaviors that characterize drugs of abuse. Kim noted, however, that students who consume large amounts of caffeine to "enhance mental capacity" should be cautioned. Excessive caffeine consumption may actually bring on "symptoms unfavorable to studying, such as restlessness, anxiety, and heart palpitations. The student may struggle and would have better study habits without the caffeine."

The Law

There are no legal consequences for caffeine sale, use, or possession, since caffeine is not a scheduled substance. In 1997, the U.S. Food and Drug Administration (FDA) required labeling of the caffeine content of foods and drinks. Soft drink manufacturers are allowed to add a maximum of 6 milligrams of caffeine per ounce of beverage, which adds up to a limit of 72 milligrams per 12-ounce serving. Coffee and tea, containing caffeine naturally rather than as an additive, are not regulated for caffeine content.

For More Information

Books

Braun, Stephen. *Buzz: The Science and Lore of Alcohol and Caffeine.* New York: Oxford University Press, 1996.

Brecher, Edward M., and others. *The Consumers Union Report on Licit and Illicit Drugs.* Boston: Little Brown & Co., 1972.

Gahlinger, Paul M. *Illegal Drugs: A Complete Guide to Their History, Chemistry, Use, and Abuse.* Las Vegas, NV: Sagebrush Press, 2001.

Kuhn, Cynthia, Scott Swartzwelder, Wilkie Wilson, and others. *Buzzed: The Straight Facts about the Most Used and Abused Drugs from Alcohol to Ecstasy,* 2nd ed. New York: W.W. Norton, 2003.

Pendergrast, Mark. *Uncommon Grounds.* New York: Basic Books, 1999.

Weil, Andrew, and Winifred Rosen. *From Chocolate to Morphine.* New York: Houghton Mifflin, 1993, rev. 2004.

Weinberg, Bennett Alan, and Bonnie K. Bealer. *The World of Caffeine: The Science and Culture of the World's Most Popular Drug.* New York: Routledge, 2001.

Periodicals

Kim, Jennie. "The Buzz on Caffeine." *The Hoya* (February 8, 2000).

Morris, Ruth. "America's Bottomless Cup." *Life* (January 14, 2005): pp. 4-9.

Reid, T. R. "Caffeine." *National Geographic* (January, 2005): pp. 3-33.

Sparano, Nicole. "Is the Combination of Ibuprofen Plus Caffeine Effective for the Treatment of Tension-type Headache?" *Journal of Family Practice* (January, 2001): pp. 312-319.

Web Sites

"Coffee Kids." *Coffee Kids: Grounds for Hope.* http://www.coffeekids.org/ (accessed June 30, 2005).

Cohen, Elizabeth. "Energy Drinks Pack a Punch, But Is It Too Much?" *CNN.com/HEALTH,* May 29, 2001. http://archives.cnn.com/2001/

HEALTH/diet.fitness/05/29/energy.drinks.02/ index.html (accessed June 30, 2005).

Kagan, Daryn. "Dr. Sanjay Gupta: Caffeine Hidden in Many Foods." *CNN.com/HEALTH,* June 27, 2003. http://www.cnn.com/2003/ HEALTH/diet.fitness/06/27/otsc.gupta/index.html (accessed June 30, 2005).

Schroeder, Karen. "Decreasing Your Caffeine Intake." *St. John Health.* http://www.stjohn.org/healthinfolib/ (accessed June 30, 2005).

"Tea and Caffeine." *Holy Mountain Trading Company.* http://www. holymtn.com/tea/caffeine.htm (accessed June 30, 2005).

"Too Much Caffeine." *Information for Health Professionals: Medsafe Prescriber Update Articles,* August 1999. http://www.medsafe.govt.nz/ profs/PUarticles/caffeine.htm (accessed June 30, 2005).

"Yes, You Really Do Need That Coffee." *MSNBC.com,* September 30, 2004. http://www.msnbc.msn.com/id/6140162/ (accessed June 30, 2005).

See also: Amphetamines; Ephedra; Herbal Drugs

Catha Edulis

Official Drug Name: *Catha edulis*
Also Known As: Khat (KOT); qat in Yemen, tschat in Ethiopia, miraa in Kenya; also, Abyssinian tea, African salad, Bushman's tea, chat, gat, kat, oat, qaadka, quat
Drug Classifications: Schedule I, cathinone; Schedule IV, cathine; both stimulants

stimulant: a substance that increases the activity of a living organism or one of its parts

amphetamines: pronounced am-FETT-uh-meens; stimulant drugs that increase mental alertness, reduce appetite, and help keep users awake

What Kind of Drug Is It?

Khat is a STIMULANT that comes from the fresh leaves of a shrubby bush known as *Catha edulis*. These leaves, along with the youngest of twigs on the bush, have both a chemical structure and an effect similar to AMPHETAMINES. As the leaves age and dry out, they lose their stimulating effect. The active ingredient in khat is cathinone. *Catha edulis* is most popular in eastern Africa and the Arabian Peninsula.

Overview

The *Catha edulis* (khat) plant is a leafy, flowering shrub that is often planted in dense rows to act as a fence or boundary. Khat is believed to have originated in Ethiopia, a farming country in eastern Africa. The khat plant also grows wild in the surrounding countries of Sudan, Eritrea, Djibouti, Somalia, and Kenya. Just across the Red Sea from these East African nations lies the Republic of Yemen. Yemen, which is located in the southern portion of the Arabian Peninsula, reportedly has the largest population of khat chewers worldwide. Legend has it that the plant was first transported from Africa to Arabia by missionaries who had discovered its abilities to ward off sleep during long, nighttime meditations.

A Hearty Plant

The khat plant has extremely long roots and is actually rather hard to kill. It grows best at elevations of 4,500 to 6,500 feet (1,370 to 1,980 meters). In areas with frost, the shrub grows no higher than 5 feet tall (1.5 meters). However, in areas where the rainfall is heavy, such as the highlands of Ethiopia and regions near the equator, khat trees can reach 20 feet (6 meters) in height. Khat is an extremely hearty plant. It grows very well in areas of plentiful rainfall but also grows during periods of drought when other crops fail.

Khat's flowers are small and white, and its leaves are oval in shape. When they are young, the leaves are shiny and reddish-green in color. They become yellowish and leathery as they age. The most prized parts of the plants are the young shoots, buds, and leaves near the top. Older leaves near the middle and lower sections of the plant are also used, as

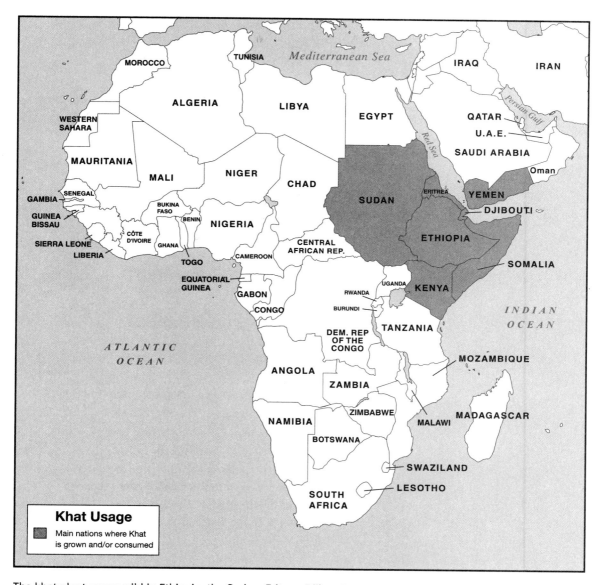

The khat plant grows wild in Ethiopia, the Sudan, Eritrea, Djibouti, Somalia, and Kenya. It is imported to Yemen, which reportedly has the largest population of khat chewers in the world. *The Gale Group.*

After a long day of work harvesting durra, a man sits and relaxes while chewing khat in Ethiopia. *Georg Gerster/Photo Researchers, Inc.*

are the stems, but these portions of the plant are considered inferior because their stimulating effects are not as great. The leaves of the *Catha edulis* are not picked until the plant is four years old.

Harvesting occurs during the dry season. Leaves gathered from plants over six years of age are most valued, possibly due to their greater ALKALOID content.

A Cultural and Traditional Influence

The ancient Egyptians considered khat to be a sacred plant—a "divine food." The Egyptians did not use khat merely for its stimulant properties but rather to unlock what they considered to be the divine aspect of their human nature.

Khat is believed to have been traded even before coffee and is used throughout Middle East countries in much the same way as coffee is used in Western culture. In addition to its use as a mild stimulant, khat use in Africa and the Arabian Peninsula is part of a daily social ritual. Its

alkaloid: a nitrogen-containing substance found in plants

intake occurs at a certain time each day and often takes place in special rooms designed strictly for that purpose.

Since ancient times, khat has also been used in religious contexts by the peoples of eastern Africa and the Arabian Peninsula. For example, khat was used, in moderation, as a stimulant to alleviate feelings of tiredness and hunger. Some members of the Islamic faith use khat during Ramadan, the ninth month of the Muslim year, which is spent fasting from sunrise to sunset.

The Economic Side

Khat growing in Ethiopia rose considerably in 2002 and 2003. The drought-ridden land and its impoverished inhabitants make far less money farming coffee than they do drugs. Sudarsan Raghavan discussed this situation in the *San Jose Mercury News.* "Faced once again with massive food shortages," some Ethiopian farmers "are uprooting their coffee trees and replacing them with khat."

Raghavan described khat as "a leafy cash crop that is chewed legally by millions of people in the Horn of Africa and the Middle East." Khat grows well even during droughts, and it resists pests that can devastate a coffee crop. "When chewed for a long time," added Raghavan, "khat has another powerful draw: It makes people feel less hungry." This could, in part, explain its use in a country with too little food to feed its people.

A similar situation exists in Yemen, where about 9 percent of the country's total cultivated area is devoted to the khat plant. Yemen also grows coffee, grapes, and maize. However, the amount of money the country makes on khat "is ten times more than those crops," explained a *Gulf News* reporter in 2002.

What Is It Made Of?

Although khat contains a number of chemicals, vitamins, and minerals, its most active ingredient is cathinone. Cathinone is an alkaloid with a chemical structure similar to amphetamines. (An entry on amphetamines is also available in this

Chewing Khat: A Yemeni Tradition

In Yemen, khat-chewing is a way of life. Traditionally, the plant's bitter leaf was chewed primarily in social situations by older men in East Africa and Yemen.

The production and consumption of khat still play key roles in Yemeni culture. In Yemen, khat has influenced everything from poetry and music to family relations and celebrations to when restaurants open and close. Workdays typically end around 2:00 or 3:00 PM, at which time groups of ten to several dozen people convene in a home to talk and chew. (Men and women hold their khat sessions separately.)

In almost every Yemeni home there is a *mafraj,* the most pleasant room in the house. It is in this room that khat sessions are held. No food is served with khat. Only water is available to help wash the leaves' juices into one's system. Between 3.5 and 7 ounces (100 and 200 grams) of leaves are chewed over three or four hours. Tea with milk is often served at the end of a khat session.

Khat vendors in Djibouti, Africa, line up along a train stopped at a station in hope of selling their product to passengers. © *Francoise de Mulder/Corbis.*

encyclopedia.) According to the *www.streetdrugs.org* Web site, "leaves less than forty-eight hours old are preferred" among khat users "to ensure a maximum potency of cathinone." As the leaves of the *Catha edulis* plant dry, cathinone turns into cathine, a far less powerful stimulant. The *www.streetdrugs.org* authors noted that "cathinone is approximately ten times more potent than cathine."

How Is It Taken?

Bitter-tasting khat leaves are typically chewed like tobacco. Users fill their mouths with fresh leaves that they chew to release the active ingredients. Khat is also sold as dried or crushed leaves, frozen leaves, or in powdered form.

Another method of ingesting khat is by chewing a paste made of khat leaves, water, and sugar or honey, sometimes flavored with herbs.

A young Kenyan man chews khat, a drug that gives people a feeling of euphoria. Scientists also are studying the plant to see if it boosts fertility in men. *AP/Wide World Photos.*

A tea made from the flowers of the khat plant—"flower of paradise" in Yemen—is considered restorative. In addition, the leaves are sometimes added to plain tea or smoked in combination with tobacco. Ethiopians often drink a juice extract made from khat leaves.

Are There Any Medical Reasons for Taking This Substance?

In the United States, khat is not approved for any medical use. Khat is mainly a RECREATIONAL DRUG used in social situations throughout Africa and the Middle East. It is sometimes used by farmers and laborers in those regions to ease fatigue and by students to improve their concentration, especially before exams. In its areas of origin, the processed leaves and roots of the khat plant are used to treat the flu, coughs, other respiratory ailments, and certain sexually transmitted diseases.

Usage Trends

For centuries, khat use was long confined to its native growing regions. This occurred because the leaves needed to reach their destination within forty-eight hours of harvesting to retain their

recreational drug: a drug used solely to achieve a high, not to treat a medical condition

President Ali Abdullah Saleh of Yemen (center) has asked citizens to follow his lead and only chew khat on weekends. Yemen reportedly has the largest population of khat chewers worldwide. *AP/Wide World Photos.*

strength. However, with improved roads and air transportation, khat use spread to many other parts of the globe.

Since the 1980s, the drug has been reported in the United States, Canada, Australia, the United Kingdom, and various countries in Western Europe. In 2002, khat was found in packages destined for U.S. cities such as Minneapolis-St.Paul, Minnesota; New York City; Kansas City, Kansas; Kansas City, Missouri; and Detroit, Michigan. Sometimes khat is smuggled into the United States by passengers on commercial jets or across the U.S.–Canadian border by car or truck.

High Use among Immigrant Populations

In the United States and the United Kingdom, khat use is most popular among immigrants from Yemen and the East African nations of Somalia and Ethiopia. In a 2004 issue of the U.K. newspaper the *Guardian,* one correspondent wrote: "In Ethiopia, Yemen, and Kenya, the plant is cultivated and several tons a week are bundled up for export; the majority ends up in Britain for use by the Somali community. Around 90 percent of Somali men in Britain are thought to chew the plant." Somalia's long history of war, political turmoil, and social unrest led many of its people to leave their homeland. Many took up residence in the United Kingdom. They report that using khat helps them deal with the chaos in their lives.

The U.S. public became more aware of khat in the 1990s, when media reports on the United Nations' mission in Somalia were broadcast regularly. According to the "Intelligence Bulletin" of the U.S. National Drug Intelligence Center (NDIC), abuse levels in the United States "are highest in cities with sizable populations" of immigrants from Somalia, Ethiopia, and Yemen. These cities "includ[e] Boston, Columbus, Dallas, Detroit, Kansas City, Los Angeles, Minneapolis, Nashville, New York, and Washington, D.C."

Khat can be purchased in the United States in various ethnic bars, restaurants, grocery stores, and smoke shops. Fresh khat leaves are most often prepared for shipment in bouquet-sized bundles, wrapped in plastic bags or banana leaves, then tied together. The bundles are sprayed with water to keep the leaves fresh and moist. Refrigeration helps to preserve them.

Effects on the Body

Like all stimulants, khat increases the users' heart rate and blood pressure, makes them feel more alert, and decreases their appetite. Chewing khat produces a "HIGH" soon after it is ingested. These effects typically lessen after one and a half to three hours, but they can last for an entire day. Users report feeling energized, content, and confident, which often leads them to talk excessively. They also claim that the drug increases their powers of concentration.

Highs and Lows

Khat has amphetamine-like effects on the body. The nerve cells activated by amphetamines are numerous in the pleasure center of the brain. When the effects of khat—or any other amphetamine-like substance—wear off, users want more.

high: drug-induced feelings ranging from excitement and joy to extreme grogginess

"Gaggers"

Around 1990, methcathinone appeared in the United States as a drug of abuse. Methcathinone, a synthetic (or laboratory-made) form of cathinone, is an even more powerful stimulant than its natural counterpart. Sometimes referred to as "bathtub speed' or "gaggers," it is manufactured in illegal labs and sold on the street in powder or capsule form. Methcathinone can be smoked, snorted, swallowed, or injected. It became illegal in the United States in 1993.

Methcathinone is an extremely dangerous drug. In addition to the numerous health risks, its use, remarked Paul M. Gahlinger in *Illegal Drugs: A Complete Guide to Their History, Chemistry, Use, and Abuse,* "causes a distinctive, very disagreeable body odor." This occurs as the products of the chemical breakdown exit the skin.

High doses or prolonged use of khat may make users appear very anxious and slightly over the edge emotionally. After the high begins to wear off, khat chewers often report feelings of drowsiness and depression. "In some cases," according to the *DrugScope* Web site, "it may make people feel more irritable and angry and possibly violent. PSYCHOLOGICAL DEPENDENCE can result from regular use so that users feel depressed and low unless they keep taking it."

Long-term khat use can also bring on extreme thirst, sleeplessness, hyperactivity, HALLUCINATIONS, and nightmares. It can even lead to paranoia, or abnormal feelings of suspicion and fear. Khat has also been known to impair intellectual abilities in those who use it.

The khat addict, according to a *Gulf News* reporter, "passes through different psychological moods" over a five-hour time span. The best of these moods occurs at the beginning of the khat-chewing cycle, and the worst come at the end. "Joy at the beginning, silence [in] the middle, depression and worry at the end ... not to mention the sleeplessness." This inability to sleep sometimes leads users to seek counteracting agents such as tranquilizers and alcohol—substances that are particularly hazardous in combination with khat.

psychological dependence: the belief that a person needs to take a certain substance in order to function

hallucinations: visions or other perceptions of things that are not really present

diabetes: a serious disorder that causes problems with the normal breakdown of sugars in the body

parasitic skin disease: infection with parasites, which are organisms that must live with, in, or on other organisms to survive

Reactions with Other Drugs or Substances

Consuming sweet beverages with khat causes blood sugar levels to rise. Therefore, the overall effect of khat on patients with DIABETES is harmful. Combining khat with some antidepressant medications may cause a potentially dangerous increase in blood pressure. In addition, several studies suggest that khat consumption is associated with reproductive problems in men and women.

Khat should not be combined with niridazole (ny-RIDD-uh-zole), a drug used in treating a PARASITIC SKIN DISEASE called schistosomiasis (SHISS-tuh-soh-MY-uh-siss), also known as snail fever. Schistosomiasis is found throughout parts of Asia, Africa, and tropical America.

Treatment for Habitual Users

There are no known physical symptoms of khat withdrawal. However, users who decide to kick the habit often need to deal with the effects of psychological dependency. Quitting khat is frequently followed by depression in the user, along with a loss of energy and an increased desire to sleep. The severity of the depression varies and may lead to agitation and sometimes to sleep disturbances.

Consequences

Khat leaves are known to contain various species of fungi. Toxic chemicals may be sprayed on the plant to ward off a wide range of insects, diseases, and weeds. When the leaves are chewed, these toxins, if present, will enter the user's bloodstream.

Overall, khat use often leads to health problems. Brian Whitaker of the *Guardian* explained that khat "may cause mouth cancers, high blood pressure and heart attacks, and may also rot the teeth." Dr. Mohamed Khodr, a native Yemeni, noted in the *New York Times* that khat chewers in his native country often indulge in cigarette smoking and tobacco chewing. He added that this "lead[s] to an epidemic of cardiovascular diseases at younger ages than in the West."

Reducing khat consumption, according to researchers, would relieve several million people, mostly men, of a costly and potentially addictive habit. "Widespread frequent use of khat impacts productivity because it tends to reduce worker motivation," noted the authors of the DEA's "Drug Intelligence Brief." Some researchers argue that khat use has increased over the years because of economic decline in Africa and Yemen.

The growing khat habit could be tied to feelings of hopelessness in the face of rising poverty and joblessness in many African and Middle Eastern countries. Khat use has also spread to a greater number of women and children, indicating that the social and economic conditions in those countries were challenging at the turn of the twenty-first century.

The Law

In 1980, the World Health Organization (WHO) deemed khat a drug of abuse. But laws governing the use and possession of khat can be difficult to understand. For instance, the latest information available from *DrugScope* as of 2005 stated that "the khat plant itself is not controlled under the [U.K.] Misuse of

A family in Somalia carries a bag of fresh khat from a cargo plane at the airport. In Somalia chewing khat after a meal is common. In the United States and Canada, it is illegal. © *Liba Taylor/Corbis.*

Drugs Act, but the active ingredients, cathinone and cathine, are Class C drugs."

Khat in any form is illegal in the United States and Canada. Under the terms of the U.S. Controlled Substances Act, cathinone is considered a Schedule I drug and cathine is considered a Schedule IV drug. Schedule I drugs (including heroin and the so-called designer drugs such as 2C-B and ecstasy) have no accepted medical value in the United States and are considered highly addictive. Penalties for distributing Schedule I drugs range from a minimum of five years to a maximum of life in prison. Schedule IV drugs have a lower potential for abuse but may lead to psychological dependence in the user. Cathinone and cathine are also controlled under the United Nations' Convention on Psychotropic Substances.

Bushman's Tea

The *U.S. Department of Justice* and the *DrugScope* Web sites, among others, provide various statistics about *Catha edulis* and khat. For example, did you know that:

- The *Catha edulis* plant is probably older than the coffee plant and the two are often planted side by side.
- The term *edulis* is derived from a Greek word meaning "edible."
- References to khat in medical literature date back to the thirteenth century.
- Khat is sometimes brewed into a tea and has acquired the street name Bushman's tea.

- As of mid-2002, about 80 percent of all men in Yemen chewed khat daily.
- Between a third and a half of the average Yemeni family's budget is spent on khat.
- The women of Yemen have taken up the habit in growing numbers, with about 40 percent of the country's female population using it almost every day.
- In the United States and the United Kingdom, khat use is most popular among immigrants from Yemen and the East African nations.

More Khat Seen in the United States

Khat leaves have been illegally bundled and shipped into the United States in increasing amounts since the 1990s. According to the statistics available from the NDIC at the beginning of 2005, "the amount of khat seized by federal law enforcement officers [in the United States] increased dramatically from 14 metric tons [about 31,000 pounds] in 1995 to 37 metric tons [about 82,000 pounds] in 2001. Moreover, in the first six months of 2002, federal officers seized nearly 30 metric tons [about 66,000 pounds] of the drug."

Khat was introduced on college campuses in the United States in the 1990s. A growing number of students began using the stimulant to stay up later at night. According to the U.S. Drug Enforcement Administration (DEA), khat has not really caught on in the United States, though, probably because the high it produces is not as intense as the high produced by amphetamines. A pill called Hagigat, made of powdered khat leaves, was on the market briefly in 2004. Hagigat originated in Israel and was used for its stimulant effects, but it was quickly banned.

More than 2,200 pounds (998 kilograms) of khat were seized at the Dublin Airport in 2003. The bundles were being sent to New York from London when they were intercepted in Ireland. Raghavan reported in late 2002 that "khat fetches as much as $200 a pound" in the United States. That translates to about $30 to $50 per bundle.

Despite these sizable seizures, law enforcement efforts directed against khat use in the United States have been minimal. The NDIC predicts that "khat likely will become increasingly available in the United States" but will not become as popular on the streets as cocaine and methamphetamines. According to the "Intelligence Bulletin," "abuse of the drug will remain most prevalent in communities with large Somali, Ethiopian, and Yemeni populations."

For More Information

Books

Gahlinger, Paul M. *Illegal Drugs: A Complete Guide to Their History, Chemistry, Use, and Abuse.* Las Vegas, NV: Sagebrush Press, 2001.

Gorman, Jack M. *The Essential Guide to Psychotropic Drugs.* New York: St. Martin's Press, 1998.

Keltner, Norman L., and David G. Folks. *Psychotropic Drugs.* Philadelphia: Mosby, 2001.

Kuhn, Cynthia, Scott Swartzwelder, Wilkie Wilson, and others. *Buzzed: The Straight Facts about the Most Used and Abused Drugs from Alcohol to Ecstasy,* 2nd ed. New York: W.W. Norton, 2003.

Periodicals

Bures, Frank. "From Civil War to Drug War." *Mother Jones* (November/December, 2001).

Jha, Alok. "Chew on This." *Guardian* (February 5, 2004).

Khodr, Mohamed. "Yemenis' Khat Habit." *New York Times* (September 22, 1999).

Lavery, Brian. "Huge Shipment of Khat Is Seized at Airport." *New York Times* (February 21, 2003).

"Pharmacological Aspects of Chewing Qat Leaves: Part I." *Yemen Times* (August 7-August 13, 2000).

"Pharmacological Aspects of Chewing Qat Leaves: Part II." *Yemen Times* (August 28-September 3, 2000).

"Qat Chewing Spreading Rapidly in Yemen." *Gulf News* (June 16, 2002).

Raghavan, Sudarsan. "Ethiopian Farmers Turn to Khat." *San Jose Mercury News* (December 29, 2002).

Whitaker, Brian. "Where the Qat Is Out of the Bag." *Guardian* (May 28, 2001).

Web Sites

"*Catha edulis.*" *PlantZAfrica.com.* http://www.plantzafrica.com/plantcd/cathedulis.htm (accessed June 30, 2005).

"Drug Intelligence Brief: Khat." *U.S. Department of Justice, Drug Enforcement Agency Intelligence Division.* http://www.usdoj.gov/dea/pubs/intel/02032/02032p.html (accessed June 30, 2005).

"Intelligence Bulletin: Khat (*Catha edulis*)." *U.S. Department of Justice, National Drug Intelligence Center (NDIC).* http://www.usdoj.gov/ndic/pubs3/3920/3920p.pdf (accessed June 30, 2005).

"Khat." *DrugScope.* http://www.drugscope.org.uk/druginfo/drugsearch/ (accessed June 30, 2005).

"Khat." *www.streetdrugs.org.* http://www.streetdrugs.org/khat.htm (accessed June 30, 2005).

See also: Amphetamines

Cocaine

Official Drug Name: Powder cocaine (cocaine hydrochloride), crack cocaine
Also Known As: Blow, C, coke, nose candy, powder, snow; crack cocaine sometimes referred to as rock
Drug Classifications: Schedule II, stimulant

What Kind of Drug Is It?

Cocaine is a natural substance that comes from the leaves of the coca (pronounced KOH-kuh) plant. This plant should not be confused with the cocoa (pronounced KOH-koh) plant, which is the source of chocolate. Cocaine acts as both a STIMULANT and an ANESTHETIC.

Overview

The coca plant grows in only one part of the world: the northwestern and central regions of South America. A huge portion of the great Andes Mountain system lies along the western coast of the continent. The warm, humid air and rich soil found among these mountain highlands are well suited for the growth of coca. More than a third of the world's supply of coca leaf is grown in Colombia, a South American coastal nation surrounded by the Pacific Ocean to the west and the Caribbean Sea to the north. The rest is grown in the nearby countries of Peru and Bolivia, which share portions of the massive mountain ranges.

Since the mid-1960s, the huge cocaine trade has been the source of violence and political unrest in Colombia. According to Paul M. Gahlinger in *Illegal Drugs: A Complete Guide to Their History, Chemistry, Use, and Abuse,* nearly 700 million pounds of coca leaf is produced in South America each year. That is enough leaves to produce well over 500 tons of cocaine. Gahlinger explained that the majority of it "is destined for the United States." The southern part of Colombia is the location of coca leaf processing laboratories. From these labs, converted cocaine powder is shipped to the United States, usually arriving through Mexico; Puerto Rico; Miami, Florida; or New York City.

A Longtime South American Tradition

South Americans in the Andes Mountains have chewed coca leaves for generations. For more than 4,000 years, the mountain people have used coca in much the same way Europeans and North Americans use coffee: for its mild stimulating effects. The leaves are not simply plucked and chewed. Rather, a bit of lime or plant ash is added to the leaves and then the mixture is chewed together. This process helps the naturally

stimulant: a substance that increases the activity of a living organism or one of its parts

anesthetic: a substance used to deaden pain

The coca plant grows in only one part of the world: the northwestern and central regions of South America. The warm, humid air and rich soil found along the Andes Mountains are well suited for the growth of coca.

The Gale Group.

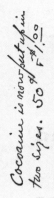

THE BEST HAIR DRESSING COCOAINE

It kills Dandruff, promotes the Growth of the Hair, cures Scald Head and all Irritation of the Scalp.

JOSEPH BURNETT & CO., BOSTON, MASS.

From the 1860s through the early 1900s, cocaine was thought to be a "cure-all." The drug was used in various products, including elixirs and hair tonics, before the dangers of the drug were known. This hair product advertisement appeared in 1886. © *Bettmann/Corbis*.

occurring cocaine ALKALOID to be released and absorbed into the user's cheek. After about a half an hour, the wad is spit out.

The leaves are also recognized for their medicinal value. When chewed or made into tea, they reportedly ease digestive troubles and reduce the symptoms of certain psychological ills. When used in whole-leaf form, cocaine does not produce a "HIGH" and is not ADDICTIVE.

Attempts to introduce coca leaves to North American and European nations were largely unsuccessful. The leaves of the coca plant tend to rot quickly. This caused considerable problems with shipping, because the stimulating effects and the medicinal value of the plant were both lost before it could reach its destination. In 1858, however, German chemist Albert Niemann managed to separate cocaine from the coca leaf. In doing so, he unleashed the world's most powerful naturally occurring stimulant. The salt form (cocaine hydrochloride), commonly known as POWDER COCAINE, travels quite well. Soon, large quantities were being consumed far beyond the Andes Mountains.

Cure-All or Curse?

From the 1860s through the early 1900s, cocaine was thought to be a "cure-all." Medical experts mistakenly believed that, like the whole-leaf form, powder cocaine was also non-addictive. For more than four decades, cocaine use was unregulated and widespread in both Europe and the United States. No prescription was necessary

alkaloid: a nitrogen-containing substance found in plants

high: drug-induced feelings ranging from excitement and joy to extreme grogginess

addictive: any substance that is habit-forming

powder cocaine: (cocaine hydrochloride) an addictive psychoactive substance derived from coca leaves; it is either snorted into the nose or mixed with water and injected into the veins

to obtain the drug, and it could easily be purchased at grocery stores, at drugstores, and through mail-order catalogs. Containers of 99.9 percent pure powder cocaine were available for sale on the open market.

Cocaine-laced beverages were extremely popular as well. One coca wine known as Vin Mariani was widely recommended by doctors for improving health. The original formula for Coca-Cola, a beverage created by John Pemberton in the 1880s, is said to have contained 60 milligrams of cocaine per serving. However, claims about the exact amount used have not been backed up by solid evidence. (Coca-Cola no longer uses any cocaine in its products.) Cocaine was seen as a remedy for many conditions, including fatigue, toothaches, hay fever, asthma, seasickness, and vomiting during pregnancy.

Although experts maintained that powder cocaine was not an addictive drug, frequent and heavy users began showing unmistakable signs of physical and PSYCHOLOGICAL DEPENDENCE. By the close of the nineteenth century, reports of nasal damage, addiction, and cocaine-related deaths had surfaced. The toxic and addictive nature of cocaine became public knowledge. By the time the U.S. government stepped in to ban cocaine in 1914, most people were already shunning it.

Usage Decreases until the 1970s

Over the next fifty or so years, cocaine use and abuse was very low. Then, in the 1970s, powder cocaine use began to skyrocket. This trend was followed in the 1980s by a surge in the use of a new form of cocaine called crack. Because CRACK COCAINE is cheaper than powder, it became more readily available to the young and the poor. Crack addiction and crime began to increase rapidly. Television coverage of the epidemic was massive. In response to public concern, the Anti-Drug Abuse Act of 1986 and 1988 was passed. This federal law includes mandatory minimum sentences for first-time offenders. The penalties are much harsher for possession of crack cocaine than powder cocaine.

Andrew Weil and Winifred Rosen noted in their book *From Chocolate to Morphine:* "Many people can't leave this drug alone if they have it, even though all they get from it after a while is the unpleasant effects characteristic of all stimulants used in excess: anxiety, insomnia, and general feelings of discomfort." Because of

---

The Real Thing

It is true that when Coca-Cola was first produced in the mid-1880s, it contained cocaine. In fact, the drink derives its name from its two main ingredients— South American coca leaves and African kola nuts. By 1905 all cocaine had been eliminated from Coca-Cola, but the term "Coca" has remained a part of the popular beverage's name for more than a century.

---

psychological dependence: the belief that a person needs to take a certain substance in order to function

crack cocaine: a highly addictive, smokable freebase cocaine made by combining powder cocaine with water and sodium bicarbonate

A police officer holds individual bags of crack cocaine seized during a drug raid in Miami, Florida. © *Steve Starr/Corbis.*

its addictive and destructive nature, a worldwide effort is under way to reduce the production and ILLICIT use of cocaine.

What Is It Made Of?

Cocaine is the most powerful naturally occurring stimulant known. It is found as an alkaloid in the leaves of the *Erythroxylon coca* trees native to the Andes Mountains. Coca leaves contain 0.5–1.8 percent cocaine, which can be refined to nearly 100 percent purity. The chemical formula for cocaine is $C_{17}H_{21}NO_4$.

Cocaine in Its Various Forms: Leaves, Paste, Powder, and Freebase

"Drugs and Chemicals of Concern: Cocaine," part of the *U.S. Department of Justice, Drug Enforcement Administration (DEA), Diversion Control Program* Web site, states that "all mucous membranes readily absorb cocaine." That is why it can be taken in so many different forms. Cocaine is ingested in its mildest form by chewing coca leaves. In addition to cocaine, the leaves contain protein, minerals, vitamins, and more than a dozen alkaloids. Instead of

illicit: unlawful

experiencing a RUSH or a high, chewers first notice numbness of the mouth followed by increased alertness and a general sense of well-being. This form of cocaine use is completely legal and socially acceptable in the mountain regions of South America. Chewing coca leaves is part of the people's religious tradition as well. The leaves can also be made into tea. Coca leaves are not smoked because the temperature needed to burn them destroys the cocaine alkaloid before it can be inhaled.

COCA PASTE is a psychoactive drug that produces a rush followed by a high in those who smoke it. (Psychoactive drugs alter the user's mental state or change behavior.) To make the paste, lime water, kerosene (a type of fuel), and sulfuric acid are added to coca leaves. After the bulky leaf matter is removed, an unpleasant-smelling residue remains. This residue, called coca paste, is usually added to tobacco or marijuana cigarettes and smoked.

With additional processing, coca paste can be converted into powder cocaine (cocaine hydrochloride), which can be more than a hundred times more powerful than coca leaves. This powder is diluted with fillers before it is sold on the street in the United States. Common fillers include cheaper drugs such as AMPHETAMINES or sugars such as lactose. Average street powder cocaine is about 60 percent pure.

The most common way to use powder is to snort it into the nose, but it can also be dissolved in water and injected into the veins. Powder cocaine cannot be smoked, but it can be turned into another substance called FREEBASE, which is smokable. Powder cocaine is addictive regardless of the way it is taken.

There are three freebase forms of cocaine, and all of them are highly addictive. The first, coca paste, has already been mentioned. It is made directly from coca leaves and is usually mixed with tobacco or marijuana before being smoked. The second form, simply called freebase, was developed in the mid-1970s. In this process, powder cocaine is converted into freebase by using water, ammonia, and a liquid anesthetic called ether.

Freebasing is a dangerous process because the chemicals are highly explosive and may ignite. Comedian Richard Pryor was badly burned while freebasing. The third and by far the most common form of freebase is crack. Crack forms when cocaine, water, and SODIUM BICARBONATE are combined.

Crack Cocaine: The Drug of the Eighties

Crack is a form of freebase cocaine made from powder cocaine combined with water and sodium bicarbonate. After the resulting

rush: a feeling of euphoria or extreme happiness and well-being

coca paste: an impure freebase made from coca leaves and used mainly in South America; coca paste is smoked and is highly addictive

amphetamines: pronounced am-FETT-uh-meens; stimulant drugs that increase mental alertness, reduce appetite, and help keep users awake

freebase: term referring to the three highly addictive forms of cocaine that can be smoked: 1) coca paste, which is made from processed coca leaves, 2) freebase, which is made with powder cocaine, ammonia, and ether, and 3) crack, which is made with powder cocaine and sodium bicarbonate

sodium bicarbonate: a fizzy, liquid, over-the-counter antacid taken by mouth to relieve upset stomachs

A U.S.-trained "Jungle Commando," a member of the National Police, takes part in an anti-drug operation on a coca plantation in Colombia in 2000. The soldier is shown here among the coca plants. © *Reuters/Corbis*.

mixture is allowed to dry, it is cut into "rocks" weighing between one-tenth and one-half a gram. These rocks resemble human teeth in size, shape, and color. Ten grams of powder cocaine will convert to 8.9 grams of nearly pure crack.

A rock of crack is smoked in a glass pipe. As the crack heats up, the vapors are released and inhaled through the pipe. Sodium bicarbonate is the ingredient that gave crack its name, since it makes a crackling sound when lit. Because crack is inexpensive and delivers large amounts of cocaine to the lungs, it became the most popular form of cocaine shortly after its creation in the 1980s. Although all forms of cocaine are addictive, crack is known as the most highly addictive.

How Is It Taken?

The speed at which cocaine reaches the brain depends on how it is taken. The faster and more intense the high produced in the user, the greater the risk of addiction. Drug researchers have determined patterns in cocaine use. Cocaine abusers are more likely to take the drug at night rather than earlier in the day. They also tend to use up whatever supply they have in one sitting, snorting or injecting the drug over several hours until all of it is gone.

Cocaine is taken in one of four ways. The leaves of the coca plant, combined with lime or plant ash, are chewed, releasing small amounts of cocaine alkaloid in the process. Some of the cocaine is absorbed by the mucous membranes of the mouth and the intestines absorb some of the juice as it is swallowed. The small amount of cocaine entering the bloodstream numbs the mouth, decreases the feeling of hunger, and has a stimulant effect. Rather than feeling a high, users report feelings of well-being that can last one to two hours.

Snorted, Injected, or Smoked—They Are All Addicting

Powder cocaine is snorted through the nose in 20 to 30 milligram doses called "lines." Lines of powder cocaine, about the width of a straw, are placed on a smooth surface and inhaled through one

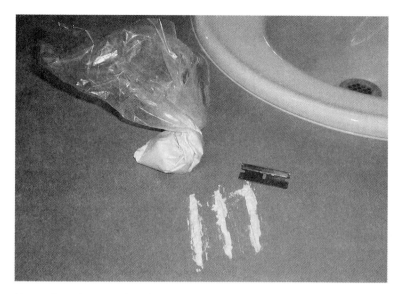

Lines of cocaine are placed on a smooth surface so they can be inhaled through one nostril at a time. In less than a minute, the cocaine travels through the network of blood vessels in the nasal cavity and reaches the brain. *Photo by Lezlie Light.*

nostril at a time. In less than a minute, the cocaine travels through the network of blood vessels in the nasal cavity and reaches the brain. The high obtained from snorting powder cocaine is the least intense of all methods of ingestion. The drug causes the blood vessels in the nose to constrict, or tighten up. Thus, the high that is produced is milder, but longer lasting than the high achieved by the remaining two ingestion methods: injecting and smoking.

Some users take powder cocaine, dissolve it in water, and inject the solution directly into their bloodstream through veins. The INTRAVENOUS, OR IV, METHOD of taking cocaine is considered the most dangerous method because it involves the use of needles. In a matter of seconds, the injected cocaine reaches the brain, resulting in an almost immediate rush. IV cocaine use is highly addictive because the rush generally lasts only a few minutes, and the remaining high drops off quickly. To maintain the high, users inject another dose after about fifteen minutes.

Cocaine is also smoked. Users change the cocaine powder into paste or rock form in order to smoke it. If inhaled deeply into the lungs, cocaine vapors will enter the bloodstream in just three seconds. The immediate brain rush occurs slightly faster than the

intravenous, or IV, method: injection of a liquid form of a drug directly into the bloodstream

Did You Know?

How much do you know about cocaine? Did you know that:

- In 2003, an estimated 2.3 million Americans were current cocaine users. That is nearly 1 percent of the U.S. population. One out of every four of those 2.3 million users was considered "hooked" or dependent on cocaine.
- Research reveals that the coca plant produces cocaine to kill insects that prey on it.
- Cocaine is the second most commonly used illicit drug in the United States, according to Heather Lehr Wagner's 2003 book *Cocaine*. About 10 percent of Americans over the age of 12 have tried cocaine at least once in their lifetimes. About 2 percent have tried crack. And nearly 1 percent of all Americans are currently using cocaine.

injection method and is achieved without the use of needles. Smoking cocaine is highly addictive because it creates the fastest and most intense rush and subsequent high.

Are There Any Medical Reasons for Taking This Substance?

The age-old tradition of chewing coca leaves continues to be part of the daily culture of South American Indians. This practice has often been compared to the American coffee break. Coca leaves are chewed to increase energy and reduce feelings of nausea in users.

After 1860, cocaine was being processed into powder and shipped to the United States and Europe. When mixed with water and taken by mouth in its liquid form, it was considered a common nonprescription remedy for hay fever, children's toothaches, asthma, and nausea. Snorting and injecting cocaine were somewhat less popular methods of ingestion through the early 1900s.

Only Acceptable Use Is as an Anesthetic

As more and more people used cocaine, it became increasingly obvious that the drug was harmful. Users were getting addicted. In 1914, the Harrison Narcotic Act banned the use of cocaine in the United States, except when used by a physician as a LOCAL ANESTHETIC.

Cocaine was the first local, or topically applied, anesthetic ever used. In 1884, physician Carl Koller (1857–1944) started using the drug as a topical anesthetic for eye surgery. Soon it was being used by dentists and veterinarians to deaden pain at the site of surgical incisions. But it was William S. Halsted, the father of modern surgery, who found that cocaine injected under the skin (rather than just rubbed on top of the skin) made an even more effective local anesthetic for surgery. When used in this way, cocaine numbs the site of application almost immediately and lessens bleeding.

Typically, a 1–4 percent cocaine solution is used for surgical purposes. This highly diluted solution does not have a psychoactive or changing effect on the brain. While cocaine is still used for ear,

local anesthetic: a painkiller applied directly to the skin or mucus membranes

nose, and throat surgery, another drug called lidocaine has replaced it as the most widely used local anesthetic of modern times.

Usage Trends

When cocaine became popular in the late 1870s, it was thought to be a non-addictive "cure-all." The drug was routinely found in family medicine cabinets, and its use was completely legal. Cocaine use was accepted among factory workers to boost energy and ensure peak efficiency. But by the 1890s, cocaine had become an increasingly abused recreational drug, taken purely for the high it produced in users. During this time of widespread use, medical journals began to report on the toxic and addictive properties of cocaine.

The Era of Prohibition

Public support turned against cocaine around the same time that efforts were being made to ban alcohol in the United States. From 1920 to 1933, a nationwide ban existed on the manufacture and sale of all alcoholic beverages. This was known as the era of PROHIBITION. At that time, alcohol was viewed as a destructive force in society. Crime, poverty, gambling, prostitution, and declining family values were blamed on excessive alcohol use. Even before this great push for Prohibition, however, the Harrison Act of 1914 was passed. This act classified cocaine as a NARCOTIC and prohibited its use in the United States except as a local anesthetic. Tough drug laws were passed between the 1930s and the 1960s, and cocaine use dropped dramatically.

It was not until the 1970s that cocaine use began to rise once more. The drug became part of the disco scene, an era well known for its glittery nightlife, brightly lit dance clubs, outrageous outfits, and distinctive music. Cocaine gave clubbers the energy to dance the night away. Powder cocaine was quite expensive, though, and by the 1980s a new and cheaper form of the drug was being manufactured. It was called crack cocaine, and it was inexpensive enough to appeal to middle- and lower-income buyers. Crack can be smoked, it delivers a more intense high than powder cocaine, and it costs about one-tenth the price. Drug dealers had opened up a whole new market, and hundreds of thousands of new users became hooked on crack.

Cocaine use peaked in 1985 when the number of Americans who had ever used cocaine soared to 25 million. In response to the increase in cocaine-related hospital emergency visits, crack gained

Prohibition: a ban on the manufacture and sale of alcoholic beverages

narcotic: a painkiller that may become habit-forming; in a broader sense, any illegally purchased drug

Crack cocaine gained a reputation as the most destructive and addictive drug of the 1980s. © Lester Lefkowitz/Corbis.

a reputation as the most destructive and addictive drug of the 1980s. The Anti-Drug Abuse Act of 1986 and 1988 was passed, making possession of crack a far more serious offense than possession of powder cocaine.

By the time the law was passed, cocaine use was already on its way down. It declined steeply until 1992, when the trend once again reversed. According to the U.S. Department of Health and Human Services, the cocaine-using population had crept back up to about 3 million people by 1993. The gradual increase continued. By 1999, reported cocaine use hit 3.7 million or 1.7 percent of Americans.

Four years later, the 2003 National Survey on Drug Use and Health (NSDUH), conducted by the Substance Abuse and Mental Health Services Administration (SAMHSA), showed a downward trend in cocaine use among Americans. About 2.3 million persons were classified as "current cocaine users" that year, and 604,000 of those users smoked crack. Rates of use were highest among people age eighteen to twenty-five, with 2.2 percent of that age group using powder cocaine.

User Characteristics

The typical cocaine user comes from a large metropolitan area rather than a small town, but these metropolitan areas span the entire country. In other words, cocaine is abused widely throughout the big cities of the United States, with no concentration of use showing up in any specific state or section of the country.

According to "Pulse Check," a report available on the *Office of National Drug Control Policy* Web site, as of January 2004, the characteristics of powder cocaine users had not changed. The crack-using population, however, was aging considerably. Only in Cleveland, Ohio, and St. Louis, Missouri, were there reports of new use among young people. The results of the Monitoring the Future (MTF) survey, a joint effort of the University of Michigan and the National Institute on Drug Abuse (NIDA), seemed to back up these results. Annual use of powder cocaine among tenth and twelfth graders rose about one-half of 1 percent between 2003 and 2004. However, increases in crack cocaine use were reported to be much lower.

No single risk factor predicts cocaine use, but a person's willingness to take risks is often a factor in his or her decision to try it for the first time. Young people who smoke cigarettes are ten times as likely to use an illegal drug than their nonsmoking peers. In the past, students who used cocaine had to be willing to be very different from the norm. The trend of acceptance began changing in the 1990s, however. According to the 2004 MTF study, the perceived risk and disapproval of powder cocaine and crack use decreased among eighth, tenth, and twelfth graders.

Effects on the Body

When smoked or injected, cocaine quickly brings on an intense rush in the user, followed by a high. Snorting the drug does not produce the rush, and the high is slightly delayed because constricted blood vessels release the cocaine into the system at a slower rate.

Small doses of cocaine can cause users to feel self-confident, uninhibited, talkative, clever, and in control. Users have reported that they feel as if they can take on and accomplish just about any task. Their energy levels increase, and their appetites decrease. Larger doses and heavy use can cause the opposite effects. Heavy users often have difficulty expressing themselves verbally. They just cannot seem to find the right words to say what they want to say. They may also suffer memory problems, become extremely confused, and show signs of aggression, antisocial behavior, and PARANOIA.

The pleasurable feelings from cocaine use last only twenty to thirty minutes if it is snorted and only five to ten minutes if it is smoked or injected into the veins. When the high is over, the user feels tired, sluggish, and low. This cycle can trigger a dangerous

paranoia: abnormal feelings of suspicion and fear

Cocaine Bugs

Heavy users of cocaine can experience paranoia, mood disturbances, and hallucinations (visions or perceptions of things that are not really there) of all sorts. A tactile hallucination (one involving the sense of touch) called "cocaine bugs" causes users to feel imaginary bugs or even snakes crawling under their skin. Users frequently scratch themselves until they bleed—using tweezers or a knife—to try to remove the imagined "bugs" from their bodies.

tolerance: a condition in which higher and higher doses of a drug are needed to produce the original effect or high experienced

strokes: loss of feeling, consciousness, or movement caused by the breaking or blocking of blood vessels in the brain

dopamine: pronounced DOPE-uh-meen; a combination of carbon, hydrogen, nitrogen, and oxygen that acts as a neurotransmitter in the brain

neurotransmitter: a substance that helps spread nerve impulses from one nerve cell to another

pattern of repeated cocaine use as the user tries to recapture the first high. As the user "takes more of the drug," explained Elaine Landau in *Cocaine,* "he or she develops a TOLERANCE for it. The same amount of cocaine will no longer make that person feel as good as it once did. Higher cocaine doses and increasingly frequent use of the drug become necessary. Many cocaine users say that in time they [need] significant amounts of the drug just to feel normal."

Harm to the Brain

In 1999, two NIDA-funded studies confirmed that heavy cocaine use could cause long-lasting brain impairment. Because cocaine reduces blood flow to the brain, some abusers develop problems with their attention span, memory, and problem-solving skills. Even a month after their last use, heavy users still found it difficult to perform tasks involving planning and reasoning. Users can become psychologically dependent on cocaine, using the drug to take the place of real-life experiences and problem-solving strategies. People who become dependent and then quit using cocaine often experience an intense craving for the drug long after the last use.

It has been known for years that cocaine use narrows blood vessels, raises blood pressure and body temperature, and increases the user's heart rate. These changes put a user at a high risk for life-threatening events. Sudden death can result from heart failure, respiratory failure, seizures, and STROKES. In 2003, even more evidence came to light about cocaine's negative effects on the heart and circulatory system. Patrick Zickler reported in *NIDA Notes* that heavy users of cocaine also seem to "have elevated levels of . . . a blood protein that increases in concentration" among people at risk for a heart attack.

The Dopamine Connection

Drug researchers found out long ago that cocaine interferes with the regulation of the brain's DOPAMINE levels. Dopamine is a NEURO-TRANSMITTER and acts on the part of the brain responsible for filtering incoming information, making choices, judging behavior, and deciding when and how to act. Dopamine levels are associated with movement, emotional response, and the ability to experience pleasure.

U•X•L Encyclopedia of Drugs & Addictive Substances

Natural Sources of Drugs

Left: Wild ephedra is shown growing in a canyon in Utah. *See* Ephedra, Vol. 3. *(© Scott T. Smith/Corbis)*

Above right: The sap of the opium poppy is used to make a variety of prescription and illegal painkillers. See Codeine, Vol. 2; Heroin, Vol. 3; Morphine, Vol. 4; and Opium, Vol. 5. *(© Vo Trung Dung/Corbis)*

Natural Sources of Drugs

Right: Some Native Americans use the hallucinogenic peyote cactus in religious rituals. *See* Mescaline, Vol. 4. *(AP/Wide World Photos)*

Below left: Tobacco is one of the most widely abused, mind-altering drugs in the world. See Nicotine, Vol. 4. *(© Kevin Fleming/Corbis)*

Natural Sources of Drugs

Top: Marijuana is the most widely used illegal controlled substance in the world. *See* Marijuana, Vol. 4. *(AP/Wide World Photos)*

Middle: Coffee is a major source of caffeine. *See* Caffeine, Vol. 2. *(© Renée Comet/PictureArts/Corbis)*

Bottom: DMT is found in the poisonous venom of the cane toad. *See* Dimethyltryptamine (DMT), Vol. 2. *(© Wayne Lawler; Ecoscene/Corbis)*

Herbal Drugs and Dietary Supplements

Top: Wild echinacea is shown growing near Mount Adams in Washington. *See* Herbal Drugs, Vol. 3. *(© Steve Terrill/Corbis)*

Middle: St. John's Wort is used to treat depression and anxiety. *See* Antidepressants, Vol. 1, and Herbal Drugs, Vol. 3. *(© Clay Perry/Corbis)*

Bottom: The bulking supplement creatine is used by weight lifters, bodybuilders, and other athletes. *See* Creatine, Vol. 2. *(© Najlah Feanny/Corbis)*

Older Illicit Drugs

Top: When snorted, cocaine reaches the brain in less than one minute. *See* Cocaine, Vol. 2. *(Photo by Lezlie Light)*

Middle: Putting tiny amounts of LSD on blotter papers is a common way to take a dose. *See* LSD (Lysergic Acid Diethylamide), Vol. 3. *(Sinclair Stammers/Photo Researchers, Inc.)*

Bottom: Heroin is a Schedule 1 drug, meaning that it has no medical value but a high potential for abuse. *See* Heroin, Vol. 3. *(Garry Watson/Science Photo Library)*

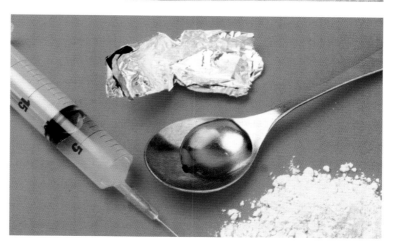

Prescription Drugs

Top row, left: Adderall®, 5 mg. *See* Adderall, Vol. 1.

Top row, middle: Darvocet-N®, 100 mg. *See* Opium, Vol. 5.

Top row, right: Demerol®, 100 mg. *See* Meperidine, Vol. 4.

2nd row, left: Dexedrine®, 5 mg. *See* Dextroamphetamine, Vol. 2.

2nd row, middle: Dilaudid®, 4 mg. *See* Hydromorphone, Vol. 3.

2nd row, right: Halcion®, 0.25 mg. *See* Benzodiazepine, Vol. 1.

3rd row, left: Lasix®, 40 mg. *See* Diuretics, Vol. 2.

3rd row, middle: MS Contin®, 15 mg. *See* Morphine, Vol. 4.

3rd row, right: Nitroglycerin, 6.5 mg. *See* Amyl Nitrite, Vol. 1.

4th row, left: OxyContin®, 40 mg. *See* Oxycodone, Vol. 5.

4th row, middle: Paxil®, 40 mg. *See* Antidepressants, Vol. 1.

4th row, right: Restoril®, 7.5 mg. *See* Benzodiazepine, Vol. 1.

5th row, left: Ritalin®, 20 mg. *See* Ritalin and Other Methylphenidates, Vol. 5.

5th row, middle: Valium®, 5 mg. *See* Tranquilizers, Vol. 5.

5th row, right: Vicodin ES®, 7.5 mg. *See* Meperidine, Vol. 4.

Bottom row, left: Wellbutrin®, 100 mg. *See* Antidepressants, Vol. 1.

Bottom row, middle: Xanax®, 2 mg. *See* Benzodiazepine, Vol. 1.

Bottom row, right: Xenical®, 120 mg. *See* Diet Pills, Vol. 2.

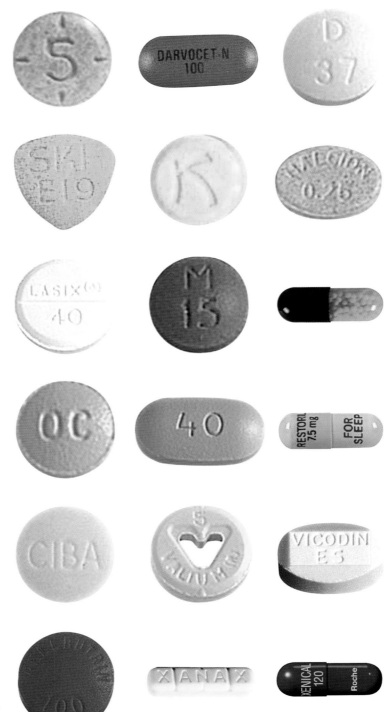

Cocaine blocks the normal flow of dopamine, allowing greater-than-normal amounts of the chemical to build up in the spaces between the neurons. Too much dopamine in the brain produces negative effects: dopamine receptors become over-stimulated, and this can cause the brain to lose the ability to produce feelings of pleasure on its own. Although a cocaine-induced high typically lasts from fifteen to thirty minutes, the low can last from one to two days. Scientists suspect that continued use of cocaine actually reduces both the amount of dopamine and the number of dopamine receptors in the brain. So, once the cocaine-induced high is over, the user can fall into a period of deep and lasting depression. "In the same way that [the] brain will interpret the presence of cocaine as one of the most pleasurable experiences," wrote Heather Lehr Wagner in *Cocaine*, "it will interpret the absence of cocaine as one of the most painful."

The Myth of Nonaddiction

As late as the 1980s, there was a myth that cocaine was not addictive. Addiction occurs when drug use is no longer a voluntary choice but an uncontrollable compulsion. Some crack users report addiction after just one use.

When a person addicted to a substance stops taking that substance, he or she experiences unpleasant WITHDRAWAL symptoms. Cocaine withdrawal symptoms include an intense and irresistible craving for the drug, along with depression, irritability, exhaustion, extreme hunger, and sometimes paranoia. It is now known that cocaine is extremely addictive. In fact, it is one of the easiest drugs to get animals to take willingly. Animal research indicates that after repeated ingestion of cocaine, nearly 100 percent of monkeys and rats tested will continue to self-administer the drug whenever they are given the chance.

The most serious effect of using cocaine is the possibility of sudden death. It can happen after the first use or anytime thereafter. Sudden death can occur with cocaine use alone, but is more common when combined with alcohol or other drugs. Other side effects include irreversible damage to the heart and liver, along with damage inflicted by strokes and seizures.

And There Is More....

The point of ingestion determines the specific side effects cocaine will cause in a user. For instance, snorting powder cocaine over time will damage the septum and ulcerate the mucous membrane of the nose. Users who snort cocaine are prone to nosebleeds.

withdrawal: the process of gradually cutting back on the amount of a drug being taken until it is discontinued entirely; also the accompanying physiological effects of terminating use of an addictive drug

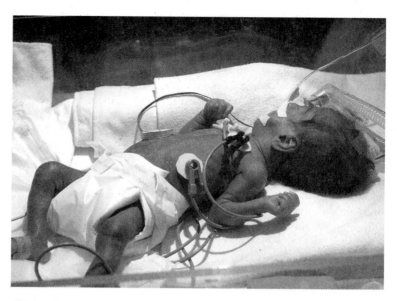

Children born to mothers who take cocaine when they are pregnant usually have lower-than-average birth weights, small heads, and the potential for more behavioral problems than other children. *John Chiasson/Getty Images.*

The bleeding may occur without warning and could cause considerable disruption if it happens in public. For instance, schools are required to evacuate and thoroughly clean areas where human blood has spilled. This precaution must be taken to decrease the risk of transmitting blood-borne viruses such as HIV (the human immunodeficiency virus), which causes AIDS (acquired immunodeficiency syndrome).

Smoking crack cocaine can cause lung trauma and bleeding. Injecting cocaine into the veins often causes inflammation and infections. It also carries a greater risk for contracting HIV/AIDS and hepatitis because users sometimes share needles. Cocaine also has a reputation for lowering users' INHIBITIONS. Users may take unusual risks that can lead to long-term consequences. These risks can range from unsafe sexual encounters to automobile crashes caused by poor judgment or aggression.

New information released by NIDA in 2004 revealed that cocaine might negatively affect a user's immune system. "Cocaine itself has a direct biological effect that may decrease an abuser's ability to fight off infections," wrote Patrick Zickler in *NIDA Notes.* This information, reported by a team of doctors at Harvard Medical School and the McLean Hospital Alcohol and Drug Abuse Research

inhibitions: inner thoughts that keep people from engaging in certain activities

DON'T LET DRUG DEALERS CHANGE
THE FACE OF YOUR NEIGHBOURHOOD
Call Crimestoppers anonymously on 0800 555 111.

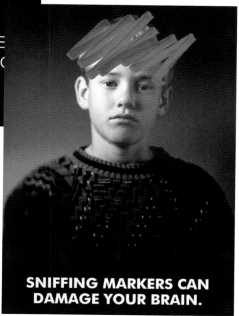

SNIFFING MARKERS CAN
DAMAGE YOUR BRAIN.

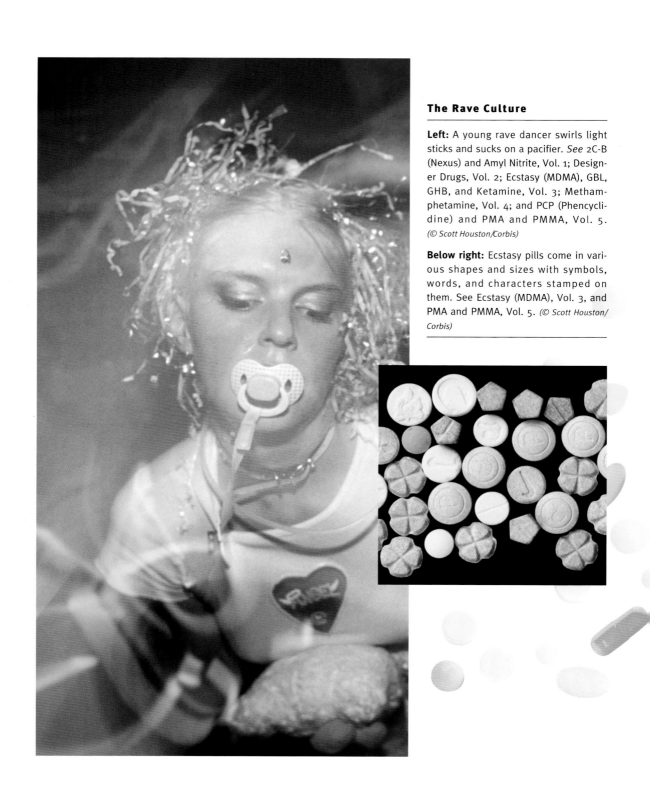

The Rave Culture

Left: A young rave dancer swirls light sticks and sucks on a pacifier. *See* 2C-B (Nexus) and Amyl Nitrite, Vol. 1; Designer Drugs, Vol. 2; Ecstasy (MDMA), GBL, GHB, and Ketamine, Vol. 3; Methamphetamine, Vol. 4; and PCP (Phencyclidine) and PMA and PMMA, Vol. 5. *(© Scott Houston/Corbis)*

Below right: Ecstasy pills come in various shapes and sizes with symbols, words, and characters stamped on them. See Ecstasy (MDMA), Vol. 3, and PMA and PMMA, Vol. 5. *(© Scott Houston/ Corbis)*

Center, could help explain why drug abusers have such a high incidence of infections.

Other research findings published in *NIDA Notes* show that cocaine has a definite negative effect on unborn babies. Children born to mothers who took cocaine when they were pregnant usually have lower-than-average birth weights, small heads, and the potential for more behavioral problems than other children. "At age two," wrote Robert Mathias, "cocaine-exposed children did significantly poorer in mental development than children" who were not exposed to cocaine.

These findings suggest that cocaine-exposed children may require extra assistance to overcome learning difficulties. Experts such as Dr. Lynn Singer of Case Western Reserve University believe that early educational programs can help these youths develop the skills they will need to succeed in school.

Reactions with Other Drugs or Substances

Cocaine is almost always used with other drugs, including alcohol, heroin, amphetamines, and marijuana. Combining drugs increases the chances of overdosing or experiencing serious side effects. The most common drug to be combined with cocaine is alcohol. Alcoholic beverages prolong the cocaine high and tend to reduce drug-induced paranoia. This combination creates a new substance, COCAETHYLENE. Cocaethylene is as powerful as cocaine, and its effects last longer. However, it can be more toxic to the heart. NIDA statistics indicate that the combination of cocaine and alcohol results in more deaths than any other illegal drug combination.

The combination of cocaine and heroin is called a "SPEEDBALL." It is especially dangerous because cocaine speeds up the respiratory system, while heroin depresses it, or slows it down. At very high doses, however, cocaine can begin to depress the respiratory system as well. In speedballing, cocaine and heroin are typically ingested at the same time, but some users ingest the drugs alternately to feel either more energetic or more relaxed. This combination can be more toxic than using either drug alone. Comedian John Belushi died from speedballing in 1982.

Amphetamines are often combined with cocaine to extend the high. Cocaine creates a rush but it is short-lived. Adding amphetamines extends the high for up to ten hours. Using these drugs together increases the chances of an overdose and increases toxic effects.

cocaethylene: a substance formed by the body when cocaine and alcohol are consumed together; it increases the chances of serious adverse reactions or sudden death from cocaine

speedball: a combination of cocaine (a stimulant) and heroin (a depressant); this combination increases the chances of serious adverse reactions and can be more toxic than either drug alone

Addicts and Addiction

Some people believe that drug addiction is a voluntary behavior—that addicts simply choose to use drugs again and again. However, with continued use over a period of weeks or months, a person can go from being a voluntary drug user to being a compulsive, out-of-control drug user. Addictive drugs can actually change the brain in ways that result in more and more drug use.

Drug use is a very hard habit to break, even for the most determined individuals. It really does not matter which drug a person is abusing. In general, many drugs of abuse have similar effects on the brain. Such effects are discussed in Alan I. Leshner's article "Exploring Myths about Drug Abuse" on the *NIDA* Web site. Among the effects are:

- changes in the chemical makeup of brain cells
- a shift in mood
- transformation in memory processes
- alteration of motor skills needed to walk and talk.

These changes greatly impact the addict's behavior. The user's biggest motivation in life becomes obtaining and using the drug. Such behavior is not the result of a weak will or a character flaw. Rather, the drug use has caused major changes in the structure and the functioning of the user's brain—changes that are beyond the user's control.

Treatment for Habitual Users

In an article for the *New York Times,* Linda Carroll reported that certain people are more likely to become addicted to cocaine than others. The reason for this seems to be some sort of inborn flaw in the brain's wiring. "The leading suspect," noted Carroll, "is a defect in the dopamine system." Studies conducted on monkeys seem to back up this theory. Five monkeys involved in a Wake Forest University medical school experiment were allowed to take cocaine whenever they wanted for a whole year. At the end of the year, the "addicted monkeys ended up with a 15 percent to 20 percent decrease in dopamine receptors," wrote Carroll. The five monkeys were reexamined nine months after the conclusion of the experiment. The brains of three of them had returned to normal, but the brains of the other two still had lower-than-normal amounts of dopamine receptors in them.

The biggest challenge to cocaine treatment and rehabilitation is preventing relapse (the return to using drugs) caused by a persistent and intense craving for cocaine. Although cocaine addiction can be treated successfully, there is no single program that is effective for

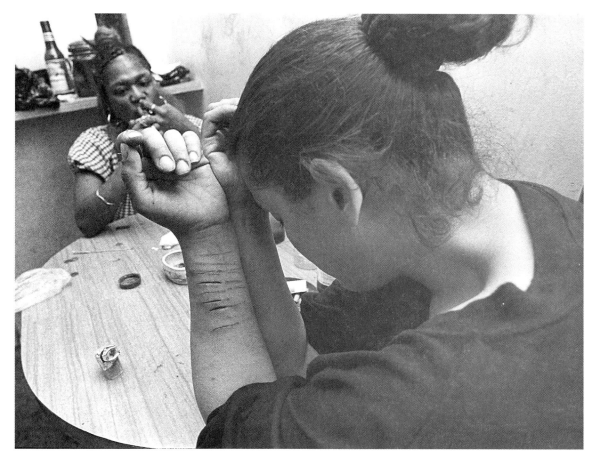

Frustrated by her failed attempts to give up crack cocaine, a young woman
intentionally cut her arm. Addiction to crack is a hard habit to break even
when the individual is determined to succeed. © *Brenda Ann Kenneally/Corbis.*

everyone. NIDA recommends a dual approach to treatment, healing
both the body and the mind. It suggests behavioral therapies, medications, rehabilitation, and social services. The idea is to treat the
whole person.

Regarding medication, NIDA research reports that medications that act on dopamine receptors might reduce the intense
craving and depression in former cocaine users. Behavioral therapies can include group and/or individual counseling, popular
twelve-step programs, and chemical dependency inpatient and
outpatient programs.

A Drug Enforcement Administration (DEA) agent stands guard next to 5,137 pounds of cocaine seized from a Panamanian vessel near Miami, Florida. *AP/Wide World Photos.*

A Simple but Promising New Treatment Approach

On January 5, 2005, the National Institutes of Health (NIH) announced that peer counseling actually helped reduce cocaine and heroin abuse. The study was conducted by doctors at Boston University Schools of Medicine and Public Health and involved 1,175 male and female drug abusers. The process took only twenty minutes and consisted of "a motivational interview with a substance abuse outreach worker who also was a recovering addict," according to the NIH press release.

Members of the study were also given referrals to drug abuse treatment programs and a list of different types of treatment methods. In addition, they received a phone call ten days later to check on their progress. These simple interventions motivated a significantly higher percentage of abusers to stay away from drugs over a six-month period.

Consequences

When cocaine use progresses to a point of dependence, it can be devastating. At this stage, drug seeking often becomes the user's first priority. Suddenly, values such as love of family and friends and commitment to work can take second place to finding, buying, and using cocaine. "Cocaine addiction almost always interferes with social and economic functioning," stated Weil and Rosen. Addicts may end up spending "phenomenal amounts of money on their habits ($15,000 a year and more)," the authors explained. "They become paranoid, isolated, and depressed, unable to stop thinking about their next dose."

Habitual users often find themselves trapped in a web of deception and criminal behavior. Users desperate for more drugs may turn to robbery or prostitution in order to finance their habit. *NIDA Notes* stated that "cocaine use in 'crack' exchanges also contribute[s] to transmission of HIV/AIDS." Conviction of an illegal drug offense can trigger minimum mandatory prison sentences. Also, students convicted of cocaine possession can be disqualified from obtaining federal college grants and loans. In addition, NIDA-funded research shows that drug abusers cost employers about twice as much in medical and workers' compensation claims than drug-free workers. As a result, more and more businesses are requiring drug screening for employees.

The Law

Under the U.S. Controlled Substance Act of 1970, cocaine is a Schedule II drug. This means that cocaine has a high potential for abuse and that abuse may lead to severe physical and psychological dependence. It also means that cocaine has accepted medical uses with severe restrictions. The only legal use of cocaine in the United States is as a local anesthetic.

The Anti-Drug Abuse Act of 1986 and 1988 established mandatory minimum drug sentencing guidelines for cocaine use and possession. Federal law carries a much harsher penalty for crack cocaine than for powder cocaine. Because more African Americans tend to use crack than powder, this law continues to result in harsher prison terms for blacks. Possession of 5 grams of crack or 500 grams of powder carries a first-offense penalty of not less than five years in prison. Despite the severity of this penalty, according to Landau, about "85 percent of those imprisoned for drug abuse" will continue to "use cocaine or other drugs after leaving prison."

In the United Kingdom, cocaine and crack are considered Class A drugs under the 1971 Misuse of Drugs Act. Possession of the drugs can result in a fine and a prison term of up to seven years. Supplying, or selling, either form of cocaine can lead to a lifetime prison sentence.

For More Information

Books

Brecher, Edward M., and others. *The Consumers Union Report on Licit and Illicit Drugs.* Boston: Little Brown & Co., 1972.

Gahlinger, Paul M. *Illegal Drugs: A Complete Guide to Their History, Chemistry, Use, and Abuse.* Las Vegas, NV: Sagebrush Press, 2001.

Landau, Elaine. *Cocaine.* New York: Franklin Watts, 2003.

Robbins, Paul R. *Crack and Cocaine Drug Dangers.* Berkeley Heights, NJ: Enslow Publishers, Inc., 1999.

Wagner, Heather Lehr. *Cocaine.* Philadelphia: Chelsea House, 2003.

Weil, Andrew, and Winifred Rosen. *From Chocolate to Morphine.* New York: Houghton Mifflin, 1993, rev. 2004.

Periodicals

Carroll, Linda. "Genetic Studies Promise a Path to Better Treatment of Addictions." *New York Times* (November 14, 2000).

Web Sites

"2003 National Survey on Drug Use and Health (NSDUH)." *U.S. Department of Health and Human Services, Substance Abuse and Mental Health Services Administration.* http://www.oas.samhsa.gov/nhsda.htm (accessed June 30, 2005).

"Brief Encounters Can Provide Motivation to Reduce or Stop Drug Abuse." *National Institutes of Health: NIH News* (press release). http://www.nih.gov/news/pr/jan2005/nida-05.htm (accessed June 30, 2005).

"Cocaine." *bbc.co.uk, A to Z of Drugs.* http://www.bbc.co.uk/crime/drugs/cocaine.shtml (accessed June 30, 2005).

"Cocaine." *U.S. Department of Justice, Drug Enforcement Administration.* http://www.usdoj.gov/dea/concern/cocaine.html (accessed June 30, 2005).

"Comparing Methamphetamine and Cocaine." *National Institute on Drug Abuse, NIDA Notes.* http://www.nida.nih.gov/NIDA_notes/NNVol13N1/Comparing.html (accessed June 30, 2005).

"Crack." *bbc.co.uk, A to Z of Drugs.* http://www.bbc.co.uk/crime/drugs/crack.shtml (accessed June 30, 2005).

"Crack and Cocaine." *National Institute on Drug Abuse, NIDA Info Facts.* http://www.nida.nih.gov/Infofax/cocaine.html (accessed June 30, 2005).

"Drugs and Chemicals of Concern: Cocaine." *U.S. Department of Justice, Drug Enforcement Administration, Diversion Control Program.* http://www.deadiversion.usdoj.gov/drugs_concern/cocaine/cocaine.htm (accessed June 30, 2005).

"Four Tonnes of Cocaine Seized in Joint Operation with UK, Spain, and Portugal." *Tackling Drugs, Changing Lives: Drugs.gov.uk,* January 7, 2005. http://www.drugs.gov.uk/News/1117623830 (accessed June 30, 2005).

Leshner, Alan I. "Exploring Myths about Drug Abuse." *National Institute on Drug Abuse: The Science of Drug Abuse and Addiction.* http://www.drugabuse.gov/published_articles/myths.html (accessed June 30, 2005).

Mathias, Robert. "Study Finds Significant Mental Deficits in Toddlers Exposed to Cocaine before Birth." *National Institute on Drug Abuse, NIDA Notes.* http://www.nida.nih.gov/NIDA_notes/NNVol17N5/Study.html (accessed June 30, 2005).

Monitoring the Future. http://www.monitoringthefuture.org/ and http://www.nida.nih.gov/Newsroom/04/2004MTFDrug.pdf (both accessed June 30, 2005).

National Institute on Drug Abuse. http://www.nida.nih.gov/ and http://www.drugabuse.gov (both accessed June 30, 2005).

"Pulse Check: Drug Markets and Chronic Users in 25 of America's Largest Cities." *Executive Office of the President, Office of National Drug Control Policy.* http://www.whitehousedrugpolicy.gov/publications/drugfact/pulsechk/january04/january2004.pdf (accessed June 30, 2005).

"Stimulants." *NIDA for Teens: The Science behind Drug Abuse, Mind over Matter.* http://www.teens.drugabuse.gov/mom/mom_stim1.asp (accessed June 30, 2005).

Swan, Neil. "Brain Scans Open Window to View Cocaine's Effects on the Brain." *National Institute on Drug Abuse, NIDA Notes.* http://www.nida.nih.gov/NIDA_notes/NNVol13N2/Brain.html (accessed June 30, 2005).

Zickler, Patrick. "Cocaine May Compromise Immune System, Increase Risk of Infection." *National Institute on Drug Abuse, NIDA Notes.* http://www.nida.nih.gov/NIDA_notes/NNVOL18N6/Cocaine.html (accessed June 30, 2005).

Zickler, Patrick. "Methamphetamine, Cocaine Abusers Have Different Patterns of Drug Use, Suffer Different Cognitive Impairments." *National Institute on Drug Abuse, NIDA Notes.* http://www.nida.nih.gov/NIDA_notes/NNVOL16N5/Meth_Coc.html (accessed June 30, 2005).

See also: Alcohol; Amphetamines; Heroin; Marijuana

Codeine

Official Drug Name: Codeine, codeine phosphate, codeine sulfate, methyl morphine

Also Known As: T-threes, schoolboy, coties, dors and fours; cough syrup with codeine is known as: syrup, barr, karo, lean, nods, down, drank

Drug Classifications: Schedule I, codeine methylbromide and codeine-N-oxide; Schedule II, methyl morphine; Schedule III, codeine combinations with acetaminophen, aspirin, or ibuprofen; Schedule V, prescription cough syrup preparations containing codeine

morphine: an addictive opiate that is used to kill pain and bring on relaxation and sleep

constipation: an inability to have a bowel movement

nausea: upset stomach, sometimes with vomiting

narcotic: a painkiller that may become habit-forming; in a broader sense, any illegally purchased drug

recreational use: using a drug solely to achieve a high, not to treat a medical condition

What Kind of Drug Is It?

Codeine is an opiate analgesic, meaning it is a pain reliever derived from the opium poppy plant. Its powers of pain relief—and its side effects—are many times weaker than the related opiates MORPHINE and heroin. (An entry for each of these drugs is available in this encyclopedia.)

Doctors sometimes prescribe pills containing combinations of codeine and over-the-counter (OTC) analgesics, such as Tylenol (acetaminophen) or aspirin, for pain relief after minor surgery, or for bone breaks and sprains, migraine headaches, or other pain that is expected to pass fairly quickly. The other most common use for codeine is in cough syrup. The drug acts on the part of the brain that controls coughing.

In the United States and many other countries, a prescription is necessary to obtain products containing codeine. This is because the drug is addictive, or habit-forming. It also can produce unpleasant side effects such as CONSTIPATION and NAUSEA. When codeine is abused, it is either ingested in its cough syrup form at greater-than-prescribed doses or extracted from prescription pills through chemical "cooking." In either case, taking a large dose of codeine can be fatal, because it can cause the user to stop breathing.

According to Paul M. Gahlinger in *Illegal Drugs: A Complete Guide to Their History, Chemistry, Use, and Abuse*, codeine "is by far the most commonly used NARCOTIC in the world," especially in the form of cough syrup. Codeine's qualities as a pain reliever have been recognized since the early 1800s. Chemically speaking, opiate medications such as codeine mimic the brain's own natural mechanisms for suppressing pain. Codeine actually reduces the ability of the brain's nerve cells to transmit pain signals. The reason it works better than the body's own mechanisms is because it floods the brain with chemical messages in a more powerful way than the brain's chemistry can on its own.

RECREATIONAL USE of codeine, in the absence of pain, can produce feelings of euphoria (pronounced yu-FOR-ee-yuh). Such feelings bring on a state of extreme happiness and well-being in users. However, when the effects of the drug wear off, the user is often

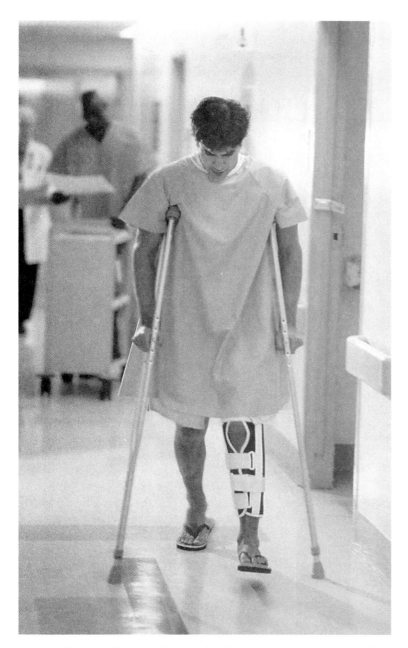

Codeine is prescribed to relieve pain after minor surgeries as well as pain resulting from broken bones, sprains, and migraine headaches.
© Steve Prezant/Corbis.

left with a sensation of depression or nervousness. This leads to a desire to take more of the drug. This is how the cycle of addiction begins. For this reason, doctors and pharmacists use caution when prescribing or dispensing medications containing codeine. Still, codeine abusers have found ways to obtain the drug illegally. In some parts of the United States, cough syrup abuse has contributed to growing numbers of emergency room visits for drug overdoses.

Overview

Humans like to experiment. They do this in art, music, medicine, technology, science, and other fields. For thousands of years, some have also experimented with using mind-altering drugs found in plants and animals. The first real evidence of opium poppy use in the historical record dates back 6,000 years to ancient Mesopotamia (the current nation of Iraq). Descriptions of poppy use for pain relief can be found in Egyptian papyrus records. Later, ancient Greek farmers learned that the most potent, or strongest, part of the poppy plant was found in the sap that oozes from the ripened seed bulbs. The word "opium" is actually derived from a Greek word meaning "sap." Historical records also reveal that ancient Romans used opium as a painkiller, a poison, and a means of suicide, varying their doses accordingly.

During the Middle Ages (c. 500–c. 1500) and the Renaissance period (spanning the fourteenth through the seventeenth centuries), physicians and ALCHEMISTS experimented with poppy sap. In 1524, Swiss scientist Paracelsus (1493–1541) created laudanum, a mixture of opium and alcohol. All by itself, laudanum is a bitter-tasting substance. When mixed with wine, better-tasting herbs, or syrups, however, it became one of the most popular cure-alls of the late 1800s and early 1900s. The use of TINCTURES and ELIXIRS containing opium became so commonplace in nineteenth-century Europe that the practice even found its way into literature. Fictional detective Sherlock Holmes, created by Sir Arthur Conan Doyle (1859–1930), even visited an OPIUM DEN to solve a crime.

Morphine, the most active ingredient in opium, was discovered in 1803 by a young German pharmacist's assistant, Friedrich Sertürner (1783–1841). The drug was far more powerful than crude opium and also far more addictive. Attempts to lessen the habit-forming aspects of morphine led to further experimentation with poppy sap. In 1832, the codeine compound was separated from the sap for the first time. Its name comes from the Greek word *kodeia*, meaning "poppy head."

alchemists: those who study or practice medieval chemical science aimed at discovering a cure for all illnesses

tinctures: combinations of an active drug and a liquid alcohol

elixirs: pronounced ih-LIK-suhrs; medicines made of drugs in a sweetened alcohol solution

opium den: darkly lit establishment, often in the Chinatown section of big cities, where people went to smoke opium; many dens had beds, boards, or sofas upon which people could recline while experiencing the effects of the drug

The name "codeine" comes from the Greek word *kodeia,* meaning "poppy head." The drug is derived from opium poppy sap. © *Vo Trung Dung/Corbis.*

At first, nineteenth-century scientists thought they had finally found what they had been seeking: a painkiller that did not produce euphoric side effects and was not addictive. However, they were wrong. When taken in large doses, codeine produces the same effects as morphine, including addiction. The only difference is that it is five to ten times weaker than morphine.

Scientists did discover some qualities of codeine that made it popular. It works as a painkiller when taken orally (by mouth). In comparison, morphine and heroin are usually injected or snorted through the nose. Codeine also was effective at suppressing coughs, and it quickly found its way into cough syrups. Like the more powerful opiates, codeine causes constipation by working on the nerves and muscles in the intestines. Therefore, it was used to treat diarrhea.

Throughout the twentieth century, knowledge about opiate analgesics increased. In 1900, codeine could be found in a variety of OTC medications for adults and children. The Harrison Narcotics Act of 1914 set new regulations on the sale of opiates, making them illegal unless prescribed to a patient by a licensed physician. Since then, drug companies have developed analgesics that contain combinations of painkillers such as aspirin and codeine, or Tylenol and codeine. A prescription for pure codeine, however, is rarely ever given.

By 2000, all OTC sales of codeine-containing products had ended in the United States. The drug is legally available in America only if prescribed by a doctor, a dentist, or a veterinarian. Nevertheless, it is still manufactured in large quantities. At the turn of the twenty-first century, total codeine production worldwide approached 300 tons.

What Is It Made Of?

Codeine is a controlled substance in the United States. This means that the U.S. Food and Drug Administration (FDA) and the Drug Enforcement Administration (DEA) supervise its manufacture and distribution. Opium is sometimes harvested by slicing the plant's seed pods and extracting the sap. In 2005, however, machines were available to slice the entire mature poppy plant into bits and grind those bits into powder. According to Gahlinger, "Each year, more than 600 tons of opium powder are legally imported into the United States for legitimate medical use."

Pure opium can be separated into three different drugs: morphine, codeine, and thebaine. Most of the codeine used in the United States is SYNTHESIZED from morphine by a process called methylation (pronounced meh-thuh-LAY-shun). Codeine is an ORGANIC, or naturally occurring, compound that contains carbon, hydrogen, nitrogen, and oxygen. Its chemical formula is $C_{18}H_{21}NO_3$. Codeine is also an ALKALOID. Curiously, while most of the prescription codeine is derived from morphine, when the drug is ingested, the human liver turns the codeine back into morphine. Therefore, the compound works on the brain in the same way morphine does.

synthesized: made in a laboratory

organic: a term used to describe chemical compounds that contain carbon

alkaloid: a nitrogen-containing substance found in plants

expectorant: a cough remedy used to bring up mucus from the throat or bronchial tubes; expectorants cause users to spit up thick secretions from their clogged breathing passages

phlegm: pronounced FLEM; thick, germ-filled mucus secreted by the respiratory system

How Is It Taken?

Prescription codeine is available in several forms. Tylenol 3, for instance, is a pill containing 300 milligrams of acetaminophen and 30 milligrams of codeine. Some oral medications containing codeine also contain low doses of caffeine to counteract the sedating effects of the codeine. Pill-form medications containing codeine are swallowed, and their pain-relieving effects can last from three to six hours.

Liquid cough syrups containing various strengths of codeine are usually combined with an EXPECTORANT agent for clearing the airways of PHLEGM. Phlegm must be spit up, or expectorated, to improve a patient's breathing. Cough remedies with codeine and expectorants are taken by the spoonful every four hours with a full glass of water.

"Tylenol by the Numbers"

People experiencing levels of pain that will not respond to over-the-counter drugs can sometimes receive prescription pain relievers containing various dosages of codeine. Tylenol-brand acetaminophen is one product that contains codeine in its prescription form. These drugs are assigned the numbers one through four to indicate their various strengths. Here's a quick rundown of "Tylenol by the Numbers":

- Tylenol with Codeine No. 1 (more commonly referred to as Tylenol 1) contains 8 milligrams of codeine and 300 milligrams of acetaminophen.
- Tylenol with Codeine No. 2 (more commonly referred to as Tylenol 2) contains 15 milligrams of codeine and 300 milligrams of acetaminophen.
- Tylenol with Codeine No. 3 (more commonly referred to as Tylenol 3) contains 30 milligrams of codeine and 300 milligrams of acetaminophen.
- Tylenol with Codeine No. 4 (more commonly referred to as Tylenol 4) contains 60 milligrams of codeine and 300 milligrams of acetaminophen.

Tylenol 3 contains codeine and is available by prescription only. *Copyright 2002 Thomson MICROMEDEX. All rights reserved.*

The brand-name product Fiorinal with Codeine contains aspirin, butalbital (a barbiturate), caffeine (a stimulant), and codeine. This prescription drug is used primarily for relief of migraine headache pain.

Are There Any Medical Reasons for Taking This Substance?

Codeine-containing medications are usually prescribed to relieve pain or control coughs. Pills containing codeine and other analgesics are typically used for mild to moderate pain that is expected to go away within days or weeks. Cough syrups containing codeine are usually prescribed for dry coughs that keep a patient up at night.

To Cough, or Not to Cough

It is important to note that cough syrups containing codeine can actually be dangerous for patients with certain kinds of respiratory illnesses. Coughing is the body's natural way of clearing fluids out of the lungs and bronchial tubes. Because codeine works on the brain to quiet a cough, users may experience a buildup of unwanted fluids that block their airways. As noted in the journal *Pediatrics,* "Cough suppression may adversely affect patients . . . by pooling of secretions, airway obstruction, [and] secondary infection." In other words, patients run the risk of choking on their own secretions, and these secretions may serve as a source of infection that can spread throughout the body. Therefore, cough syrups with codeine are not prescribed for patients with asthma, allergies, cystic fibrosis, or pneumonia.

In the early part of the twentieth century, codeine was commonly prescribed for diarrhea. However, it is rarely used for that purpose anymore. Likewise, the use of codeine-enhanced products for migraine headaches is being phased out with the introduction of more effective non-narcotic medications for migraine pain.

How Effective Is Codeine?

Reports in *Chemist & Druggist* and the *Western Journal of Medicine* both cited recent studies comparing codeine-containing and noncodeine-containing pain relievers. The evidence suggests that pain relievers with codeine prove no more effective than plain, over-the-counter analgesics. In addition, "patients receiving codeine were more likely to stop therapy because of side effects," wrote Sanjay Arora and Mel E. Herbert in the *Western Journal of Medicine.* The researchers went on to state that codeine's pain-relieving powers are largely a "myth."

Usage Trends

The continued research on opiates, both natural and SYN-THETIC, has produced a new generation of pain-fighting drugs that are related to but more powerful than codeine. Brand-name pills such as Percocet, Percodan, and OxyContin contain oxycodone, which is synthesized from thebaine. (An entry on oxycodone is available in this encyclopedia.) Hydrocodone, another relative of codeine, is six times stronger than codeine and can be found in generic form or in brand-name pills such as Vicodin, Lortab, and Lorcet.

According to a 2003 online report by the Drug Abuse Warning Network (DAWN), abuse of prescription painkillers "has risen

synthetic: made in a laboratory

dramatically in the U.S. Of particular concern is the abuse of pain medications containing opiates." Unlike club drugs or DESIGNER DRUGS, opiates can be obtained from a doctor legally. This has led to addiction among senior citizens, who sometimes fail to understand the dosage directions, as well as upper- and middle-class users of any age who would tend to shun illegal street drugs. Celebrities such as political commentator Rush Limbaugh and comedian George Carlin have made the news for undergoing treatment for prescription opiate addiction.

Although prescription opiate abuse is rising, the trend of codeine abuse, in particular, fell more than 60 percent between 1994 and 2001, according to the 2003 *DAWN Report*. Because codeine is dispensed most commonly in combination with other agents, it is less likely to be a drug of choice for an abuser, particularly if that abuser can obtain OxyContin, Vicodin, or other stronger medications.

In certain regions of the United States, however, codeine abuse continues to be a problem. In Houston, Texas, an entire culture has sprung up around cough syrup abuse, including a type of rap music called "screw." In this type of rap, songs are re-mixed, slowed down, and chopped to sound like a skipped recording. One of the pioneers of SCREW MUSIC, Robert Davis Jr. (1971–2000), also known as DJ Screw, died of a codeine overdose at his recording studio.

In Houston, Texas, an entire culture has sprung up around cough syrup abuse, including a type of rap music called "screw." © *Chris Coxwell/Corbis.*

The popularity of screw music—and cough syrup abuse—is reported to be spreading across the southern United States. Kristen Mack noted in the *Houston Chronicle* that a Memphis, Tennessee-based rap group, Three 6 Mafia, had a locally popular single called "Sippin on Syrup." Mack wrote that in 2001, Houston-area "police confiscated 125 gallons of illegal codeine. Each year, they say, they encounter more abuse and more people coming to Houston looking for 'syrup.'... Everyone agrees that Houston is ground zero for this 'quiet epidemic.'"

designer drugs: harmful and addictive substances that are manufactured illegally in homemade labs

screw music: an engineered music inspired by codeine use that uses existing songs but slows them down and makes certain segments repetitive

Cough syrup with codeine is more readily available in Texas because codeine is sold in small quantities over-the-counter in Mexico. Smugglers stockpile as many doses as they can, take them across the Mexican-U.S. border, and sell them on the street. Mack reported that in 2002, eight ounces of cough syrup could fetch $200 on the BLACK MARKET. Users typically mix the medication with soft drinks or alcohol.

Effects on the Body

Most people who use codeine for its prescribed purposes experience few side effects. A bothersome cough disappears, perhaps with some drowsiness. Post-surgical pain decreases, perhaps with some nausea. When the medical problem goes away, the patient stops using the pills or cough syrup with no significant after-effects.

Ingesting the drug at higher-than-prescribed doses, some users may experience a sense of well-being, along with a loss of INHIBITIONS and feelings of drowsiness or light-headedness. Other users have reported the opposite effect: a sense of discomfort and restlessness. Because codeine is taken orally, the user might not feel the effects of the drug for a half an hour to an hour after ingestion. The sensations last several hours and then slowly diminish. Users might feel nauseated or their skin might itch. An overdose can cause users—especially children—to stop breathing. In the event that a codeine abuser stops breathing, rapid administration of the drug naloxone (Narcan) will reverse the effects of the opiate. However, the patient must be diagnosed by a doctor very quickly.

The most profound effect of codeine and other related opiates is psychological. Flooding the brain with opioids from drug use causes the brain to stop producing naturally occurring ENDORPHINS, or pleasure-enhancing hormones. Then, when the effects of the drug wear off, the user may feel uncomfortable, anxious, and irritable. He or she might have trouble relaxing or sleeping. Many abusers take another high dose of the opiate in order to restore that feeling of well-being. Such abuse leads to serious problems with addiction.

Addiction to opiates like codeine can happen swiftly; WITHDRAWAL can be a difficult and lengthy ordeal. Almost immediately, the codeine abuser who stops taking the drug experiences a host of unpleasant symptoms, including restlessness, anxiety, INSOMNIA, muscle and bone pain, diarrhea, chills that produce goose bumps (hence the term "cold turkey"), and leg tremors ("kicking the habit"). The patient may yawn frequently and feel more sensitivity to pain. These flu-like symptoms usually last for a few days.

black market: the illegal sale or trade of goods; drug dealers are said to carry out their business on the "black market"

inhibitions: inner thoughts that keep people from engaging in certain activities

endorphins: a group of naturally occurring substances in the body that relieve pain and promote a sense of well-being

withdrawal: the process of gradually cutting back on the amount of a drug being taken until it is discontinued entirely; also the accompanying physiological effects of terminating use of an addictive drug

insomnia: difficulty falling asleep or an inability to sleep

What makes opiate addiction so hard to beat is the lasting effects on the brain. The recovering codeine abuser will just "not feel good" psychologically as the brain readjusts to producing its own endorphins. Cynthia Kuhn, Scott Swartzwelder, and Wilkie Wilson described this situation in *Buzzed: The Straight Facts about the Most Used and Abused Drugs from Alcohol to Ecstasy.* "There is a DYSPHORIA (the just-feeling-lousy feeling), which may be the reverse of opiate-induced euphoria. Withdrawing opiate addicts just feel *bad,* and they feel bad in a way that they know [taking more] opiates will solve. The craving for a fix can last for months, long after the physical symptoms have abated," or gone away.

Reactions with Other Drugs or Substances

Pharmacists dispensing drugs containing codeine usually warn users that side effects can include drowsiness, dizziness, nausea, and constipation. These substances should not be used with other tranquilizers or SEDATIVES, with BENZODIAZEPINES, with the antidepressant drugs known as monoamine oxidase inhibitors (MAOIs), or with ANTIHISTAMINES, AMPHETAMINES, or alcohol. Patients taking products that contain codeine must use care when operating automobiles or machinery. When used briefly and specifically for its prescribed purpose, a product containing codeine will not produce extreme side effects.

Doctors prescribing pain relievers containing codeine must carefully check the patient's records for other medications that will adversely interact with codeine. These substances include sleeping pills, tranquilizers, antihistamines, anti-anxiety medications, and any other medicine that produces sedation. Using alcohol and codeine at the same time greatly increases the likelihood of breathing problems. Mixing codeine with illegal substances such as HALLUCINOGENS or designer drugs can be fatal.

Additionally, higher doses of prescription pain relief pills containing codeine and/or acetaminophen, ibuprofen, and aspirin can cause severe, sometimes fatal, reactions. Over-the-counter analgesics taken in large doses can lead to stomach bleeding, liver failure, and other organ damage.

Treatment for Habitual Users

As previously described, stopping opiate use abruptly (or going "cold turkey") takes both a physical and psychological toll on the user. Someone wishing to end a codeine addiction can find

dysphoria: pronounced diss-FOR-ee-yuh; an abnormal feeling of anxiety, discontent, or discomfort; the opposite of euphoria

sedatives: drugs used to treat anxiety and calm people down

benzodiazepines: a type of drug used to treat anxiety

antihistamines: drugs that block *histamine,* a chemical that causes nasal congestion related to allergies

amphetamines: pronounced am-FETT-uh-meens; stimulant drugs that increase mental alertness, reduce appetite, and help keep users awake

hallucinogens: substances that bring on hallucinations, which alter the user's perceptions of reality

Words from a "Junkie"

Experimental American author William S. Burroughs (1914–1997) was very honest and open about his experiences as an opiate addict. Here, in a passage from his novel *Junkie,* he describes the process of drug withdrawal.

"The last of the codeine was running out. My nose and eyes began to run, sweat soaked through my clothes. Hot and cold flashes hit me as if a furnace door was swinging open and shut. I lay down on the bunk, too weak to move. My legs ached and twitched so that any position was intolerable, and I moved from one side to the other, sloshing about in my sweaty clothes." Burroughs added: "Almost worse than the sickness is the depression that goes with it. One afternoon I closed my eyes and saw New York in ruins. Huge centipedes and scorpions crawled in and out of empty bars and cafeterias and drugstores on Forty-second Street. Weeds were growing up through cracks and holes in the pavement. There was no one in sight."

assistance from a licensed physician who may prescribe methadone to ease the symptoms of withdrawal. Methadone is itself an opiate, but it works differently in the body. It releases slowly, so that the user does not feel a rush of euphoria or a backlash when the euphoria ends. Recovering addicts slowly reduce the dosage of methadone under a doctor's care until they become drug-free. (An entry on methadone is available in this encyclopedia.) Another drug, buprenorphine, also provides some sedating effects while blocking the brain's absorption of opiates.

Any successful drug-treatment program requires some sort of psychological intervention. Former users have reported remarkable benefits from talk therapy and the support of other recovering addicts. Narcotics Anonymous is built on the philosophy of the better-known Alcoholics Anonymous. The organization offers free group therapy, online information, telephone hotlines, and other services to recovering addicts worldwide, no matter what type of drug abuse led to their addiction.

Consequences

Interestingly enough, opiate use alone does not produce any lasting damage to the brain or other organs. But that does not mean that codeine can be abused without harmful consequences. Codeine users are likely to combine the drug with other substances ranging from alcohol to hallucinogens, sometimes with fatal results. Attraction to codeine may encourage users to try its stronger relatives, heroin and morphine. Even if the user restricts ingestion simply to codeine, addiction changes behavior in self-destructive ways. In order to obtain their supply of drugs, users may engage in burglary, theft, drug dealing, or prostitution. Under the influence of opiates, addicts eat poorly and ignore symptoms of bad health. So while codeine abuse may not lead to organ damage, its effect on the overall level of good health can be devastating.

The Law

Codeine is a controlled substance. The FDA and the DEA strictly oversee its legal production. Therefore, possession of codeine without a prescription is illegal. Laws for possession and distribution of codeine vary from state to state and may even vary depending on the strength of the dose. For instance, in Massachusetts, possession of pure codeine is a "Class A" offense, carrying a penalty of up to two years in prison and $2,000 in fines. But Massachusetts also has a "Class C" distinction, with lesser penalties, for some prescription opiates containing lower dosages of the drug. In 2002, possession of small quantities of codeine in Texas was considered a misdemeanor with a minimal fine.

Federal penalties for possession of a controlled substance include up to a year in jail for the first conviction, and between $1,000 and $100,000 in fines. A second conviction carries the penalty of fifteen days to two years in prison with up to $250,000 in fines. A third conviction requires ninety days to five years in prison with a maximum $250,000 fine.

Fact or Fiction: Codeine's Reputation

Some people think that prescription opiates are always addictive, and those who use them for any amount of time will become drug addicts. This is not true. Studies show that when prescription painkillers are used as directed, and discontinued when no longer needed, they carry no danger of addiction.

Over time, certain drugs begin to lose their effectiveness, and users need to take more and more of the drug to achieve the original results. Some critics think that codeine users with chronic pain will develop a tolerance to opiates, but this theory has not been proven. Increased doses of codeine only seem to be necessary if the degree of pain experienced by patients worsens as a serious disease progresses.

Prescription painkillers containing codeine have a reputation for bringing on troublesome side effects. Some of the side effects are rumored to be so horrible that patients refuse to take the drug. This is not necessarily the case. In fact, carefully supervised use of prescription painkillers results in a few, easily tolerated side effects.

There are other ways to break the law in search of codeine. It is illegal to "doctor shop." This is a process whereby a user seeks multiple prescriptions by visiting more than one doctor and "fakes" a set of symptoms that might lead those doctors to prescribe the drug the user wants. It is illegal to bring over-the-counter purchases of codeine into the United States from other countries that sell it. It is also illegal to extract the codeine from analgesic compounds like Tylenol 3. Again, jail time and fines vary from state to state.

Drug Tests

Because the liver turns codeine into morphine, the use of prescription products containing codeine can produce a positive urine test for codeine *and* morphine. Positive tests for the drug can be obtained as many as three to four days after the last use. Curiously enough, as much as a teaspoon of poppy seeds used in baking and on

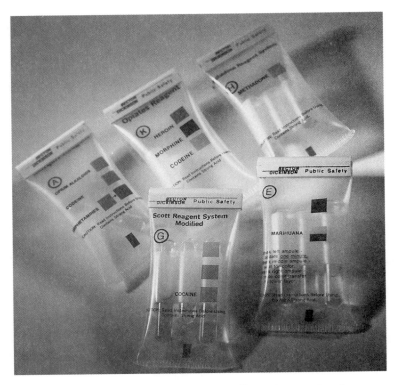

Various drug kits are available to determine if people are using drugs illegally. Tests are available for codeine, amphetamines, cocaine, heroin, marijuana, methadone, morphine, and opium alkaloids, among others.

TEK Image/Photo Researchers, Inc.

bagels can also produce a positive drug test for opiates. According to Gahlinger, there is "no direct way to be sure whether a urine test positive for morphine or codeine is due to poppy seeds or to drugs. Eating a single poppy seed bagel can result in a positive drug test for up to three days."

For More Information

Books

Burroughs, William S. *Junkie.* New York: Ace Books, 1953. Reprinted as *Junky.* New York: Penguin Books, 2003.

Clayman, Charles B. *The American Medical Association Encyclopedia of Medicine.* New York: Random House, 1989.

Gahlinger, Paul M. *Illegal Drugs: A Complete Guide to Their History, Chemistry, Use, and Abuse.* Las Vegas, NV: Sagebrush Press, 2001.

Kuhn, Cynthia, Scott Swartzwelder, and Wilkie Wilson. *Buzzed: The Straight Facts about the Most Used and Abused Drugs from Alcohol to Ecstasy,* 2nd ed. New York: W. W. Norton, 2003.

Silverman, Harold M. *The Pill Book,* 11th ed. New York: Bantam Books, 2004.

Periodicals

Arora, Sanjay, and Mel E. Herbert. "Myth: Codeine Is a Powerful and Effective Analgesic." *Western Journal of Medicine* (June, 2001): p. 428.

"Avoid Codeine Combinations." *Chemist & Druggist* (May 22, 1999): p. 9.

Harris, Mikal. "Cough Syrup Becomes Addictive Street Drug." *St. Louis Post-Dispatch* (July 21, 2000).

Mack, Kristen. "From Bayou City to 'City of Syrup': 'Quiet Epidemic' of Codeine Abuse Centered in Houston, Officials Say." *Houston Chronicle* (February 10, 2002): p. 37.

Monaco, John E. "Uncommonly Common Poisonings in Children." *Pediatrics for Parents* (September, 1997): p. 6.

"Use of Codeine- and Dextromethorphan-Containing Cough Remedies in Children." *Pediatrics* (June, 1997): p. 918.

Walling, Anne D. "Codeine Plus Acetaminophen: Benefits and Side Effects." *American Family Physician* (November 15, 1996): p. 2302.

Web Sites

"Controlled Substances Schedules." *U.S. Department of Justice, Drug Enforcement Administration, Diversion Control Program.* http://www.deadiversion.usdoj.gov/schedules/schedules.htm (accessed June 30, 2005).

"Legal Penalties for Drug Offenses: Commonwealth of Massachusetts Penalties and Federal Penalties." *University of Massachusetts, Lowell.* http://www.uml.edu/student-services/dean/policies/ (accessed March 8, 2005).

"Narcotic Analgesics: In Brief." *The DAWN Report.* http://www.oas.samhsa.gov/2k3/pain/DAWNpain.pdf (accessed June 30, 2005).

"Texas Study Warns of Codeine Cough Syrup Abuse." *U.S. Department of Justice, Drug Enforcement Administration, Diversion Control Program.* http://www.deadiversion.usdoj.gov/pubs/nwslttr/spec2000/texas.htm (accessed June 30, 2005).

See also: Heroin; Methadone; Morphine; Opium; Oxycodone

Creatine

Official Drug Name: Creatine monohydrate (KREE-uh-teen *or* KREE-uh-tin mon-oh-HY-drate)
Also Known As: Dietary supplements, supps
Drug Classifications: Creatine is not a controlled substance

What Kind of Drug Is It?

Creatine monohydrate can be found in numerous DIETARY SUPPLEMENTS, in pill, powder, liquid, or even chewing gum form. It is a combination of three AMINO ACIDS that are found in the muscles of humans and all animals with backbones. Creatine provides fuel to muscles during moments of rapid exertion, working within the muscle cells as a substance called creatine phosphate. Some studies suggest that it helps to repair and restore muscles after intense physical activity.

Human beings and other animals store creatine naturally in their muscle cells. The body manufactures it in the liver, kidneys, and pancreas. Additionally, creatine can be absorbed from natural outside sources such as meat and fish during the digestion process. According to Robert Monaco and Terry Malloy in *Creatine and Other Natural Muscle Boosters,* "the average man has about 120 grams [or 4 ounces] of creatine in his body, with about 95 percent in skeletal muscles." New creatine is created within the body at a rate of about two grams per day.

Safety Concerns, Especially for Teens

Some athletes have begun to use dietary supplements containing creatine to build muscle mass and reduce recovery times between workouts. Creatine supplements can be found in health food stores, on the Internet, and through mail-order companies. No one breaks the law by buying or selling creatine. It is not a controlled substance. Short-term studies have proven that creatine does contribute in a small way to increased strength during short bursts of activity, such as weight lifting, shot put, or batting a baseball.

Since creatine is not regulated by the U.S. Food and Drug Administration (FDA), many questions remain not only on its true effectiveness, but also on the possible damage it can do to the body, especially with prolonged use. How it affects the growing bodies of teenagers and younger children is not known. Although it is legal, creatine should be used by adults

dietary supplements: products including vitamins, herbal extractions, and synthetic amino acids sold for specific uses such as weight loss, muscle building, or prevention of disease

amino acids: any of a group of chemical compounds that form the basis for proteins

with extreme caution, under the close supervision of a medical doctor. Children and adolescents should avoid it.

Overview

Creatine was first isolated and named in 1832 by French chemist Michel-Eugène Chevreul (1786–1889). By the end of the nineteenth century, scientists had determined that intense muscular activity caused concentrations of creatine to build up in—and strengthen—muscle tissue. Further study determined that creatine levels could be raised in the body by eating a diet rich in meat. Eating great quantities of meat is not considered a healthy habit, so in the 1950s an Illinois company named Pfanstiehl Laboratories created and marketed the first synthetic, or manufactured, creatine.

Creatine was first isolated and named in 1832 by French chemist Michel-Eugène Chevreul. *Photo courtesy of the Library of Congress.*

Use by Olympic Athletes

As early as the 1960s, competitive athletes in the former Soviet Union were using creatine, along with anabolic STEROIDS, to increase their strength and durability. (An entry on steroids is available in this encyclopedia.) In those years competitors were not tested for drugs prior to the Olympic Games. However, the apparent physical superiority of the Soviet, Eastern European, and Chinese athletes raised many suspicions. As the 1970s progressed, sports authorities in many nations, as well as the International Olympic Committee, instituted blood tests to check for performance-enhancing substances.

It is possible to test athletes for elevated levels of ANABOLIC AGENTS such as testosterone, androstenedione (ann-druh-STEEN-dee-ohn), and dehydroepiandrosterone (dee-HY-droh-epp-ee-ann-DROSS-tuh-rone). No tests, however, exist for measuring creatine levels. By the end of the twentieth century, a number of famous professional and amateur athletes and bodybuilders were using creatine supplements legally. In fact, they were even touting the substance's powers. Home run champions Mark McGwire and Sammy Sosa

steroids: drugs that mimic the actions of testosterone, a hormone found in greater quantities in males than in females, and help build muscle mass and strength

anabolic agents: substances that promote muscle growth

Creatine is known as a bulking supplement that is used by weightlifters, bodybuilders, and other athletes. © Najlah Feanny/Corbis.

have both admitted taking creatine. Use of the supplement has been linked to former professional quarterbacks Troy Aikman and John Elway and Olympic runner Michael Johnson, to name only a few.

A June 2000 article for *Time* magazine discussed the safety of creatine. The writer reported that half of the athletes surveyed by the magazine, "many of them Olympians, admitted ... that they'd be willing to take a drug even if it was sure to kill them eventually, so long as it would let them win every event they entered five years in a row." This "win at all costs" mindset filters down from the professional and Olympic level to high school and even middle school athletes. Many youth are feeling that they will have no chance of succeeding at the highest levels if they do not use supplements such as creatine.

What Is It Made Of?

ENDOGENOUS, or natural, creatine is produced from three amino acids: arginine (AHR-juh-neen), glycine (GLY-seen), and methionine (meh-THY-uh-neen). It can be found in most of the body's organs. However, the vast majority of it resides within the muscle cells that power the body's movements.

Creatine is part of a complex chemical process that creates and restores ADENOSINE TRIPHOSPHATE (ATP), the fuel that muscles feed on as they contract. In quick movements, ATP converts to adenosine phosphate (ADP), releasing a burst of energy in the process. As Monaco noted in his book, "Normally, muscles contain only enough ATP to provide energy for between five and ten seconds, depending on the amount of effort required for the activity. Then, the muscles need creatine to make more ATP."

About two-thirds of the creatine in the body is creatine phosphate. This chemical comes into play when the muscle's store of ATP has been depleted, or used up. Creatine phosphate breaks down into creatine and phosphate, restoring the levels of ATP. The reason muscles ache after a difficult workout is that levels of ATP and creatine have fallen. As the body restores the chemical balance, the aches fade and the muscles become stronger.

Endogenous creatine is manufactured in the liver, kidneys, and pancreas. A normal, active human being manufactures about two grams of creatine daily, taking in perhaps one or two grams more through foods. Vegetarians tend to store less creatine in their bodies, since they do not eat meat.

How Is It Taken?

Supplemental creatine is available in pill form, as a powder dissolved into beverages, or as a gum or candy. Because it is not considered a drug, the substance is not regulated for purity

---

Mark McGwire

In September of 1998, while working toward setting a new single-season home run record, St. Louis Cardinals slugger Mark McGwire talked with reporters at his locker in the stadium clubhouse. A photographer snapped a shot of McGwire's locker, showing a bottle of creatine supplements.

On March 17, 2005, McGwire was called to testify in Washington, D.C., before the House Committee on Governmental Reform. Facing tough questions from members of Congress, McGwire dodged the issue about whether he used performance-enhancing products. As reported in the *Philadelphia Daily News,* McGwire stated: "I cannot answer these questions without jeopardizing my friends, my family, and myself." McGwire wept when parents whose sons had died of complications of steroid abuse told the committee that their sons idolized McGwire and wanted to be like him.

---

endogenous: pronounced en-DAH-juh-nuss; produced within the body

adenosine triphosphate (ATP): an important energy-carrying chemical, created with the assistance of creatine

Fast Facts about Creatine

Did you know the following facts about creatine supplements?

- Half of the athletes surveyed by *Time* magazine in 2000 said they would be willing to take a deadly drug if it would allow them to win every event they entered for five years.
- In 2001, $400 million worth of creatine supplements were sold in the United States.
- Creatine supplements have not been banned by any professional or amateur sports authority, except the National Collegiate Athletic Association (NCAA), where it is classified as a "non-permissible" substance.
- In 2001, survey findings suggested that 390,000 children between the ages of ten and fourteen had tried some sort of performance-enhancing product.

in its many different products. Sometimes the dosage per unit varies from the information printed on the label. Sometimes extra ingredients are added to the pills or powders, and some of these can act as steroids in the body.

Two athletes, American bobsledder Pavle Javanovic and Norwegian wrestler Fritz Aanes tested positive for steroid use prior to the Olympic Games and received two-year suspensions. Both men claimed they used only creatine. A test of Aanes's dietary supplement revealed that it contained a banned substance called nandrolone, which was not listed on the label. In a random test of creatine supplements conducted by *ConsumerLab.com* in 2003, only half of the products tested were found to have the ingredients they listed at the dosages they claimed. The other half made false claims of dosages or were found to contain other unlabeled ingredients.

Are There Any Medical Reasons for Taking This Substance?

A very small number of children are born with a condition called guanidinoacetate methyltransferase deficiency (GMAT; pronounced GWAN-ih-deen-oh-AH-suh-tate METH-uhl-TRANZ-fuh-rase). This extremely serious illness causes muscle wasting and seizures from the time of birth onward. Some of its symptoms are eased by high doses of supplemental creatine.

Small research studies show creatine supplements benefit people who have diseases that cause muscle degeneration, such as amyotrophic (ay-my-oh-TROH-fik) lateral sclerosis (ALS, or "Lou Gehrig's Disease"), myasthenia gravis (my-us-THEE-nee-uh GRAH-vuss), muscular dystrophy, Huntington's disease, Parkinson's disease, and McArdle's disease. It is important to note that creatine supplementation may slow the symptoms of these diseases, but it does not cure them.

People who face long periods in bed recovering from surgery or from multiple broken bones may speed the restoration of their muscles by taking extra creatine. Creatine also appears to improve the exercise capacity in patients suffering from heart problems. Also, there is some evidence to suggest that the supplement helps elderly people retain balance and muscle control later in life.

Usage Trends

Since the late 1990s, there has been a huge surge in the purchase of creatine supplements. According to the *Knight Ridder/ Tribune Business News,* Americans purchased $400 million worth of creatine in 2001. A *Sports Illustrated* piece claimed that over-the-counter dietary supplements for sports nutrition were a $1.7 billion industry in 2003. Most of the buyers are teenagers and grown men and women who want to build muscle. Some creatine products are especially targeting "the upmarket youth," according to Suhit Kelkar in the *Asia Africa Intelligence Wire.*

In a survey conducted by *Time* magazine in 2000, 44 percent of high school seniors said they used creatine to improve athletic performance. No legal restrictions exist on the purchase of creatine, so teenagers can buy it without the advice or consent of their parents. Peer pressure, along with the desire to win in competition, can be powerful agents of persuasion for those considering creatine supplementation.

When Norwegian wrestler Fritz Aanes (top) tested positive for steroid use prior to the Olympic Games, he claimed he had used only creatine. © *Reuters/Corbis.*

Effects on the Body

Creatine supplement use has been shown to raise the levels of stored creatine in muscles. Plus, research has revealed it does lead to modest gains in strength during ANAEROBIC EXERCISE. In most people, use of creatine supplements does not improve performance in AEROBIC EXERCISES or sustained periods of activity. Creatine users claim that the substance helps them to "bulk up,"

anaerobic exercise: short, strenuous exercises that require sudden bursts of strength, such as weight lifting and batting a baseball

aerobic exercises: exercises performed to increase heart health and stamina, such as jogging, biking, and swimming, usually lasting between twenty minutes and an hour

or gain muscle mass. This is the case, but the weight gain stems only from retained water within muscle cells.

Small research studies show creatine supplements benefit people who have diseases that cause muscle degeneration, such as muscular dystrophy. © *Gerhard Gscheidle/Peter Arnold, Inc.*

Not Enough Information Available

The water retention is just one of the dangers of creatine use. One of the most common side effects of using creatine supplements is dehydration, or a drying-out of body tissues. Taking creatine mixed in a caffeinated beverage, such as coffee or some soft drinks, increases the risk of dehydration. Athletes who work out briskly at higher temperatures risk HEAT STROKE and, ultimately, kidney damage due to dehydration. Other reported side effects of high doses of creatine include nausea, diarrhea, indigestion, and an increased risk of muscle strain.

Whether muscle strain is linked to creatine use is highly debated. Some studies suggest that creatine use encourages athletes to work out harder and longer, while their bodies reap little benefit from the extra creatine. This psychological component of creatine use can be a factor in painful muscle strains or cramping.

How does using creatine affect children and teens who are still growing? As of 2005, no answers were available. Long-range studies of creatine use had not been completed. Doctors recommend that children and teens avoid all use of creatine, no matter how tempted they might be to "bulk up." A *Sports Illustrated* story on sports supplements quoted Dr. Arthur Grollman of the State University of New York at Stony Brook. He observed: "Basically, anyone who uses these products is a human lab rat."

Case in point: In the *Journal of Toxicology: Clinical Toxicology,* Christine A. Haller and her colleagues discussed whether seizures are linked to dietary supplements. They noted that although creatine has not been linked with seizures in published studies, "the California Poison Control System has received a few . . . reports of seizures in young athletes who were allegedly taking only creatine. This potential association between creatine use and seizures requires further investigation."

heat stroke: a condition resulting from longtime exposure to high temperatures; symptoms include an inability to sweat, a very high body temperature, and, eventually, passing out

Creatine Chronology

1832 French chemist Michel-Eugène Chevreul isolates creatine within muscle cells and names it after the Greek word for "flesh."

1926 An article in a British medical journal links creatine consumption in meats to weight gain as muscle mass.

1954 Pfanstiehl Laboratories Inc. of Illinois produces synthetic creatine in bulk and markets it to catalog resellers.

1992 British sprinters Linford Christie and Sally Gunnel win Olympic gold medals after having trained using creatine supplements.

1998 Mark McGwire, working toward breaking the single-season home run record for Major League Baseball, is photographed with a bottle of creatine supplements in his stadium locker.

2005 Mark McGwire testifies before Congress about steroid use in Major League Baseball. He dodges questions about whether he used performance-enhancing products.

Reactions with Other Drugs or Substances

Creatine and caffeine do not mix well. Both tend to dehydrate the body. Taken together, they can lead to heat stroke. Few studies have been done about the body's reaction to creatine supplements when taken with prescription medications, over-the-counter medications, or even other dietary supplements. Some fitness magazines warn against mixing creatine powder with drinks that are high in sugar or glucose content. Sweetened beverages carry their own dangers, including encouraging DIABETES and weight gain.

Although the purchase of creatine is legal, the substance has not been proven safe, even for adults. Before taking creatine supplements, adults should first consult a licensed doctor and carefully review any other medications that they are using daily. People with kidney problems should never take creatine supplements. Doctors will take periodic blood tests to make sure that creatine use is not damaging internal organs such as the liver and kidneys. Coaches, personal trainers, and sports nutritionists are not qualified to recommend creatine supplementation. They do not have the extensive medical education and training that licensed medical doctors have.

Treatment for Habitual Users

The use of creatine supplements has not been shown to cause the human body to stop making its own endogenous

diabetes: a serious disorder that causes problems with the normal breakdown of sugars in the body

Home run champion Mark McGwire was photographed with a bottle of creatine in his locker in 1998. In 2005 he appeared before Congress to discuss steroid use in baseball. The use of performing-enhancing products by star baseball players is a subject of much debate.

AP/Wide World Photos.

psychological dependence: the belief that a person needs to take a certain substance in order to function

creatine. Also, creatine monohydrate is not a habit-forming substance. Withdrawal from creatine supplements does not plunge the user into a period of muscle weakness or other difficulties. Still, users can develop a PSYCHOLOGICAL DEPENDENCE on the drug and become convinced that extra creatine will make them better athletes. This may cause them to use the substance longer, or in higher doses, than anyone would recommend.

As of 2005, no studies had been done on the long-term use of creatine supplements. Experts suggest that young athletes never begin using creatine supplements at all. Those who have already begun should consult a doctor about continued use.

Consequences

Are creatine supplements safe? As of 2005, the bodybuilding industry and its periodicals claimed creatine was safe. However, various medical journals offered a different opinion. They noted that nothing was known about the long-term effects of creatine use, particularly for young people. Plus, since creatine was already available on the market and fairly inexpensive, drug companies have been reluctant to conduct trials to prove the medical benefits of taking the supplement.

What this means is that those using creatine supplements in the early twenty-first century will provide the only long-term data on creatine's possible ill effects, since these users were the first to buy the supplement in great numbers. Because the long-term effects of creatine are not yet known, users could learn one day that the substance has various health risks.

Building Muscles without Supplements

All athletes should be wary of any substance that promises quick results. Health professionals note that there is simply no substitute for a carefully chosen exercise program and good dietary habits. In its August 2003 edition, *Prevention* magazine offered teens various tips for building muscle without the pills and the powders. For example, the editors recommended:

- When exercising vigorously, add twenty-eight grams of protein to your diet daily. Instead of protein powders, consume larger quantities of milk, eggs, lean meats, and beans.
- After exercising, eat a snack high in carbohydrates, such as trail mix, apples, fruit juices, or whole grain breads.
- Cramped, sore, or stiff muscles are the body's sign that it is being overworked. Take longer breaks between intense workouts, and vary the types and duration of exercise routines. A long run or bike ride one day might be followed by some weight lifting the next day.

The Law

Anyone of any age can buy creatine supplements and use them. They are legal. The burden of keeping them out of the hands of growing children and young adults falls on parents, doctors, coaches, and the young people themselves. Nutritional supplements have not been proven to turn an average, or even above-average athlete, into a sports star, like Mark McGwire. The odds of receiving a contract to play professional sports—in any sport—are very slim. A study published in *NCAA News Online* in 2000 stated that only 2 percent of college football players go on to play professional football. The percentage of high school players who win pro contracts is far smaller than that.

Since the long-term effects of creatine use are unknown, experts suggest that young athletes never begin using the supplements at all. Hard work and exercise should be used instead. © *Jose Luis Pelaez, Inc./Corbis.*

For More Information

Books

Clayman, Charles B., editor. *The American Medical Association Encyclopedia of Medicine.* New York: Random House, 1989.

Monaco, Robert, and Terry Malloy. *Creatine and Other Natural Muscle Boosters.* New York: Dell Publishing, 1999.

Periodicals

Anderson, Nicki. "Creatine for a 14-Year-Old? It's Not a Good Idea, Parents." *Arlington Heights, IL Daily Herald* (December 13, 2004): p. 2.

Beckham, Lauren. "Your S.T.U.F.F.: Healthy or Health Hazard?: Teens and Families Need to Do Their Homework When It Comes to Dietary Supplements." *Boston Herald* (November 27, 2000): p. 40.

Christie, Tim. "Eugene, Oregon-Area High School Athletes Use Performance Booster with Creatine." *Knight Ridder/Tribune Business News* (November 20, 2003).

"Crazy for Creatine: Everyone from Mark McGwire to Kiddie Jocks Is Using This Muscle Builder. But Is It Safe?" *Time* (June 12, 2000): p. 93.

Donnellon, Sam. "Swearing Thin." *Philadelphia Daily News* (March 18, 2005).

Fauber, John. "Performance Enhancers Might Harm Your Child." *Milwaukee Journal Sentinel* (September 3, 2001): p. 1.

Fragakis, Allison Sarubin. "Your Teen: The Terminator: Pills Promise Kids Bulging Muscles—but at a Price." *Prevention* (August, 2003): p. 66.

Haller, Christine A., Kathryn H. Meier, and Kent R. Olson. "Seizures Reported in Association with Use of Dietary Supplements." *Journal of Toxicology: Clinical Toxicology* (January, 2005): p. 23.

Kelkar, Suhit. "Creatine a Monster." *Asia Africa Intelligence Wire* (August 24, 2004).

Kubetin, Sally Koch. "Demand Swells for Sports Supplements." *Family Practice News* (February 15, 2002): p. 1.

"A Little Chip on His Big Shoulder." *Time* (September 7, 1998): p. 23.

O' Neil, John. "Creatine and Boys in Pursuit of Bulk." *New York Times* (December 19, 2000): p. F8.

Schneider, Mary Ellen. "Screen Teens for Use of Performance Enhancers: Steroids, Ephedra, Creatine, More." *Family Practice News* (February 15, 2004): p. 62.

Song, Bonita. "Stanford U.: Creatine May Be More Hype than Help, Doctor Says." *America's Intelligence Wire* (February 5, 2004).

Splete, Heidi. "Creatine Popular with Student Athletes." *Family Practice News* (February 15, 2002): p. 5.

Wertheim, L. Jon. "Jolt of Reality: Following the Lead of Elite Athletes, Teenagers Are Increasingly Juicing Their Workouts with Pills and Powders—Sometimes with Tragic Results." *Sports Illustrated* (April 7, 2003): p. 68.

Web Sites

"A History of Innovation." *Ferro.* http://www.ferro.com/Our+Products/Pharmaceuticals/About+Us/_Time+Line.htm (accessed June 30, 2005).

"Probability of Competing in Athletics Beyond the High-School Interscholastic Level." *NCAA News Online.* http://www.ncaa.org/news/2000/20000814/digest.html (accessed June 30, 2005).

"Product Review: Muscular Enhancement Supplements: Creatine, HMB, and Glutamine." *ConsumerLab.com.* http://www.consumerlab.com/results/creatine.asp (accessed June 30, 2005).

U.S. Food and Drug Administration, Center for Food Safety and Applied Nutrition. http://www.cfsan.fda.gov/ (accessed June 30, 2005).

See also: Diuretics; Ephedra; Melatonin; Steroids

What Kind of Drug Is It?

Designer drugs are illicit (unlawful) and dangerous substances made in illegal labs. It is against the law to make, possess, sell, or use them. The designer drugs discussed here include 2C-B (nexus), ecstasy (MDMA), GHB, ketamine, methamphetamine, and PCP (phencyclidine). (Separate entries on each of these drugs with more in-depth information are available in this encyclopedia.)

Overview

Designer drugs were deliberately created by underground chemists to get around the laws set forth in the U.S. Controlled Substances Act (CSA) of 1970. The CSA called for the federal regulation of certain drugs. Under the terms of the act, all federally regulated substances must be categorized into one of five schedules. These schedules are based on a substance's medicinal value, possible harmfulness, and potential for abuse and addiction.

Schedule I is reserved for the most dangerous drugs that have no recognized medical use. 2C-B, ecstasy (MDMA), and GHB are all Schedule I drugs. Schedule II and Schedule III drugs have limited medical uses when prescribed by a physician, but the possibility of abuse and addiction among users remains a cause for concern. Methamphetamine and PCP are Schedule II drugs, and ketamine is a Schedule III drug.

Gary Henderson, a University of California professor, came up with the term "designer drug" back in the early 1980s. These designer drugs are synthesized, meaning that they are made in labs. As Lawrence Clayton explained in his book *Designer Drugs,* these synthetic substances "are made to mimic the feeling and the 'high' caused by other drugs." However, they "cost less than the drugs they are modeled after."

Illegal Labs

Amateur drug makers sought to create homemade drugs that would not qualify as controlled substances but would still appeal to

Official Drug Name: 2C-B (4-bromo-2, 5-dimethoxyphenethylamine; pronounced BROH-moh dy-meth-OCK-sy-FENN-eh-THY-luh-meen)
Also Known As: Afro, bees, bromo, cloud-9, eve, nexus, toonies, utopia, venus
Drug Classifications: Schedule I, hallucinogen

Official Drug Name: Ecstasy (MDMA; 3, 4-methylenedioxymethamphetamine; pronounced METH-uhl-een-die-OCK-sy-meth-am-FETT-uh-meen)
Also Known As: Adam, disco biscuit, E, hug drug, Stacy, X, XTC
Drug Classifications: Schedule I, hallucinogen

Official Drug Name: GHB (gamma hydroxybutyrate; pronounced GAMM-uh hy-DROK-see-BYOO-tuh-rate)
Also Known As: Cherry meth, Georgia home boy, goop, grievous bodily harm, max, soap
Drug Classifications: Schedule I, depressant

Official Drug Name: Ketamine (pronounced KEET-uh-meen; brand names include Ketaset and Ketalar)
Also Known As: Cat valium, jet, K, ket, special K, vitamin K
Drug Classifications: Schedule III, hallucinogen

Official Drug Name: Methamphetamine (pronounced meth-am-FETT-uh-meen)
Also Known As: Chalk, crank, crystal, crystal meth, ice, glass, meth, speed
Drug Classifications: Schedule II, stimulant

Official Drug Name: PCP (phencyclidine; pronounced fenn-SICK-luh-deen or fenn-SIKE-luh-deen)
Also Known As: Angel dust, cadillac, dust, embalming fluid, fry
Drug Classifications: Schedule II, hallucinogen

Designer drugs are popular at all-night dance parties called raves. The illegal drugs are said to intensify the rave experience and help the user dance longer. Such drugs have been known to cause death among party-goers. © *Lawrence Manning/Corbis.*

illegal drug users. With a slight change to the chemical structure of a controlled substance, a newly created designer drug would no longer be considered "controlled"—at least not technically. For more than fifteen years after the passage of the CSA, more and more illegal labs sprang up. These labs were "where new drugs that would bypass the CSA could be made," explained Elizabeth Russell Connelly in *Psychological Disorders Related to Designer Drugs.*

In the middle and late 1980s, however, further laws were passed that made designer drugs illegal as well. The U.S. government added existing designer drugs to the Drug Enforcement Administration's (DEA) list of controlled substances. In addition, the 1988 Chemical Diversion and Trafficking Act cut down on the availability of some of the ingredients necessary to concoct designer drugs. "Yet," commented Connelly, "designer drugs continue to be manufactured and sold for profit."

The popularity of RAVES in Europe and the United States contributed significantly to the increase in designer drug use. Raves generally appeal to young audiences. The term "club drugs" was coined to describe the many drugs that are often used by ravegoers to heighten the party experience. It is important to note, however, that not all "club drugs" or "rave drugs" are designer drugs, although the terms are often used interchangeably.

What Is It Made Of?

Designer drugs are often made with common household substances by inexperienced drug makers. Connelly reported that "illegal labs have been found in remote mountain cabins and rural farms, as well as in single and multifamily homes in city and suburban neighborhoods. These operations can be moved fairly quickly to new locations, in order to avoid detection by police or federal Drug Enforcement Administration (DEA) agents."

Although the ingredients in them are often quite ordinary, the illegal production of designer drugs is a dangerous business for both the producer and the user. Secret labs have been known to blow up during the drug-making process, and botched batches of drugs can be deadly when ingested. Myra Weatherly, writing in *Ecstasy and Other Designer Drug Dangers,* commented: "These imitation drugs mixed by 'BATHTUB CHEMISTS' can be much more POTENT than the real thing. Not only are these drugs dangerous in themselves, but a goof in the lab—such as overheating a substance—can mean death."

The chemical compositions for the six drugs discussed in this entry are listed below.

- 2C-B: $C_2H_8NO_2Br$
- ecstasy: $C_{11}H_{15}NO_2$
- GHB: $C_4H_3O_3$
- ketamine: $C_{13}H_{16}ClNOHCl$
- methamphetamine: $C_{10}H_{15}N$
- PCP: $C_{17}H_{25}N$

Shocking Ingredients

People are often shocked to learn what ingredients are used in designer drugs. Many of the ingredients are products that one would never dream of consuming. One good example is GHB. Few people realize that GHB is synthesized in household laboratories by mixing ingredients such as floor cleaning products, nail polish, and super glue removers with sodium hydroxide in the form of lye. Lye is made from wood ashes and used to make soap. Unintentional poisonings from bad homemade batches of GHB are not uncommon.

---

raves: wild overnight dance parties that typically involve huge crowds of people, loud techno music, and illegal drug use

bathtub chemists: inexperienced and illegal drug makers who concoct homemade drugs; also referred to as "kitchen chemists" or "underground chemists"

potent: powerful

How Is It Taken?

2C-B, ecstasy, and methamphetamine are usually sold and distributed in tablets or capsules that are swallowed. Users have also been known to crush the tablets and snort these drugs. Methamphetamine addicts often liquefy the powdered form of the drug and inject the mixture directly into their veins.

GHB is usually sold and consumed as a liquid in small glass or plastic bottles (about 30 milliliters in size). This reportedly provides enough of the drug for three moderate doses. GHB can also be purchased in capsule form or as a powder packaged in a bag. Because it is both odorless and colorless, GHB often goes undetected when added to a drink. It has been used in cases of date rape.

When used by physicians or veterinarians as an ANESTHETIC, ketamine comes in liquid form and is packaged in small glass vials. Illicit drug users often inject the liquid into their veins, but some abusers dry out the substance by cooking it, then crush and snort it.

PCP is available in the form of tablets, capsules, liquid, and powder. In its base form, PCP is a white crystalline powder that is snorted, pressed into tablets, or mixed together with water or alcohol. The liquid form is often sprayed on leafy material such as oregano, mint, or marijuana and sold to users in the form of joints to be smoked. (Separate entries on alcohol and marijuana are included in this encyclopedia.)

Are There Any Medical Reasons for Taking This Substance?

The Schedule I drugs 2C-B, ecstasy, and GHB had no known medical uses for humans as of 2005.

Ketamine, a Schedule III drug, was approved for use as an anesthetic in animals and humans in 1970. About 90 percent of legally sold ketamine is intended for veterinary use.

Methamphetamine produced by legal drug companies is available with a doctor's prescription for the treatment of NARCOLEPSY and ATTENTION-DEFICIT/HYPERACTIVITY DISORDER (ADHD). It is categorized as a Schedule II stimulant.

PCP is also a Schedule II drug. At one time, it was given to surgical patients as an anesthetic. Because of disturbing psychological side effects, however, it is no longer used for that purpose. As of the early 2000s, PCP was being investigated for potential use in patients who have suffered a heart attack or a stroke.

anesthetic: a substance used to deaden pain

narcolepsy: a rare sleep disorder characterized by daytime tiredness and sudden attacks of sleep

attention-deficit/hyperactivity disorder (ADHD): a disorder characterized by impulsive behavior, difficulty concentrating, and hyperactivity that interferes with social and academic functioning

Erin Rose, left, appears with her mother, Maryanne, at a press conference to warn others about the dangers of ketamine use. Rose suffered brain damage after using ketamine. *AP/Wide World Photos.*

Usage Trends

"New designer drugs are being developed all the time," noted Clayton, as are new ways to market these drugs. According to "Pulse Check," a publication of the Executive Office of the President, the Internet is playing an increasingly large part in the sale of designer drugs. The "Pulse Check," report, which was published in 2004, states that "law enforcement is way behind dealers and users technologically, especially at the local and state levels."

Designer drug use seemed to explode between the 1990s and 2002. Drug Abuse Warning Network (DAWN) statistics tell the story. According to DAWN, annual hospital emergency room visits associated with club and designer drug use jumped from a few hundred or less in 1995 to several thousand or more in 2002. Most statistics available on designer drug use are delayed by a year or two.

As of 2005, however, reports showed that designer drug usage was going down. The 2004 Monitoring the Future (MTF) survey and the 2003 National Survey on Drug Use and Health (NSDUH) both reported an overall decrease in users of drugs such as ecstasy and GHB.

Effects on the Body

"Every designer drug," noted Weatherly, "has the potential to kill the user." Strength and purity of dosages varies from batch to batch, and from dealer to dealer. So, a user who feels that a particular designer drug is "safe" based on prior use can never be sure what the next dose will be like. In addition, the long-term effects of these drugs on the body remain unknown. According to a 2005 report from "NIDA InfoFacts," however, "current science ... is showing changes to critical parts of the brain" from the use of ecstasy, GHB, and ketamine, among other drugs.

2C-B

Small doses of 2C-B reportedly produce relaxation in the user, but larger doses may bring on HALLUCINATIONS. Recreational users—those who use the drug to get high—say that 2C-B greatly heightens their reaction and sensitivity to music and enhances the enjoyment of dancing. At high doses, however, some users report seeing horrifying images, and others experience panic attacks. Such attacks are unexpected episodes of severe anxiety that can cause physical symptoms such as shortness of breath, dizziness, sweating, and shaking.

2C-B is also associated with increased feelings of anger and PARANOIA. The mood-altering effects of the drug can last for days. Unpleasant physical side effects of 2C-B use include nausea, diarrhea, cramps, and gas.

Ecstasy

Ecstasy probably has the highest name recognition among designer drugs. Known to many as the "hug drug," ecstasy lowers INHIBITIONS and encourages people to act on their impulses. Its use has been linked to casual sexual encounters, which can contribute to the spread of HIV (the human immunodeficiency virus) and eventually AIDS (acquired immunodeficiency syndrome).

The side effects of ecstasy may include nausea, dizziness, confusion, and anxiety. The drug acts on the body's muscular system, causing muscle tension, involuntary teeth clenching, and rapid eye movement. "Ecstasy deaths are a fact of life," noted Decca Aitkenhead in the *Independent*. High doses of the drug can bring on

hallucinations: visions or other perceptions of things that are not really present

paranoia: abnormal feelings of suspicion and fear

inhibitions: inner thoughts that keep people from engaging in certain activities

Ecstasy is classified as a Schedule I drug, meaning that it is illegal and has no recognized medical value. © Andrew Brookes/Corbis.

hyperthermia, a dangerously high increase in body temperature. This condition can damage internal organs such as the liver, kidneys, heart, and even the brain. Drug researchers have confirmed that ecstasy has the potential to cause permanent brain damage.

Because of high demand, ecstasy pills are frequently mixed with fillers and other active substances, most commonly amphetamines and caffeine. (Separate entries on these drugs are available in this encyclopedia.)

GHB

GHB was sold over-the-counter in the mid-1980s and used mainly by bodybuilders seeking to bulk up their muscles. The DEA later banned the drug. Recreational users report increased sociability, relaxation, and a positive mood while on GHB. People taking the substance often become talkative and giddy. They may become incoherent or hard to follow. Slurred speech is also common.

To help people test their drinks for possible date rape drugs such as GHB, various companies have developed testing kits. The effectiveness of such tests is highly debated, however. *AP/Wide World Photos.*

Because it is a depressant, GHB can bring on breathing difficulties, seizures, brain damage, and even comas in users who overdose. The drug becomes even more toxic when mixed with alcohol or other nervous system depressants such as BENZODIAZEPINES, painkillers, allergy medications, or sleeping pills. Combining even a low GHB dose with alcohol can trigger an overdose, leaving the user unconscious and barely breathing. Such effects have led to the use of GHB as a date rape drug.

Ketamine

benzodiazepines: a type of drug used to treat anxiety

The effects produced by ketamine are intense, but they do not last for long. This drug is often used as a booster to draw out the desired effects of other drugs. Because ketamine is an anesthetic, it produces significant effects when taken alone. Abusers of ketamine report immediate effects including numbness all over the body, altered vision, muffled hearing, and a floating sensation. The drug takes effect so quickly that users may collapse suddenly, injuring themselves in the process. After using the drug once, many people will never use it again, at least not knowingly. At higher doses, ketamine leads to hallucinations, the onset of a dreamy state, and so-called "out-of-body experiences." Some users have claimed they saw visions of angels after taking ketamine.

Combining ketamine with drugs such as alcohol or BARBITURATES can create a life-threatening situation. (A separate entry on barbiturates is included in this encyclopedia.) Users mixing these drugs risk slowing their breathing and heart rates to dangerously low levels. This can starve the brain of oxygen, thus increasing the chances of permanent brain damage, coma, or death.

Methamphetamine

Methamphetamine is taken illicitly for its HALLUCINOGENIC "feel-good" effects. Even small amounts of the drug are said to produce extreme alertness, increased energy, decreased appetite, and EUPHORIA. Such effects are those generally sought by users.

Methamphetamine reduces users' inhibitions and increases their sensitivity to sound, light, and touch. Because it is a stimulant, which increases activity, this drug gives club-goers energy to dance well into the morning hours. Some users stay awake for two to three days while on a meth binge. People also report feeling especially witty, clever, and in control while under the influence of methamphetamine.

Methamphetamine users often want to extend the high brought on by the drug. The so-called "crash" that results when the effects wear off is quite unpleasant. Irritability, confusion, anxiety, and difficulty sleeping are common side effects.

Methamphetamine is highly addictive, and users who try to quit typically suffer from WITHDRAWAL symptoms. These include severe depression, extreme anxiety, tiredness, tremors, convulsions, aggression, and intense drug cravings. Long-term abuse of methamphetamine may cause dangerously high blood pressure, INSOMNIA, paranoia, and violent behavior that sets the stage for users to harm themselves or others.

barbiturates: pronounced bar-BIH-chuh-rits; drugs that act as depressants and are used as sedatives or sleeping pills; also referred to as "downers"

hallucinogenic: ability to bring on hallucinations, which alter the user's perception of reality

euphoria: pronounced yu-FOR-ee-yuh; a state of extreme happiness and enhanced well-being; the opposite of dysphoria

withdrawal: the process of gradually cutting back on the amount of a drug being taken until it is discontinued entirely; also the accompanying physiological effects of terminating use of an addictive drug

insomnia: difficulty falling asleep or an inability to sleep

When police raid methamphetamine labs, they have to wear protective suits because the chemicals used in the product are considered hazardous materials. Bottles of the drug seized in a raid in Tennessee are shown here. *AP/Wide World Photos.*

PCP

PCP is another veterinary anesthetic used illicitly as a PSYCHEDELIC DRUG. Individual responses to PCP at low and moderate doses are varied. Users generally feel detached and distant when they first take the drug, and later experience a surging sense of power and strength.

Some users report having bizarre hallucinations—seeing people with enlarged or detached heads and limbs—and disturbing feelings of isolation and numbness. Because PCP users typically cannot feel pain when under the influence of the drug, they may engage in acts of self-mutilation or violence. Self-mutilation involves deliberately cutting or injuring oneself in some way.

At high doses, PCP prompts a drop in blood pressure, pulse rate, and breathing. These reactions may be accompanied by nausea, vomiting, blurred vision, uncontrolled eye movement, drooling, loss of balance, seizures, coma, and death. Taking PCP in combination

psychedelic drug: a drug that can produce hallucinations and distort reality with depressants such as alcohol or benzodia-zepines increases the risk of overdose.

Reactions with Other Drugs or Substances

Designer drugs are rarely taken alone. This complicates matters for paramedics, emergency room doctors, and nurses in cases of overdose. If medical personnel cannot pinpoint which drugs the user has taken, it makes treatment of the overdosing patient much more difficult.

Dosage Confusion

The effects of many designer drugs can be tripled or quadrupled in intensity with only minor increases in dosage. A 150-milligram dose of ecstasy, for example, can produce double the effects of a 120-milligram dose. Because most designer drugs are manufactured in illegal laboratories and are usually cooked up by inexperienced drug makers, the concentration of active ingredients in each batch can vary significantly.

Treatment for Habitual Users

Drug addiction is curable. Common forms of treatment include individual therapy, group therapy, day-long outpatient programs, and short-term inpatient programs. The National Institute on Drug Abuse (NIDA) confirms that the most successful drug rehabilitation programs are those that tailor treatment to the user. Connelly pointed out that "individual therapy may uncover issues of poor self-esteem, depression, severe family problems, and/or preexisting psychological disorders" that are at the root of an individual's drug use. The primary goals of therapy include helping the patient to quit drugs, improving the patient's coping abilities and outlook on life, and reducing the risk of relapse.

Consequences

Frequent drug users often find that their habit damages their relationships with family members and friends who do not use drugs. School-related and work-related performance may also suffer as physical or PSYCHOLOGICAL DEPENDENCE on drugs progresses. Repeated use of certain drugs brings about dramatic changes in both the structure and function of the brain. Methamphetamine use leads to extreme dependence that can quickly turn a recreational user into an addict. Many designer drugs (ecstasy, GHB, ketamine, and PCP) have the potential to produce hallucinations that can trigger traumatic emotional episodes in some users.

psychological dependence: the belief that a person needs to take a certain substance in order to function

Designer Drug Lingo

Designer drug talk has its own vocabulary. Here are some examples:

- Ketamine is frequently mixed with a stimulant like cocaine or methamphetamine. When taken at the same time, this combination is referred to as "trail mix."
- "Candy flipping," or the practice of using ecstasy and the hallucinogenic drug LSD together, has landed many users in the hospital.
- "Embalming fluid" is a common street slang term for PCP. Confusion about the origin of the term may have led to a dangerous trend: experimental drug users have actually mixed PCP with formaldehyde (or other embalming chemicals) and used it as a recreational psychoactive drug—a drug that alters the user's mental state or changes behavior.
- Hospitals report that the physical effects of highs associated with "wet" or "dipsticks" (marijuana rolled into joints that are then dipped in embalming fluid) are nearly identical to those long associated with PCP use.

The Law

Under the Controlled Substances Act, the manufacture, distribution, and possession of designer drugs carries the same penalties as the manufacture, distribution, and possession of controlled substances.

Anyone who possesses, manufactures, or sells a Schedule I drug risks hefty fines and a prison sentence of twenty years. Repeat offenders receive even harsher punishment. If the drug manufactured or sold by someone results in a user's death, the drug maker and dealer risk life in prison. 2C-B, ecstasy, and GHB are considered Schedule I drugs.

Involvement with Schedule II and Schedule III drugs is also illegal and can result in jail terms and thousands of dollars in fines. The designer drugs methamphetamine and PCP are Schedule II drugs. Ketamine is a Schedule III drug.

For More Information

Books

Clayton, Lawrence. *Designer Drugs.* New York: Rosen Publishing Group, 1998.

Connelly, Elizabeth Russell. *Psychological Disorders Related to Designer Drugs.* Philadelphia, PA: Chelsea House, 2000.

Weatherly, Myra. *Ecstasy and Other Designer Drug Dangers.* Berkeley Heights, NJ: Enslow Publishers, 2000.

Periodicals

Aitkenhead, Decca. "Independent Decade: Smiling Face of the Chemical Generation, Rave Culture." *Independent* (October 7, 1996): p. 12.

Web Sites

"2003 National Survey on Drug Use and Health (NSDUH)." *U.S. Department of Health and Human Services, Substance Abuse and Mental Health Services Administration.* http://www.oas.samhsa.gov/nhsda.htm (accessed June 30, 2005).

"Controlled Substances Act." *U.S. Drug Enforcement Administration.* http://www.usdoj.gov/dea/agency/csa.htm (accessed June 30, 2005).

DAWN: Drug Abuse Warning Network. http://dawninfo.samhsa.gov/ (accessed June 30, 2005).

"GHB." *Parents. The Anti-Drug.* http://www.theantidrug.com/drug_info/drug_info_ghb.asp (accessed June 30, 2005).

"NIDA InfoFacts: Club Drugs." *National Institute on Drug Abuse.* http://www.drugabuse.gov/Infofax/Clubdrugs.html (accessed June 30, 2005).

"Pulse Check: Drug Markets and Chronic Users in 25 of America's Largest Cities." *Executive Office of the President, Office of National Drug Control Policy.* http://www.whitehousedrugpolicy.gov/publications/drugfact/pulsechk/january04/january2004.pdf (accessed June 30, 2005).

See also: 2C-B; Ecstasy (MDMA); GHB; Ketamine; Methamphetamine; PCP (Phencyclidine)

Dextroamphetamine

Official Drug Name: Dextroamphetamine (DEKS-troh-am-FETT-uh-meen),
D-amphetamine, dextroamphetamine
sulfate (Dexedrine [DEKS-uh-dreen],
DextroStat [DEKS-troh-statt])
Also Known As: Copilots, dexies,
go-pills, pep pills, speed, uppers
Drug Classifications: Schedule II,
stimulant

What Kind of Drug Is It?

Dextroamphetamines are stimulants—substances that increase
the activity of a living organism or one of its parts. Stimulants create
a temporary "HIGH" that elevates users' moods, but these effects do
not last long. A "low," which can sometimes be overwhelming,
follows once the drug's effects wear off.

Like other AMPHETAMINES, dextroamphetamines also give people
more energy, allowing them to do more and stay awake longer without
getting tired. This effect of "speeding up" people's actions explains
how the drugs came to be known by the street names "go-pills,"
"pep pills," "speed," and "uppers."

Overview

Dextroamphetamines are addictive drugs that have a high rate
of abuse. The prefix "dextro" in the drug name dextroamphetamine
refers to dextrose, a type of sugar. Dextroamphetamines are simply
amphetamines that contain sugar molecules. (An entry on amphetamines is also available in this encyclopedia.)

The history of amphetamines stretches back to the late nineteenth
century. The drug was first synthesized, or made in a laboratory, in
1887. However, it was not used until 1932 when the drug manufacturer Smith, Kline and French introduced Benzedrine. Packaged as an
over-the-counter inhaler, the amphetamine drug Benzedrine helped
relieve nasal congestion.

high: drug-induced feelings ranging
from excitement and joy to extreme
grogginess

amphetamines: pronounced
am-FETT-uh-meens; stimulant drugs
that increase mental alertness, reduce
appetite, and help keep users awake

narcolepsy: a rare sleep disorder
characterized by daytime tiredness
and sudden attacks of sleep

Dextroamphetamine: The Drug with Multiple Uses

Throughout the 1930s, doctors in Europe prescribed amphetamines to treat colds, hay fever, and asthma. That same decade, amphetamines became available in tablet form for the treatment of the
daytime sleeping disorder known as NARCOLEPSY, a fairly rare condition
that causes people to fall asleep quickly and unexpectedly. Later,
many Americans became hooked on amphetamines—specifically the
dextroamphetamine sulfate Dexedrine—after finding that users could
lose weight quickly and effortlessly. Only then did researchers begin to
realize that these drugs could be dangerous and addictive.

One of dextroamphetamine's street names is "copilot." The drug is still routinely used by Air Force pilots on long missions to help keep them awake and alert. © *Aero Graphics, Inc./Corbis.*

During World War II (1939–1945), amphetamines were distributed among soldiers from the United States, the United Kingdom, Germany, and Japan to keep them awake and alert on the battlefield. Back on the home front, people who worked in factories manufacturing goods for the war effort were also using the drug to boost their productivity. After the war, use of the drug continued, both in the United States and abroad.

Access to Amphetamines Is Restricted
Amphetamines and dextroamphetamines became the drug of choice for people who needed a lift or who needed to stay alert.

Night-shift workers, students cramming for exams, and truck drivers on long hauls were among the most common users. The addictive nature of the drugs contributed to the growing demand for them. In 1970, drug companies in the United States produced about 12 million amphetamine tablets. A large percentage of these drugs fell into the wrong hands and made their way to the BLACK MARKET. That year, the U.S. Congress passed the Controlled Substances Act (CSA) in an effort to stop the huge increase in drug use. The new law restricted the use of amphetamines and classified them as Schedule II drugs—drugs with genuine medical uses that nevertheless possess a high potential for abuse and dependency.

What Is It Made Of?

All amphetamines are SYNTHETIC, or manufactured, substances. They cannot be grown in a garden or dug up from the ground. The composition of amphetamine pills or capsules is actually a combination of various types of crystalline compounds called amphetamine salts. The difference between amphetamine and dextroamphetamine is a few molecules of dextrose, which is a type of sugar.

The chemical formula for dextroamphetamine is $(C_9H_{13}N)_2$. The chemical formula for dextroamphetamine sulfate is $C_{18}H_{28}N_2O_4S$.

How Is It Taken?

Dextroamphetamine sulfate is manufactured in capsule and tablet form and is usually swallowed. Dexedrine capsules have one brown end and one clear end and are filled with two types of tiny drug pellets. One type of pellet dissolves shortly after the capsule is ingested. The other type is time-released, allowing for a gradual release of the rest of the medication throughout the day. The capsules are available in 5-milligram, 10-milligram, and 15-milligram doses. Dexedrine also comes in tablet form. The 5-milligram pills are triangular and orange. DextroStat, another dextroamphetamine sulfate, is only available in 5-milligram and 10-milligram tablets. The pills are yellow and round.

For the treatment of narcolepsy, patients are typically prescribed 5 milligrams to 60 milligrams of dextroamphetamine per day. Patients age six or older with ATTENTION-DEFICIT/HYPERACTIVITY DISORDER (ADHD) usually take 5 milligrams to 40 milligrams per day, depending on their age and response to the drug. The youngest ADHD patients—ages three to five—may be given half of a 5-milligram tablet.

black market: the illegal sale or trade of goods; drug dealers are said to carry out their business on the "black market"

synthetic: made in a laboratory

attention-deficit/hyperactivity disorder (ADHD): a disorder characterized by impulsive behavior, difficulty concentrating, and hyperactivity that interferes with social and academic functioning

Dextroamphetamine is prescribed for the treatment of narcolepsy, a rare sleeping disorder characterized by daytime tiredness and sudden attacks of sleep. People with narcolepsy have been known to fall asleep while driving, talking, and eating, among other things. *Photograph by Leitha Etheridge-Sims.*

Are There Any Medical Reasons for Taking This Substance?

Amphetamines such as Dexedrine and DextroStat (dextroamphetamine sulfate) and Adderall (a combination of amphetamine and dextroamphetamine sulfate referred to as a "mixed amphetamine") are used to treat ADHD and narcolepsy. (An entry on Adderall is also available in this encyclopedia.) Dextroamphetamines are useful in the treatment of ADHD because they improve the user's ability to concentrate. The drug helps patients with narcolepsy by speeding up bodily functions and increasing alertness.

In the 1970s, dextroamphetamines were approved for use as anti-obesity drugs. Because they decrease feelings of hunger in people who

Some students use dextroamphetamines to help them stay alert when cramming for tests. Other students believe that using drugs to improve school performance is cheating. Should students be checked for drugs before taking tests? This question is of concern to many students, parents, and teachers. © *Gabe Palmer/Corbis.*

take them, dextroamphetamines and other amphetamines have often been abused by dieters. This is exactly what happened with Dexedrine. By the start of the twenty-first century, research was underway on a variety of different diet pills. Dextroamphetamines like Dexedrine, however, were no longer being prescribed for weight loss in the United States.

Usage Trends

Problems undoubtedly develop when dextroamphetamine pills and capsules are taken by individuals who have no medical need for the drug. All amphetamines are PSYCHOSTIMULANTS, meaning that they act primarily on the brain. Amphetamines are extremely addictive, and high doses can affect the brain in negative ways. Regardless of the dangers, their power to increase concentration and decrease the need for sleep has led to a new trend known as stimulant "sharing." (See separate entries in this encyclopedia on "Adderall" and "Ritalin and Other Methylphenidates.")

Reports from the United States, Canada, and the United Kingdom in the first five years of the twenty-first century indicate that prescription dextroamphetamines are being shared—or sold—among adolescents and college students. ILLICIT drug users claim they receive the stimulants from other young people who use them for medical purposes. In some cases, the drugs are stolen or simply lifted from the family medicine cabinet.

The reasons for the abuse of dextroamphetamines at the high school and college levels vary. Nicholas Zamiska commented in the *Wall Street Journal* that the "unapproved use" of drugs like Adderall seem to stem from increased pressure on students to perform well on standardized tests. Illicit RECREATIONAL DRUG USE occurs as well.

Major Studies on Amphetamine Use and Abuse

DAWN and NSDUH: The Drug Abuse Warning Network (DAWN) operates through the Substance Abuse and Mental Health Services Administration (SAMHSA), a division of the U.S. Department of Health and Human Services. DAWN monitors drug-related visits to hospital emergency departments (EDs). In the last two quarters of 2003, the DAWN report estimated that the use of stimulants resulted in 42,538 emergency department visits in 260 hospitals across the United States. Of those visits, 18,129 of them were attributed directly to amphetamines and dextroamphetamines.

SAMHSA's own annual study, known as the National Survey on Drug Use and Health (NSDUH), tracks nonmedical drug use among

psychostimulants: pronounced SY-koh-STIM-yew-lents; stimulants that act on the brain

illicit: unlawful

recreational drug use: using a drug solely to achieve a high, not to treat a medical condition

Americans of all ages. The latest statistics available from SAMHSA as of mid-2005 were from 2003. That year, 4 percent of all youths age twelve to seventeen reported using prescription-type drugs, including stimulants. The percentage was higher among eighteen- to twenty-five-year-olds. Six percent of this age group admitted to using prescription drugs for nonmedical reasons. About 1.9 percent of adults age twenty-six and older reported illicit prescription drug use.

Generation Rx?: On April 21, 2005, the Partnership for a Drug-Free America (PDFA) released the findings of its 2004 study on the abuse of drugs among U.S. teenagers. The PDFA's Partnership Attitude Tracking Study, better known as PATS, indicated that the trend in teen drug use in the early part of the twenty-first century involves prescription (Rx) and over-the-counter (OTC) medications. The authors of the study see this as a sign that "Rx and OTC medicine abuse has penetrated teen culture."

Millions of teens are using prescription drugs without a doctor's order, prompting the media to dub these young adults "Generation Rx." According to PATS, 10 percent of American teenagers, or 2.3 million young people, have tried prescription stimulants like Adderall without a doctor's prescription. The teens in the study reported that they obtained the stimulants from fellow classmates or from their own home medicine cabinets.

Monitoring the Future ... and Beyond: The PATS statistics mirror the results of the 2004 Monitoring the Future (MTF) study. An annual survey of drug use among eighth, tenth, and twelfth-grade students, the MTF is performed by the University of Michigan and funded by the National Institute on Drug Abuse (NIDA). Although amphetamine use was down slightly among eighth and tenth graders, about 10 percent of high school seniors reported recreational use of the drug in 2004.

A study conducted by University of Michigan Substance Abuse Research Center scientists, detailed in the journal *Addiction* in 2005, tracked the usage of amphetamines beyond high school. Of nearly 11,000 randomly selected college students, 6.9 percent of them reported nonmedical prescription stimulant use at least once in their lives. About 4.1 percent admitted using prescription stimulants in the past year, and 2.1 percent used them in the past month. The authors of the study concluded that "high-risk behavior" such as this "should be monitored further." They added, "intervention efforts are needed to curb this form of drug abuse."

Blurred vision is one of the side effects of taking high doses of dextroamphetamine. Other medical problems that can result include fever, an unusually fast heartbeat, chest pain, nervous tics, tremors, moodiness, and even aggression. © *Tom & Dee Ann McCarthy/Corbis.*

Effects on the Body

Common side effects of dextroamphetamine use include dry mouth, headache, nausea, dizziness, restlessness, increased blood pressure and pulse rate, loss of appetite, difficulty sleeping, and either diarrhea or constipation. Higher doses can result in fever, an unusually fast heartbeat, chest pain, blurred vision, TICS, tremors, moodiness, and even aggression.

tics: repetitive, involuntary jerky movements, eye blinking, or vocal sounds that patients cannot suppress on their own

Amphetamine Psychosis

High-dose dextroamphetamine abusers can develop "amphetamine psychosis" after a week or so of continuous use. Amphetamine PSYCHOSIS affects the way the mind functions, causing feelings of severe PARANOIA, and all kinds of hallucinations—visual, auditory, and tactile. Tactile hallucinations make the user feel as if bugs, worms, or snakes are crawling on their skin. Such

psychosis: pronounced sy-KOH-sis; a severe mental disorder that often causes hallucinations and makes it difficult for people to distinguish what is real from what is imagined

paranoia: abnormal feelings of suspicion and fear

Finding the Right Treatment

Dextroamphetamines such as Dexedrine and amphetamine/dextroamphetamine mixtures such as Adderall are commonly prescribed by physicians to treat ADHD. Finding the right drug to treat a child or an adult with ADHD is often a process of "trial and error." Doctors try one drug, observe the effects, and decide whether an alternate form of treatment is advisable.

Establishing a safe and effective drug treatment can be especially difficult when it comes to children. Some evidence indicates that children experiencing ADHD-like symptoms may actually be suffering from severe anxiety, or a severe state of fear or worry, which is worsened by the use of stimulants. In these very rare cases, amphetamines and dextroamphetamines can cause overstimulation in the child.

In one case reported in the May 2004, issue of *Pediatrics,* doctors raised the question about whether dextroamphetamines may have contributed to psychotic behavior in a seven-year-old ADHD patient. His symptoms, including extreme agitation, an elevated temperature, ranting and raving, and hallucinations, all disappeared when the stimulant prescription was discontinued and an anti-anxiety drug was administered. Results such as these suggest that the child was suffering from severe anxiety rather than ADHD, even though his symptoms mirrored those of a typical ADHD patient.

sensations are very real, and therefore extremely frightening, to the individual who is experiencing them. As a result, violent reactions sometimes occur during amphetamine psychosis. Once the amphetamine abuser is free of the drug, however, the psychosis goes away. Symptoms such as mental confusion and memory problems may linger, however.

Monitoring Dosage

When used for medical purposes, dextroamphetamines are prescribed at the lowest possible dosage. The dosage is then raised gradually by a doctor until the desired action is achieved. All amphetamines are highly addictive. According to the 59th edition of the *Physicians' Desk Reference:* "There are reports of patients who have increased the dosage to many times that recommended," leading to "tolerance, extreme PSYCHOLOGICAL DEPENDENCE, and severe social disability."

Tolerance occurs when it takes more and more of the drug to achieve the effect or high originally produced by smaller doses. Tolerance to amphetamines can occur quickly and often leads to overdose. Symptoms of dextroamphetamine overdose include extreme confusion and anxiety, hallucinations, severe tics or shaking, an irregular heartbeat, extremely high blood pressure, vomiting, stomach cramps, convulsions, and coma. An overdose of dextroamphetamine—or any other amphetamine, for that matter—can be fatal.

Dextroamphetamine as a Treatment for ADHD

Amphetamines and dextroamphetamines typically give the user a boost of energy. In people with attention-deficit/hyperactivity disorder (ADHD), however, these very same drugs help to calm them down, allowing them to better focus their energy. Individuals with ADHD typically have a short attention span, and they tend to get distracted quite easily. They may also show signs of

psychological dependence: the belief that a person needs to take a certain substance in order to function

hyperactivity, impulsive behavior, and emotional instability. It can be a challenge for people with untreated ADHD to concentrate their attention and control their behavior. Drugs like Dexedrine, a dextroamphetamine sulfate, and Adderall, a combination of amphetamine and dextroamphetamine salts, help manage the symptoms of ADHD by acting on the part of the brain that decides when and how to act.

According to an article in *Phi Delta Kappan,* it is essential that parents or caregivers of children and teens with ADHD: 1) be informed about the effects of the drugs that have been prescribed for treatment; 2) know the consequences that might arise if these drugs are discontinued; and 3) accept the responsibility to stay in close touch with the child's doctor and therapist. In most cases, drug treatment for ADHD must be combined with some sort of counseling or therapy to achieve the highest success rates. One of the most popular and successful therapeutic methods as of 2005 was COGNITIVE BEHAVIORAL THERAPY (CBT), or "talk" therapy. Cognitive behavioral therapy helps patients develop better coping skills and change their negative patterns of thinking and behavior into positive ones.

Reactions with Other Drugs or Substances

The stimulating effects of dextroamphetamine can be intensified when the drug is combined with other stimulants such as cocaine or nicotine. (Entries on cocaine and nicotine are also available in this encyclopedia.) Dextroamphetamines should never be mixed with alcohol or other depressants.

Some medications can cause severe reactions in the user when mixed with stimulants. In addition, people with certain medical conditions should stay away from these drugs. Specifically, dextroamphetamines should not be taken by pregnant women, nursing mothers, or individuals with any of the following conditions:

cognitive behavioral therapy (CBT): a type of therapy that helps people recognize and change negative patterns of thinking and behavior

thyroid: an important gland, or group of cells, in the body that secretes chemical messengers called hormones; these hormones control metabolism, the process by which food is converted to energy that the body uses to function

Tourette's syndrome: a severe tic disorder that causes distress and significant impairment to those affected by it

- heart disease
- high blood pressure
- THYROID disease
- TOURETTE'S SYNDROME, or any other tic disorder
- a history of drug abuse
- depression that is being treated with prescription drugs
- severe pain that is being treated with the prescription drug meperidine. (A separate entry on meperidine is available in this encyclopedia.)

Patti Davis (right), daughter of Nancy Reagan (left) and former U.S. President Ronald Reagan, battled a drug addiction when she was younger. During her husband's presidency, Nancy Reagan became a spokesperson for the "Just Say No" to drugs campaign. *AP/Wide World Photos.*

Treatment for Habitual Users

WITHDRAWAL from amphetamines can be a long and difficult process for many users. Psychological dependence is made even worse by the intense cravings for the drug that users experience. Unpleasant and sometimes frightening symptoms develop as the body tries to adjust to the absence of the stimulant. The withdrawal process causes depression and may also bring on fatigue, vivid dreams, irregular sleep patterns, and increased appetite.

Experts in the treatment of substance abuse and addiction report that behavioral therapy and emotional support are essential for the successful rehabilitation of amphetamine abusers. An individual recovering from drug addiction must avoid all psychoactive drugs, including alcohol. Amphetamine and dextroamphetamine cravings can be extremely powerful and may last for years after a former user has kicked the habit.

Patti Davis, daughter of former U.S. President Ronald Reagan and his wife, Nancy, talked about her past drug addiction in the article "Dope: A Love Story" in *Time* magazine. In the article, Davis wrote that she often wondered "why the world is so hard for some

withdrawal: the process of gradually cutting back on the amount of a drug being taken until it is discontinued entirely; also the accompanying physiological effects of terminating use of an addictive drug

people" that they "run for the refuge of drugs." This observation shows why an effective drug rehabilitation program must help patients identify and deal with the underlying emotional issues surrounding their drug use.

The reasons for drug use are numerous. *The Merck Manual of Medical Information* noted that "some amphetamine abusers are depressed and seek the mood-elevating effects of these stimulants to temporarily relieve the depression." Davis pointed out that some people are afraid of the world. Drugs "take you away—far away; they let you hide, which is what frightened people do," she commented. Recovering drug abusers need a solid support system to remain drug free.

Consequences

Amphetamine addicts frequently allow their need for the drug to take over their lives. Users can become so obsessed with satisfying their drug habit that they ignore the most important people in their lives. Relationships with family and friends frequently deteriorate, and money problems may begin to develop as the addiction grows. In general, substance abuse is associated with increased rates of school failure, theft (usually to fund the drug habit), domestic violence, sexual assault, unemployment, and homelessness. People who are high on amphetamines are more likely to engage in risky behavior than people who do not take drugs. This can contribute to the spread of sexually transmitted diseases, including HIV (the human immunodeficiency virus, which can lead to acquired immunodeficiency syndrome [AIDS]).

The Law

Abuse of any amphetamine can have serious legal consequences. Amphetamines are controlled substances, meaning their use is regulated by certain federal laws. Under the terms of the Controlled Substances Act (CSA) of 1970, amphetamines are classified as Schedule II drugs. Schedule II drugs are prescription medications that have genuine medical uses but also pose a high risk for abuse and addiction. Schedule II drugs like dextroamphetamines require a doctor's prescription and carry a warning that states they "should be prescribed or dispensed sparingly." Pharmacies and hospitals that dispense Schedule II drugs must register with the U.S. Drug Enforcement Administration. In addition, limits are placed on the amount of dextroamphetamine produced by manufacturers for the United States each year.

"Go-Pills" and the Military

Dextroamphetamines have a long history of use by the military and were even given to astronauts to fight motion sickness and fatigue during space flights. The drug's routine use by air force pilots has given new meaning to the term "copilot," one of several street names for dextroamphetamine.

The U.S. Air Force has used Dexedrine, known in military circles as "go-pills," since 1960. A 1995 report from Langley Air Force Base revealed widespread amphetamine use in Operation Desert Storm. Gene Collier, writing in the *Post-Gazette,* reported that 60 percent of U.S. pilots in the Gulf War said they took Dexedrine during their missions. In a study performed by the U.S. Army Aeromedical Research Laboratory in 2000, one pilot was able to stay awake for sixty-four hours straight by taking Dexedrine.

Dextroamphetamine reportedly improves alertness and flight performance by fighting fatigue, confusion, and air sickness in the cockpit. It has been shown to increase accuracy, improve short-term memory, and speed up reaction time. But Dexedrine, like all amphetamines, is a habit-forming drug with potentially serious side effects. A tragic incident occurred in 2002 involving two American pilots who were taking the drug. This incident called the use of Dexedrine by the military into serious question.

Deadly Consequences

The two pilots, Major Harry Schmidt and Major William Umbach, were flying separate F-16s back from a mission in Afghanistan. On the night of April 17, 2002, twelve Canadian soldiers in Afghanistan were hit by a quarter-ton bomb dropped by Major Schmidt from his F-16. Four of the soldiers were killed, the other eight were wounded. The Canadians had been conducting a live-fire exercise with anti-tank guns that night—an exercise that U.S. Air Force officials apparently had been told about earlier. According to the Canadian inquiry report on the case, as reported by *CBC News,* "Until the moment the bombs struck, Canadian forces had no knowledge of impending danger."

Both U.S. pilots stated that they believed they were under attack when they saw the flashes of gunfire on the ground below. Schmidt wanted

Since the passage of the CSA, according to Andrew Weil and Winifred Rosen in *From Chocolate to Morphine,* "most cases of amphetamine abuse have involved legally manufactured and prescribed drugs." Most of the illicit dextroamphetamine supply, then, comes from actual prescriptions that are obtained, used, and sold illegally.

Anyone convicted of transporting or dealing in dextroamphetamine in the United States faces up to twenty years in prison and a hefty fine for a first offense. Repeat offenders face even stiffer penalties. In the United Kingdom, amphetamines are designated a class B drug under the 1971 Misuse of Drugs Act. Possession carries a penalty of imprisonment for three months to five years, and dealing carries a sentence of six months to fourteen years, along with a possible fine.

U.S. Air Force pilots Harry Schmidt (left) and William Umbach were involved in a "friendly fire" incident in Afghanistan. *AP/Wide World Photos.*

The American pilot who dropped the 500-pound bomb had taken a 20-milligram dose of Dexedrine about an hour before the incident. Some observers felt that the drug "may have been a factor in the decision to drop a bomb on allied soldiers," noted *CBC News.* American Air Force officials argued that hundreds of earlier patrols had been flown safely and successfully over Afghanistan by pilots on Dexedrine.

The outcome of the so-called "friendly fire" case was decided on July 6, 2004. According to *CBC News,* the text of the U.S. Air Force verdict stated that Schmidt exhibited "arrogance and a lack of flight discipline" for not taking "a series of evasive actions and remain[ing] at a safe distance to await further instructions." Instead, he "closed on the target and blatantly disobeyed the direction to 'hold fire.'" Schmidt's actions were deemed "inexcusable," and he was found guilty of dereliction of duty—abandoning duty or showing negligence—for his actions.

to return fire, but, according to the *Post-Gazette,* was told by Umbach, "Let's just make sure that it's not friendlies, that's all." By "friendlies," Umbach was referring to soldiers fighting on the same side as the Americans. Cockpit voice recordings indicate that Major Schmidt was instructed to hold his fire, but he remained convinced that he was under attack and responded, "I am rolling in in self-defense."

The use of Dexedrine by the military remains a hot topic of debate.

For More Information

Books

Beers, Mark H., and others. *The Merck Manual of Medical Information,* 2nd home ed. New York: Pocket Books, 2003.

Brecher, Edward M., and others. *The Consumers Union Report on Licit and Illicit Drugs.* Boston: Little Brown & Co., 1972.

Clayton, Lawrence. *Amphetamines and Other Stimulants.* New York: Rosen Publishing Group, 1994.

Gahlinger, Paul M. *Illegal Drugs: A Complete Guide to Their History, Chemistry, Use, and Abuse.* Las Vegas, NV: Sagebrush Press, 2001.

Kuhn, Cynthia, Scott Swartzwelder, Wilkie Wilson, and others. *Buzzed: The Straight Facts about the Most Used and Abused Drugs from Alcohol to Ecstasy,* 2nd ed. New York: W.W. Norton, 2003.

Physicians' Desk Reference, 59th ed. Montvale, NJ: Thomson PDR, 2004.

Weil, Andrew, and Winifred Rosen. *From Chocolate to Morphine.* New York: Houghton Mifflin, 1993, rev. 2004.

Periodicals

"Attention Deficit Disorder: Generic Dexedrine Spansule Capsules Approved." *Medical Letter on the CDC & FDA* (February 17, 2002): p. 6.

Calello, Diane P., and Kevin C. Osterhoudt. "Acute Psychosis Associated with Therapeutic Use of Dextroamphetamine." *Pediatrics* (May, 2004): p. 1466.

Collier, Gene. "Pilots on the Go Might Not Know When to Stop." *Post-Gazette* (January 19, 2003).

Davis, Patti. "Dope: A Love Story." *Time* (May 7, 2001): p. 55.

Emonson, D., and R. Vanderbeek. "The Use of Amphetamines in U.S. Air Force Tactical Operations during Desert Shield and Storm." *Aviation Space and Environmental Medicine,* volume 66, number 3 (1995): p. 802.

Grady, Denise. "History Counsels Caution on Diet Pills." *New York Times* (May 25, 1999).

Hewitt, Bill. "Clipped Wings." *People* (February 3, 2003): pp. 103-104.

Jurgensen, John. "Military Researchers Focus on Pilot Fatigue." *Detroit News* (January 25, 2003).

McCabe, S. E., and others. "Non-medical Use of Prescription Stimulants among U.S. College Students." *Addiction* (January, 2005): pp. 96-106.

"Negligence Is a Two-Way Street." *Phi Delta Kappan* (November, 1995): pp. 259-260.

"Sex, Drugs, and Rock 'n' Roll." *Independent* (January 28, 1996): p. 8.

Shute, Nancy, and others. "The Perils of Pills: The Psychiatric Medication of Children Is Dangerously Haphazard." *U.S. News & World Report* (March 6, 2000): p. 44.

Zamiska, Nicholas. "Pressed to Do Well on Admissions Tests, Students Take Drugs; Stimulants Prescribed for Attention Disorders Find New Unapproved Use." *Wall Street Journal* (November 8, 2004): p. A1.

Web Sites

"2003 National Survey on Drug Use and Health (NSDUH)." *U.S. Department of Health and Human Services, Substance Abuse and Mental*

Health Services Administration. http://www.oas.samhsa.gov/nhsda.htm (accessed June 30, 2005).

"Drug Abuse Warning Network, 2003: Interim National Estimates of Drug-Related Emergency Department Visits." *DAWN, 2003: Office of Applied Studies, Substance Abuse and Mental Health Services Administration.* http://DAWNinfo.samhsa.gov/ (accessed June 30, 2005).

"Generation Rx: National Study Reveals New Category of Substance Abuse Emerging: Teens Abusing Rx and OTC Medications Intentionally to Get High." *Partnership for a Drug-Free America.* http://www.drugfree.org/ (accessed June 30, 2005).

"Grieving Canadians Stunned U.S. Pilots Took Drugs." *CBC News,* December 21, 2002. http://www.cbc.ca/stories/2002/12/21/clooney_021221 (accessed June 30, 2005).

"Indepth: Go-Pills, Bombs & Friendly Fire." *CBC News,* November 17, 2004. http://www.cbc.ca/news/background/friendlyfire/gopills.html (accessed June 30, 2005).

"Indepth: The 'Friendly Fire' Reports." *CBC News,* October 22, 2003. http://www.cbc.ca/news/background/friendlyfire/reports.html (accessed June 30, 2005).

"Indepth: U.S. Air Force Verdict." *CBC News,* July 6, 2004. http://www.cbc.ca/news/background/friendlyfire/verdict.html (accessed June 30, 2005).

Monitoring the Future. http://www.monitoringthefuture.org/ and http://www.nida.nih.gov/Newsroom/04/2004MTFDrug.pdf (both accessed June 30, 2005).

National Institute on Drug Abuse. http://www.nida.nih.gov/ and http://www.drugabuse.gov (both accessed June 30, 2005).

"Shepperd: 'Go-Pills' Common for Pilots." *CNN.com,* January 3, 2003. http://www.cnn.com/2003/US/01/03/cnna.shepperd/index.html (accessed June 30, 2005).

"Teens Becoming 'Generation Rx'." *CNN.com.* http://www.cnn.com/2005/HEALTH/parenting/04/21/drug.survey.ap/index.html (accessed June 30, 2005).

"U.S. Pilots Took Amphetamines before 'Friendly Fire' Incident." *CBC News,* December 21, 2002. http://www.cbc.ca/story/world/national/2002/12/20/friendlyfire021220.html (accessed June 30, 2005).

See also: Adderall; Amphetamines; Methamphetamine; Ritalin and Other Methylphenidates

Dextromethorphan

Official Drug Name: d-3-methoxy-N-methylmorphinan (commonly called dextromethorphan, pronounced deks-troh-meth-ORR-fan); sometimes referred to by shortened name DXM

Also Known As: DM, DXM, dex, drex, red devils, robo, robo-tripping, skittles, triple-C, tussin, velvet, vitamin D

Drug Classifications: The U.S. Department of Justice, Drug Enforcement Administration Diversion Control Program does not list dextromethorphan as a controlled substance; it has no Schedule listing

opiates: drugs derived from the opium poppy or synthetically produced to mimic the effects of the opium poppy; opiates tend to decrease restlessness, bring on sleep, and relieve pain

psychotic behavior: a dangerous loss of contact with reality, sometimes leading to violence against self or others

What Kind of Drug Is It?

Dextromethorphan (DXM) is an ingredient in more than 100 over-the-counter (OTC) cold, flu, and cough remedies. It is used specifically to suppress coughs. The drug is widely used in OTC medications because, at normal dosages, it does not produce side effects in most people. Dextromethorphan is a synthetic drug, meaning that it is manufactured in a laboratory.

The chemical is derived from levomethorphan—a synthetic substance that mimics the behavior of OPIATES such as heroin, morphine, or codeine. In its pure form, levomethorphan shows many similarities to the opiates, including the potential for addiction. Separated from the levomethorphan, dextromethorphan loses its painkilling component and is also thought to be non-addicting.

Higher Doses and Dangerous Combinations

Because so many easily purchased products contain dextromethorphan, it can be obtained legally for abuse in higher doses. It is not a controlled substance, and no one needs a prescription to purchase it. Nevertheless, emergency doctors, pharmacists, and law enforcement officials are aware of the problems that the drug can cause when abused. They warn of the drug's potential for producing a whole host of dangerous effects on the brain and central nervous system when taken in high doses or in combination with other drugs or alcohol.

Dextromethorphan has been described as a "dissociative anesthetic." This means that it is a substance that alters perception. As one young user told *People Weekly* magazine in 2004, "You start feeling numb. And finally, you're gone. You're out of your body. You're not there anymore." This is a basic description of "dissociative" feelings.

The drug is also well known for producing: 1) hallucinations—visions or other perceptions of things that are not really present; and 2) an inability to walk or communicate. In worse case scenarios, the drug has caused PSYCHOTIC BEHAVIOR.

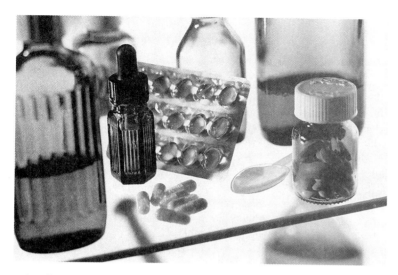

Using dextromethorphan with other drugs from one's medicine cabinet can be dangerous. © *Andrew Brookes/Corbis.*

Robert Finn compared the use of dextromethorphan to the use of the HALLUCINOGENIC drug PCP (phencyclidine) in a 2004 article for *Family Practice News.* Finn wrote: "While some symptoms of DXM intoxication are similar to those of PCP intoxication, there's one important difference: People on PCP are able to walk and they're able to become violent. On the other hand, people on DXM become immobilized." (An entry on PCP [phencyclidine] is also available in this encyclopedia.)

One of the greatest dangers of dextromethorphan use is that it is commonly sold in combination with other medications. These include: 1) acetaminophen (pronounced uh-SEE-tuh-MINN-uh fenn), a non-aspirin pain reliever, such as Tylenol; 2) antihistamines, drugs that block *histamine,* a chemical that causes nasal congestion related to allergies; and 3) guaifenesin (pronounced gwy-FENN-ess-inn) or other EXPECTORANTS. Multi-symptom cold and cough medications are formulated for correct use by the proper dosage. The use of larger doses not only delivers high quantities of dextromethorphan, it can also deliver large doses of the other ingredients. This can lead to nausea, anxiety, and organ damage.

Abusers of dextromethorphan try to find it in preparations that do not contain these other ingredients, sometimes even purchasing it in powdered form from Internet sites. In this

hallucinogenic: ability to bring on hallucinations, which alter the user's perception of reality

expectorants: a cough remedy used to bring up mucus from the throat or bronchial tubes; expectorants cause users to spit up thick secretions from their clogged breathing passages

Dangerous in High Doses

Medications available in the local drug store can be very dangerous, even deadly, when taken in high doses or combined with other drugs. Over-the-counter medications sometimes combine dextromethorphan with other ingredients meant to ease the multiple symptoms of colds and flu. Some of these other ingredients, and their potential as poisons, include:

- Acetaminophen (uh-SEE-tuh-MINN-uh-fenn), a pain reliever such as Tylenol. In high doses, this substance causes severe damage to the liver and other internal organs. It can lead to death.

- Guaifenesin (gwy-FENN-ess-inn), a mucus-thinner and expectorant. In high doses, it causes nausea and vomiting.
- Pseudoephedrine hydrochloride (SUE-doh-ih-FEH-drinn high-droh-KLOR-ide), a decongestant. Overdoses of this medication can lead to nervousness, insomnia, heart palpitations, and breathing problems.
- Chlorpheniramine maleate (KLOR-fenn-ear-uh-mene MAL-ee-ate), an antihistamine such as Chlor-Trimeton. This drug is broken down by the same liver enzyme as dextromethorphan. Overdoses of the two drugs taken together can be fatal.

case, problems arise with doses. Unlike many abused drugs, which act predictably as dosage increases, dextromethorphan works as a "PLATEAU" drug. High doses cause a different set of reactions in the brain than low doses. Thus, a mismanaged use of dextromethorphan can cause an inexperienced abuser to undergo a bewildering hallucination-filled TRIP, possibly ending in a seizure or a coma.

Overview

In 1949, American chemists applied for a patent on dextromethorphan, after having isolated it from its parent drug, levomethorphan, a synthetic OPIOID. During the 1950s, abuse of cough syrups containing codeine was a serious problem for adults and teenagers. This led manufacturers of cough and cold remedies to search for a product that would suppress coughs without causing drowsiness or promoting addiction. Dextromethorphan seemed to be the answer. By 1959, it had won approval by the U.S. Food and Drug Administration (FDA) for use as a cough remedy. In the 1960s, a dextromethorphan-only pill, Romilar, was introduced as an over-the-counter medication. However, it was pulled from the market when its potential for abuse became known.

plateau: a level or step

trip: an intense and usually very visual experience produced by an hallucinogenic drug

opioid: a substance created in a laboratory to mimic the effects of naturally occurring opiates such as heroin and morphine

The World Health Organization (WHO) classified dextromethorphan as a non-analgesic, non-addictive substance in the late 1960s. (An analgesic is a drug that relieves pain.) Yet, pharmaceutical companies decided to use the drug in combination form with other agents. The era of multi-symptom cough, cold, and flu remedies was born, with a variety of products for adults and children.

So Easy to Get

Modern pharmacies, grocery stores, and even convenience stores stock cough remedies with dextromethorphan. The drug can be found in brand-name products such as Coricidin, Robitussin, Vicks NyQuil, Dimetapp DM, Alka-Seltzer Plus Cold and Cough, Sudafed cough products, Tylenol cold products, and Vicks Formula 44. The street names "triple-C" and "skittles" have been coined to describe Coricidin. "Robo-tripping" is slang for abuse of liquid cough syrups such as Robitussin.

According to the Cleveland *Plain Dealer,* reported cases of teen dextromethorphan abuse more than doubled nationwide between 2000 and 2003. An increase of dextromethorphan abuse among teenagers sparked parent

Cough syrup abuse can lead to many side effects, including double vision. The side effects get worse when dextromethorphan is taken in combination with other drugs.
Lauren Shear/Photo Researchers, Inc.

groups, legislators, and pharmacies to take action. *Drug Topics* magazine noted that some national chain pharmacies, such as CVS and Wal-Mart, have programmed their computer scanners to ask for an age identification before selling DXM products. Others, including Walgreens, restrict the number of packages a customer can buy. Some drugstores have even moved these medications from the main aisles into the pharmacy area, so the sale of these drugs can be monitored. By September of 2004, several states were considering legislation that would prohibit anyone under the age of eighteen from buying products containing dextromethorphan.

The easy availability of dextromethorphan sometimes makes it the first choice for abuse among teens who might feel uncomfortable buying illegal drugs. However, in high doses it is as dangerous and unpredictable in its effects as PCP and ketamine. (An entry on ketamine is also available in this encyclopedia.)

In the *Palm Beach Post*, Carolyn Susman detailed the "laundry list" of side effects from dextromethorphan abuse, including "DISSOCIATION ... confusion, dizziness, double or blurred vision, slurred speech, impaired physical coordination, abdominal pain, nausea and vomiting, rapid heart beat, drowsiness, numbness of fingers and toes, and disorientation." This list does not include the even more dangerous symptoms associated with use of dextromethorphan in combination with other drugs.

What Is It Made Of?

Dextromethorphan is a synthetic substance, meaning it is manufactured in a lab. It was first developed by modifying levomethorphan, a non-carbon-containing opioid. While the brain "reads" levomethorphan like an opiate, it does not "read" dextromethorphan the same way. Thus, at recommended doses, dextromethorphan does not cause drowsiness, dizziness, or sedation.

Some people—about seven in every one hundred—have a genetic trait called CYP2D6 deficiency. This is the lack of a liver ENZYME that works to break down dextromethorphan. For these people, even the recommended dose of products containing dextromethorphan can produce unpleasant feelings of anxiety, restlessness, or "jitters." Anyone with the CYP2D6 deficiency who abuses dextromethorphan can experience a psychotic episode, or a period of intense fear, PARANOIA, and powerlessness. People with this enzyme deficiency also face a greater risk of fatal poisoning by dextromethorphan.

How Is It Taken?

Products containing dextromethorphan include pills, cough syrups, and liquid cold and flu medications. Dextromethorphan is not snorted through the nostrils or injected, even in its pure powdered form. Over-the-counter cold and flu remedies list all active and inactive ingredients as well as specific dosage charts. Physicians and pharmacists recommend that patients taking liquid medications use precise measuring cups, often provided with the products, rather than teaspoons or tablespoons from a kitchen drawer. If the product does not come with a measuring cup, pharmacies have them in stock and will provide one upon request.

dissociation: a psychological syndrome in which the mind seems detached from the body; sometimes referred to as an "out of body" experience

enzyme: a substance that speeds up chemical reactions in the body

paranoia: abnormal feelings of suspicion and fear

When taking cough medicine, it is important to measure it precisely to avoid taking too much. Measuring cups are usually provided by the product's manufacturer. *Photograph by Leitha Etheridge-Sims.*

Are There Any Medical Reasons for Taking This Substance?

Dextromethorphan is recommended for quieting coughs. It does not work on the nose or the throat, but rather on the brain and the central nervous system, to lessen the body's chemical signals to cough.

According to a 1997 report in the journal *Pediatrics*, dextromethorphan may not be safe for use in children even though it can be found in pediatric products. First, parents may administer too much medicine to a child, leading to negative side effects. Second, very young children also have immature livers that cannot properly METABOLIZE dextromethorphan and other cold remedies.

Most important, for children *and* adults, coughs serve a practical purpose. They clear the airways of fluids, allowing for better breathing. Some illnesses, including asthma, cystic fibrosis, allergies, and pneumonia, can actually be made worse by the use of dextromethorphan. The drug is only recommended for brief episodes of coughing, such as those accompanying colds and flu. Patients with chronic, or long-term coughing, should be seen by a doctor.

Usage Trends

Between 2000 and 2003, the number of dextromethorphan abuse cases reported to national poison control centers more than doubled, from 1,623 to 3,271, according to the Cleveland *Plain Dealer.* The vast majority of dextromethorphan abusers are teenagers or young adults. The main way they get the drug is by buying it in over-the-counter medications.

Deaths from Over-the-Counter Drugs?

Since 2000, newspapers and magazines have reported numerous deaths associated with dextromethorphan abuse. A twenty-year-old Colorado man was found dead in his bed of a Coricidin HBP overdose in May of 2004, as reported in the *Rocky Mountain News.* A few months earlier, *People Weekly* magazine detailed the similar death of a twenty-two-year-old college honor student who overdosed on powder he bought on the Internet. The same *People Weekly* article mentioned a fourteen-year-old Colorado boy who was killed by an automobile when trying to cross a busy highway to purchase more pills.

Two mothers who found their teenagers abusing dextromethorphan have started a parents' awareness group in Oregon. One of those mothers told the Eugene, Oregon *Register-Guard:* "What parents should do if their child is on these pills, they need to take them to the doctor or the hospital because of the damage that can be done. Definitely get medical help."

In a scientific study published in the journal *Adolescence,* Momodou N. Darboe suggested that cough syrup provides "an attractive choice for experimental abuse or misuse." Darboe found several reasons for the abuse of over-the-counter cough syrups. First, of course, is availability, then *affordability.* Teens with limited

metabolize: break down to provide energy

spending money—and perhaps a fear of breaking the law—can purchase cough syrups with dextromethorphan.

The second reason for cough syrup abuse, according to Darboe, is the "fear factor." The author explained: "Taking three or more pills of anything bears the threat ... of suicide. Powders or needles, if not prescribed, are often associated with harder, more addictive, illicit, and dangerous drugs and substances. Since cough syrup, on the other hand, [does not have] these qualities or connotations, it is relatively easier for a curious teenager to [want] to experiment with it."

Darboe made another observation in the *Adolescence* report. According to the author, "other studies show abuse of licit [legal] drugs to be a precursor of illicit drug use." Put simply, a person who takes chances abusing dextromethorphan, an easily obtainable drug, may be more likely to begin taking illegal and more addictive drugs.

> ## Signs of DXM Abuse
>
> To help people know if someone they care about is abusing DXM, health professionals note the following warning signs:
>
> - Stockpiles of cold and cough medications, more than anyone would need for a bout of the flu.
> - Empty pill packets or bottles of cough syrup found in odd places, such as under beds, in dresser drawers, or in wooded areas near homes or schools.
> - The presence of strange-looking tablets in various shapes and colors, evidence of purchase from the Internet.
> - Bookmarked Web sites or emails that encourage DXM use.
>
> Various Web sites, such as *Kids Health for Parents* (http://kidshealth.org/parent/), provide information on DXM and other drug abuse warning signs.

Effects on the Body

Taken in its recommended doses, dextromethorphan sends a chemical signal to the brain to quiet a persistent cough. The medicine's effects begin about fifteen to thirty minutes after taking it, and they last between three and six hours. Most doctors do not recommend using over-the-counter cold medications for more than a week. Cold symptoms that last longer than a week might be the first signs of a more serious illness and a doctor should be consulted. At its normal dosage level, dextromethorphan does not cause any side effects, and it is not habit-forming.

What Are the Plateaus for Dextromethorphan Overdose?

As an abused drug, dextromethorphan has been compared to HALLUCINOGENS such as ketamine and PCP. Four "plateaus" have been identified for dextromethorphan overdose. Each plateau carries a different set of symptoms and behaviors. The higher the plateau of abuse, the greater the chances of permanent brain damage, PSYCHOLOGICAL ADDICTION, or lasting behavioral problems in the user.

hallucinogens: substances that bring on hallucinations, which alter the user's perception of reality

psychological addiction: the belief that a person needs to take a certain substance in order to function

DXM Plateaus

The symptoms of dextromethorphan abuse are categorized according to the strength of the dosage taken by the user. These categories are called plateaus. According to the article "What Every Parent Needs to Know about Cough Medicine Abuse," available on the *Drug Free AZ* Web site, common symptoms of abuse at the various plateaus include:

- First plateau: mild euphoria, mild dizziness, mild distortions of color or sound.
- Second plateau: visual hallucinations, blurred vision, slurred speech, drowsiness, nausea, and vomiting.
- Third plateau: double vision, disorientation, hallucinations, rapid movements of the eyes, paranoia, difficulty speaking and walking.
- Fourth plateau: "out of body" experiences, complete loss of motor control, altered sense of time and altered sense of reality, hallucinations involving vision, hearing, and touch.

Users undergoing withdrawal from dextromethorphan may have difficulty sleeping and suffer from depression or feelings of hopelessness.

At the first plateau, users report mild sensations of dizziness or EUPHORIA. They might perceive music as either more pleasant or as strangely distorted. A first-plateau dextromethorphan abuser can still move and carry on conversations, but perceptions are altered to the point where driving a car or making other value judgments might be very difficult.

At the second plateau, users begin to experience visual hallucinations—colors swirling through the vision field with eyes closed. At this level, users also experience nausea, often with vomiting, and they have more trouble walking and communicating. To an outside observer, second plateau dextromethorphan abusers are clearly "on something." They behave as if drunk or stoned. Double vision can also occur.

Upon reaching the third plateau, users experience a wider variety of hallucinations. All sensory input is altered to some degree. An abuser might see visions that are not there or misunderstand what he or she is actually seeing. Walking and talking become very difficult, and the user becomes disoriented and out of touch with reality. This can lead to bouts of paranoia (a feeling of great personal danger) or to the recall of forgotten memories, both pleasant and unpleasant. Because motor skills become seriously impaired at this level, abusers can be a danger to themselves just from tripping and falling. Judgment is altered, leading to the possibility of self-destructive behavior.

The fourth plateau experience is extremely dangerous and sometimes deadly. At this level, the dissociation, or split between mind and body, occurs. Bizarre thoughts and hallucinations abound. Meanwhile, the abuser has little or no motor control and simply cannot move. An immobilized user may choke on his or her vomit and suffocate, or suffer seizures and brain damage. Those who abuse dextromethorphan at these highest dosages are at the greatest risk of sudden death. Survivors of fourth plateau use may become psychologically addicted to dextromethorphan and continue abusing it in search of more hallucinations and that "out of body" feeling.

euphoria: pronounced yu-FOR-ee-yuh; a state of extreme happiness and enhanced well-being; the opposite of dysphoria

Reactions with Other Drugs or Substances

As previously stated, over-the-counter multi-symptom cold and cough products contain several ingredients that can be poisonous at high doses. The dextromethorphan abuser may unknowingly risk fatal organ damage by taking too much acetaminophen. Breathing problems can occur if too much DECONGESTANT is consumed with DXM. Combining dextromethorphan with prescription drugs, controlled substances, or alcohol can prove fatal.

Even at normal doses, dextromethorphan can react negatively with prescription sedatives, antidepressant drugs known as MAO inhibitors, and the antidepressant family of drugs that includes Desyrel (trazadone) or Serzone (nefazodone). Any amount of dextromethorphan combined with a selective serotonin reuptake inhibitor (SSRI), such as Prozac, Paxil, or Zoloft, can cause chemical imbalances in the brain. Dextromethorphan is also to be avoided by anyone taking tricyclic antidepressants or medication for BIPOLAR DISORDER, such as lithium carbonate or Depacote. (A separate entry on antidepressants is available in this encyclopedia.)

Occasionally, drug dealers will pass dextromethorphan pills or powders off as ketamine, ecstasy (MDMA), or even heroin. (An entry on each of these drugs is available in this encyclopedia.) Unsuspecting users can suddenly find themselves with a whole series of symptoms for which they are not prepared. In the *New York Times,* Jacob Sullum reported that this substitution of dextromethorphan for other illicit drugs has led some dance clubs to test pills and powders on-site in order to protect customers from unknowingly taking overdoses of the dangerous DXM.

The combination of dextromethorphan products and alcohol can cause extreme nausea and vomiting, as well as a greater loss of motor control.

Treatment for Habitual Users

The FDA does not consider dextromethorphan an addictive substance. However, press coverage of dextromethorphan abuse has uncovered cases of psychological dependence, or an addiction created by an emotional need for the substance. A young user told *Teen People* magazine in 2003: "I thought I could just use Coricidin for fun, that it didn't matter. I never expected to get hooked." This user reported months of daily abuse that led to physical problems, including blood in her urine and a complete loss of interest in school and friendships. "I'll never be able to get that time back," she said. "If I could erase it and make it go away, I would."

decongestant: a drug that relieves nasal congestion

bipolar disorder: a psychological disorder that causes alternating periods of depression and extreme elevation of mood

In order to kick a drug habit, some people seek treatment at an inpatient rehab facility. At such centers, drug users get counseling to overcome their dependence. © Bojan Brecelj/Corbis.

The antidote drugs that work on opiate overdoses, such as naloxone (Narcan), do not ease the symptoms of dextromethorphan overdose. According to the *American Journal of Emergency Medicine,* the emergency medical response to dextromethorphan overdose is to administer oral medications to induce vomiting and use intravenous fluids to combat dehydration. Usually the abuser simply has to ride out the symptoms under observation at a hospital.

Those abusers motivated to end their use of dextromethorphan will find no physical symptoms of withdrawal. However, the psychological pull of the drug may be difficult to overcome. Serious abusers may have to spend time at inpatient rehab facilities, fighting depression, insomnia, and feelings of worthlessness. Counseling with a licensed addiction therapist or psychiatrist will help the recovering abuser to identify the underlying reasons for attraction to the drug. Additionally, dextromethorphan abusers are welcome in twelve-step programs such as Narcotics Anonymous, where they can meet other recovering substance abusers and find twenty-four-hour support through meetings and telephone hotlines.

Consequences

Long-term abuse of over-the-counter products containing dextromethorphan can lead to organ damage, brain damage, and permanent damage to the central nervous system. Deaths have been reported from dextromethorphan alone, as well as in situations where the user combined dextromethorphan with alcohol, sedatives, or controlled substances. The changes in judgment that come with dextromethorphan abuse can lead to accidental injuries, automobile crashes, and "date rape" situations.

The Law

Dextromethorphan is not a controlled substance. It can be purchased legally in pharmacies, grocery stores, and convenience stores. Some national pharmacy chains have opted to sell cough and cold products only to those over the age of eighteen, or in small quantities. The ability to purchase products containing dextromethorphan varies from store to store. Powdered dextromethorphan is sold on some Internet sites. However, the quality of the product, even its chemical composition, is not regulated. The Internet auction site *eBay* voluntarily decided not to allow listings of DXM for sale.

Intoxication

Police officers have pulled over drivers under suspicion of drunk driving, only to find that the drivers were under the influence of dextromethorphan. In those cases, the drivers have been prosecuted under the same statutes that apply to drunk driving. "Driving While Intoxicated" and "Driving under the Influence" do not apply strictly to alcohol, but rather include substances such as dextromethorphan.

In a report on the *Greater Dallas Council on Alcohol & Drug Abuse* Web site, the legal aspects of DXM abuse were discussed. "Even though [DXM] is not regulated as a prescription drug, or as a controlled substance, being intoxicated on ANY drug in a public place can subject a user to prosecution for disorderly conduct, disturbing the peace, and similar violations."

Police stop drivers if they suspect the person is drinking and driving. If the driver is found to be under the influence of dextromethorphan or other drugs instead, he or she faces prosecution under the same statutes that apply to drunk driving. © *Kim Kulish/Corbis.*

Furthermore, anyone who distributes nonprescription doses of an over-the-counter drug to a minor can face prosecution under laws that protect children.

Some pharmacies have reported thefts of cold and cough products. Anyone caught trying to steal dextromethorphan products from a store can be prosecuted for shoplifting.

In 2003, the states of Texas and North Dakota refused to pass legislation that would make the purchase of certain cold products illegal for persons under the age of eighteen. A similar measure was struck down in California in 2004. As of 2005, legislation was pending in New Jersey. The state of New York passed a bill creating misdemeanor charges for anyone who gives a minor two or more products containing dextromethorphan. The mindset of most state legislators seems to be that the benefits of proper use of over-the-counter cold and cough remedies outweigh the dangers of dextromethorphan abuse.

The tide of opinion could change, however. In a worst case scenario, a widespread epidemic of dextromethorphan abuse may lead the Drug Enforcement Administration (DEA) to add the drug to its list of controlled substances. Then the products containing dextromethorphan would require a prescription from a licensed doctor. In the meantime, the burden for preventing dextromethorphan abuse falls on parents and concerned friends who detect changes in behavior, motivation, and overall health in their loved ones.

For More Information

Books

Clayman, Charles B., editor. *The American Medical Association Encyclopedia of Medicine.* New York: Random House, 1989.

Physicians' Desk Reference, 55th ed. Montvale, NJ: Medical Economics Company, 2001, rev. 2005.

Periodicals

Bane, Jason. "The Scariest Drug Epidemic You've Never Heard Of: The Latest Craze for Teens Looking to Get High Doesn't Involve Illegal Drugs." *Teen People* (December 1, 2003): p. 136.

Bishop, Bill. "Teen Abuse of Cold Pills on the Rise." *Register-Guard* (February 23, 2003): p. A1.

Blum, Agnes. "Cough Syrup Abuse on Rise, Internet Sites Exacerbate Problem." *Capital* (January 6, 2000): p. C1.

"Cold Medicine High." *State Legislatures* (September, 2004): p. 11.

Darboe, Momodou N. "Abuse of Dextromethorphan-based Cough Syrup as a Substitute for Licit and Illicit Drugs: A Theoretical Framework." *Adolescence* (spring, 1996): p. 239.

Dignam, John. "Police Warn of Cough Syrup Abuse." *Worcester Telegram & Gazette* (December 3, 2003): p. B1.

Fields-Meyer, Thomas, and Melinda Janiszewski. "Over the Counter Killer: It's Cheap, It's Legal, and It's Available at Any Drugstore. DXM, a Cough Medicine Ingredient, Is the Latest Craze for Teens Who Want to Get High—or Die Trying." *People Weekly* (February 2, 2004): p. 48.

Finn, Robert. "Dextromethorphan Presents Increasing Abuse Problems." *Family Practice News* (October 1, 2004): p. 39.

Horton, John. "Kids Find They Can Start High at a Store." *Plain Dealer* (September 27, 2004): p. B1.

Levy, Sandra. "R.Ph.s Keeping Eyes Peeled for Dextromethorphan Buyers." *Drug Topics* (May 17, 2004): p. 44.

Scanlon, Bill. "Cough Syrup Abuse Rises: Center Notes 20 Percent Increase in '03, Reports One Death in '04." *Rocky Mountain News* (June 21, 2004): p. A4.

Sloat, Bill. "Teens Abusing Cold Pills, Officials Warn Parents." *Plain Dealer* (February 19, 2000): p. B1.

Strickland, Leif B. "Drug Fad Catching Parents, Professionals by Surprise: Teens Abusing Cough Medicine Ingredient." *Dallas Morning News* (July 15, 1999): p. A1.

Sullum, Jacob. "When Holding a Party Is a Crime." *New York Times* (May 30, 2003): p. A27.

Susman, Carolyn. "Doctors Worried about Cough-Syrup Abuse." *Palm Beach Post* (December 15, 2004): p. E3.

"Use of Codeine- and Dextromethorphan-Containing Cough Remedies in Children." *Pediatrics* (June, 1997): p. 918.

Wolfe, Timothy R., and E. Martin Caravati. "Massive Dextromethorphan Ingestion and Abuse." *American Journal of Emergency Medicine* (Volume 13, 1995): pp. 174-176.

Web Sites

"Cough and Cold Medicine Abuse." *Kids Health for Parents.* http://kidshealth.org/parent/ (accessed June 30, 2005).

"Dextromethorphan." *U.S. Department of Justice, Drug Enforcement Administration: Diversion Control Program.* http://www.deadiversion.usdoj.gov/drugs_concern/ (accessed June 30, 2005).

"DXM (Dextromethorphan)." *Greater Dallas Council on Alcohol & Drug Abuse.* http://www.gdcada.org/statistics/dxm/ (accessed June 30, 2005).

Wall, Andrea L. "Abuse of OTC Drugs in Adolescence." *Nonprescription Medicines Academy.* http://www.nmafaculty.org/ (accessed June 30, 2005).

"What Every Parent Needs to Know about Cough Medicine Abuse." *Drug Free AZ.* http://www.drugfreeaz.com/ (accessed June 30, 2005).

See also: Over-the-Counter Drugs

Diet Pills

What Kind of Drug Is It?

Prescription diet pills are stimulants—substances that increase the activity of a living organism or one of its parts. Diet pills that can only be prescribed by physicians fall into one of two categories: 1) appetite suppressants; or 2) lipase inhibitors. Lipase is a substance that speeds up the breakdown of fats in the body.

Appetite suppressants, also known as ANORECTICS, decrease feelings of hunger. These drugs were created to replace AMPHETAMINES, which proved to be an extremely dangerous method of weight control. (A separate entry on amphetamines is included in this encyclopedia.) Lipase inhibitors work by keeping fats from being absorbed in the digestive tract.

Note to the Reader

This entry deals specifically with diet pills that were being prescribed by physicians for weight control as of 2005.

Generations of people attempting to lose weight have tried nonprescription remedies to achieve their goals. Many dieters drink cup after cup of caffeinated coffee in an effort to suppress their hunger cravings. Caffeine is an ingredient in many over-the-counter (OTC) diet pills. Some dieters use herbal remedies, which are not regulated by the U.S. Food and Drug Administration (FDA). (Entries on over-the-counter drugs, caffeine, and herbal drugs are also available in this encyclopedia.)

Overview

The obsession with thinness seen throughout Europe and North America in the twentieth and early twenty-first centuries is a trend that developed during the late 1800s. The concept of beauty prior to that time was completely different. In fact, a full figure for women was actually quite desirable. Art from the 1700s and 1800s depicts women as well-endowed, curvaceous, and quite proud of their bodies. A few extra pounds on an individual were considered a sign of good health and high economic status. Fine French chocolates were all the rage among the rich, while the less fortunate and painfully thin lower classes barely had enough food or money to sustain themselves.

Official Drug Name: Benzphetamine (benz-FETT-uh-meen; Didrex), diethyl-propion hydrochloride (dy-eth-uhl-PROH-pee-onn high-droh-KLOR-ide; Tenuate, Tenuate Dospan), orlistat (OAR-liss-tat; Xenical), phendimetrazine (fenn-dih-MEH-trah-zeen; Bontril), phentermine (FENN-ter-meen; Adipex-P, Ionamin), sibutramine (sih-BYOO-truh-meen; Meridia)
Also Known As: None
Drug Classifications: Schedule III (benzphetamine and phendimetrazine), Schedule IV (diethylpropion, phentermine, and sibutramine); stimulants.

anorectics: pronounced ah-nuh-RECK-ticks; diet pills that cause a loss of appetite; they were developed to replace amphetamines

amphetamines: pronounced am-FETT-uh-meens; stimulant drugs that increase mental alertness, reduce appetite, and help keep users awake

The image of beauty has changed over the centuries. A full figure for women was actually quite desirable in the 1700s and 1800s. Art from this era depicts women as well-endowed, curvaceous, and proud of their bodies. The painting shown here was created by Franz Xavier Winterhalter in 1855 and depicts Empress Eugenie and her friends.
© Archivo Iconografico, S.A./Corbis.

Early Diet Pills

By the late 1800s, however, attitudes about weight were beginning to change, especially among women. The first diet pills, referred to at that time as "fat reducers," showed up on the market in 1893. These pills were thyroid extracts.

The thyroid is an important gland in the body. It secretes chemical messengers called hormones that control metabolism. Metabolism is the process by which food is converted to energy

Diet Fads

Dieting has a long and somewhat curious history. The use of diet pills to lose weight began around the turn of the twentieth century and has carried over into the twenty-first. With the dawn of the 1920s, the ideal body type became a thin one (although not as extreme as the "model thin" type that started gaining popularity in the 1980s).

Throughout the 1920s, new weight-loss trends developed. One was the use of laxatives—medicines that relieve constipation by loosening the bowels—to clean out the lower digestive tract. This can be a very risky practice, though, since overuse of laxatives can cause dehydration and chemical imbalances in the body. Laxative abuse continues to this day.

Around the same time as the laxative boom began, other unusual weight-loss products hit the market. One of the best known was called La-Mar Reducing Soap. This product promised to "wash away fat and years of age," according to an advertisement from the London, England, soap manufacturer.

Gimmicky weight-loss products continue to be marketed to people desperate to lose weight. Illegal Internet pharmacy Web sites started popping up in the 1990s, offering controlled substances for sale without a prescription. Another fad involved remedies that promised weight loss "without diet or exercise." Doctors caution patients against falling for scams like these.

that the body uses to function. Thyroid extracts are used to correct problems with the thyroid gland. Their use causes people to lose weight, but produces dangerous side effects in people with normal thyroids. These effects include muscle weakness, chest pains, an increased heart rate, abnormal heart rhythms, high blood pressure, and even death. Despite the risks, overweight people continued to seek out the thyroid hormone as a weight-loss remedy until the 1950s.

The "New" Drug of the 1930s: Dinitrophenol

"Weight-loss pills in general have a rather alarming history," wrote Denise Grady in the *New York Times*. In 1933, a drug called dinitrophenol (DY-NY-troh-FEE-noll) went on the market. It became a popular weight-loss remedy, despite the fact that it was originally used as a PESTICIDE. "During the 1930s," noted Grady, "about 100,000 Americans took . . . dinitrophenol, which prevented food energy from being turned into fat." But the drug turned out to be poisonous for humans as well as pests. It caused damage to the taste buds, blindness, serious skin rashes, extremely high fevers, and even death.

pesticide: a chemical agent designed to kill insects, plants, or animals that threaten gardens, crops, or farm animals

Despite all the dieting fads that come and go, one method remains the most successful and healthy—regular exercise and limiting calorie intake.
© *Roger Ressmeyer/Corbis.*

Dangerous and sometimes fatal side effects associated with drugs like dinitrophenol led the U.S. Congress to enact the Food, Drug, and Cosmetics Act in 1938. The act gave the U.S. government powers to regulate substances marketed as drugs. However, some people still managed to purchase dinitrophenol through mail-order companies through the 1940s.

From Dinitrophenol to Amphetamines to "Amphetamine-Like" Diet Drugs

The use of dinitrophenol dropped as dieters discovered amphetamine, a medication developed in 1887. Historically, doctors prescribed amphetamines as an appetite suppressant. Amphetamines tend to decrease feelings of hunger in people who take them, making them an often-abused drug among dieters. Although the use of amphetamines for weight control was popular in the 1950s and again in the 1980s and part of the 1990s, this practice is no longer very common. Amphetamine use for weight loss is dangerous because it can become addictive. Some overweight individuals may resort to illegal means to obtain prescription-only amphetamines and even methamphetamine. (An entry on methamphetamine is also available in this encyclopedia.) Most doctors agree that the best way to regulate weight is through moderate exercise and a healthy diet.

The dangers of amphetamine addiction prompted drug companies to develop "amphetamine-like" diet pills—medicines containing chemicals similar to amphetamines. Although not quite as powerful as amphetamines, these pills did reduce users' appetites and were considered safer, with less potential for misuse or abuse.

Into the Twenty-first Century

As of 2005, "in weight-obsessed America ... two-thirds of adults are overweight or obese," wrote the authors of an *MSNBC.com* article on fitness. In the same article, Dr. JoAnn Manson, chief of preventive medicine at Boston's Brigham and Women's Hospital, stated: "A prescription for exercise may be the most important prescription a physician writes all day."

Dozens of prescription diet pills have come and gone over the years. A large number of them are no longer available for use by patients. Physicians can no longer write prescriptions for them because they have been "discontinued." As of 2005, according to the FDA, approximately twenty-five prescription diet pills had been categorized as "discontinued." A discontinued drug product is one that has been removed from the market in the United States for reasons other than safety or effectiveness. The exact reason or reasons for their removal are not stated on the *FDA* Web site.

The large number of these drugs only serves to highlight America's cultural obsession with weight. For a list of discontinued prescription drugs, see the table on this page.

Discontinued prescription diet pills, 2005

Diet pill type (listed by active ingredient)	Drug name
Diethylpropion hydrochloride	Depletite
Diethylpropion hydrochloride	Diethylpropion-HCL
Diethylpropion hydrochloride	Tepanil; Tepanil Ten-Tab
Mazindol	Mazanor
Mazindol	Sanorex
Phendimetrazine	Adphen
Phendimetrazine	Alphazine
Phendimetrazine	Cam-Metrazine
Phendimetrazine	Di-Metrex
Phendimetrazine	Melfiat; Melfiat-105
Phendimetrazine	Metra
Phendimetrazine	Phenazite; Phenazine-35
Phendimetrazine	Plegine
Phendimetrazine	SPRX-105; SPRX-3
Phendimetrazine	Statobex; Statobex-G
Phentermine	Fastin
Phentermine	Obsetin-30
Phentermine	Oby-Trim
Phentermine	Ona-Mast
Phentermine	Pre-Sate
Phentermine	Tora
Phentermine	Wyamine Sulfate

SOURCE: Compiled by Barbara C. Bigelow for Thomson Gale, from "Drugs@FDA," Center for Drug Evaluation and Research, U.S. Food and Drug Administration, Rockville, MD [Online] http://www.accessdata.fda.gov/scripts/cder/drugsatfda/ [accessed May 24, 2005]

What Is It Made Of?

Most diet pills are SYMPATHOMIMETICS, or amphetamine-like drugs. They stimulate the sympathetic nervous system in a way similar to amphetamines. The sympathetic nervous system is responsible for the body's "fight or flight" responses in the face of danger. The body releases a burst of energy that increases blood pressure, makes the heart beat faster, and slows digestion. These types of actions decrease hunger in users. Diet pills included among the sympathomimetics are benzphetamine, diethylpropion, phendimetrazine, and phentermine.

Orlistat is a lipase inhibitor. Lipase is a substance that speeds up the chemical breakdown of fats. By "inhibiting" the action of lipase, orlistat blocks fat absorption in the intestine. An estimated 30 percent of fat that would normally be absorbed by the intestines is allowed instead to pass right through the body undigested.

How Is It Taken?

The weight-loss medications described in this entry cannot be dispensed without a doctor's prescription. They are manufactured in both pill and capsule form and are taken by mouth. The patient follows a dosage schedule set by the physician. Most prescription diet pills are taken before meals to take the edge off a person's hunger.

Are There Any Medical Reasons for Taking This Substance?

Prescription diet pills are not recommended for people who are only slightly overweight. These drugs are used to treat obesity, a medical condition characterized by excess fat stored in the body. People who are considered overweight or obese weigh more—generally 20 percent or more—than is considered healthy for their heights and ages. Obese people are at risk for such medical conditions as DIABETES, STROKE, and heart disease. Obesity contributes to the deaths of about 300,000 Americans annually, according to the FDA.

Body Mass Index

A more specific standard called body mass index (BMI) is used to determine whether an overweight or obese individual is a candidate for prescription diet pill therapy. Body mass

sympathomimetics: pronounced SIMM-path-oh-muh-MEH-ticks; medications similar to amphetamines but less powerful and with less potential for addiction

diabetes: a serious disorder that causes problems with the normal breakdown of sugars in the body

stroke: a loss of feeling, consciousness, or movement caused by the breaking or blocking of a blood vessel in the brain

Health Risk Re-evaluated

In an interesting spin on the over-emphasis given to obesity in the United States, the Centers for Disease Control and Prevention (CDC) announced in April of 2005 that being "modestly overweight" might not be as dangerous as once thought. According to *CNN.com*, the CDC's study revealed that "people who are modestly overweight have a lower risk of death than those of normal weight." The key term here is "modestly," meaning slightly.

CDC director Dr. Julie Gerberding cautioned that severe obesity remains a major health risk but pointed out that the definition of obesity is evolving. The CDC's new report changes obesity's ranking among "the nation's leading preventable causes of death" from number two to number seven, behind smoking, alcohol, germs, toxins and pollutants, car crashes, and guns.

It could take awhile for the CDC's new vision of a healthy weight to take hold throughout a weight-loss-obsessed culture. *MSNBC.com* reported that girls as young as nine years old are "using bodybuilding steroids—not necessarily to get an edge on the playing field, but to get the toned, sculpted look of models and movie stars." Steroids aid in this quest by helping replace fat with muscle. (A complete entry on steroids and their dangers is available in this encyclopedia.) In many cases, the girls taking steroids suffer from eating disorders such as bulimia and anorexia as well.

index is a calculation that expresses the relationship between a person's weight and height in a single number. It is used as an indicator of health risk due to excess weight. Diet drugs may be prescribed to a person with a body mass index (BMI) of at least 30 and no medical conditions related to obesity. A BMI of 30 is assigned to a 5-foot-5-inch-tall (1.65-meters tall) person weighing 180 pounds (81.65 kilograms), a 5-foot-7-inch-tall (1.7-meters tall) person weighing about 190 pounds (86.18 kilograms), and a 6-foot-tall (1.83-meters tall) person weighing about 220 pounds (99.79 kilograms).

Length of Treatment

The biggest problem with prescription diet pills is that some users develop a dependence on them. Most diet pills are prescribed for short-term use, which ranges from a few weeks to several months. The goal of this treatment is for patients to lose weight at a steady rate and keep the weight off. Diet pills are only part of the treatment that focuses on changing patients' behavior. These changes generally consist of establishing and sticking to an exercise routine as well as following a healthy diet.

New Obesity Drug

The quest for a better prescription diet pill continues. According to *MSNBC.com*, the drug company Sanofi-Aventis was seeking FDA approval in the spring of 2005 for a new obesity drug called rimonabant (RIM-oh-NAB-ant), which was likely to be marketed under the name Acomplia. After extensive testing, rimonabant was found to help severely obese individuals keep off the weight they lost for up to two years. For long-term success, though, cardiologist Dr. Sidney C. Smith was quoted by *MSNBC.com* as saying: "There have got to be some improved behavioral and diet changes going on beyond taking a pill."

Side effects of rimonabant in test users include nausea, dizziness, and increased cases of diarrhea. One unexpected effect: the drug may also help people stop smoking.

Usage Trends

CNN.com reported that in the United States, "prescription drug sales totaled $235 billion nationally in 2004, a historic high that was up 8.3 percent from 2003." Hundreds of millions of those dollars are spent on prescription diet pills each year.

Prescription diet pills are manufactured for the treatment of obesity, an increasingly common medical problem. However, overweight people are not the only ones using diet pills. Some people obtain prescription-only diet pills to lose a few pounds quickly. Others have eating disorders and develop a PSYCHOLOGICAL DEPENDENCE on the pills. People who lose weight using diet pills run the risk of regaining those pounds once they stop taking the drugs. This contributes to an endless cycle of weight loss followed by weight gain.

Effects on the Body

The diet pills developed to replace amphetamines became known as anorectics or appetite suppressants. Anorectics are sometimes referred to as sympathomimetic drugs. They are stimulants that "mimic" the body's natural energy-releasing mechanisms. The FDA has approved a variety of anorectics over the years for the short-term treatment of obesity. Phentermine was approved in 1959, fenfluramine (FENN-FLOOR-uh-meen) in 1973, and dexfenfluramine (deks-FENN-FLOOR-uh-meen) in 1996. Other anorectic diet pills include benzphetamine, diethylpropion, and phendimetrazine.

A different type of prescription diet pill received FDA approval in 1999. The lipase inhibitor orlistat (Xenical) is said to block about 30 percent of the fat absorbed by the body.

The Fen-Phen Craze

In the 1990s, doctors in the United States and other countries began prescribing low doses of fenfluramine (Pondimin) or dexfenfluramine (Redux) along with low doses of phentermine. The combination, known informally as "Fen-Phen," was never approved

psychological dependence: the belief that a person needs to take a certain substance in order to function

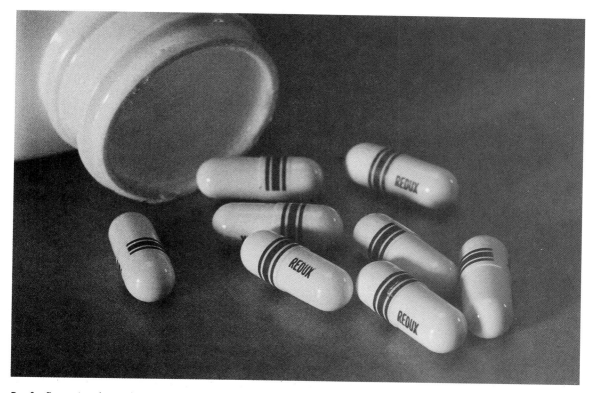

Dexfenfluramine (Redux) was part of the drug combination known as Fen-Phen. Never approved by the FDA, Fen-Phen use led to serious heart problems for some users. © *James Leynse/Corbis.*

by the FDA. Seven million prescriptions for Fen-Phen were written in 1996. "The rationale for using the two drugs," according to a *Seattle Times* contributor, "was that they might work more effectively together with fewer side effects."

Soon, however, the safety of Fen-Phen was called into question. The appetite-suppressant mixture was thought to be the cause of some severe health problems, including serious heart valve malfunctions. As a result, both fenfluramine and dexfenfluramine were withdrawn from the market in September of 1997. Phentermine is still sold because no cases of heart valve disease have been reported when that drug is taken alone, according to an FDA report.

There Are No Magic Cures

Prescription diet pills help with weight reduction by suppressing the user's appetite and increasing the feeling of fullness in the

FDA-approved prescription diet pills, 2005

Diet pill type (listed by active ingredient)	Drug name	Dosage
Benzphetamine hydrochloride	Didrex	50 mg tablet
Diethylpropion hydrochloride	Tenuate	25 mg tablets
Diethylpropion hydrochloride	Tenuate Dospan	75 mg extended release tablets
Orlistat	Xenical	120 mg capsule
Phendimetrazine	Bontril	105 mg extended release capsule
Phendimetrazine	Bontril PDM	35 mg tablet
Phendimetrazine	Phendimetrazine Tartrate	35 mg tablet or capsule; 105 mg extended release capsule
Phendimetrazine	X-Trozine	35 mg capsule
Phendimetrazine	X-Trozine-LA	105 mg extended release capsule
Phentermine	Adipex-P	37.5 mg tablet or capsule
Phentermine	Ionamin	Extended release capsules; multiple strengths
Sibutramine hydrochloride	Meridia	Capsules available in multiple strengths

SOURCE: Compiled by Barbara C. Bigelow for Thomson Gale, from "Drugs@FDA," Center for Drug Evaluation and Research, U.S. Food and Drug Administration, Rockville, MD [Online] http://www.accessdata.fda.gov/scripts/cder/drugsatfda/ [accessed May 24, 2005]

insomnia: difficulty falling asleep or an inability to sleep

withdrawal: the process of gradually cutting back on the amount of a drug being taken until it is discontinued entirely; also the accompanying physiological effects of terminating use of an addictive drug

stomach. But diet pills alone will not make excess weight disappear. According to Patricia Dwyer Schull in the *Nursing Spectrum Drug Handbook,* prescription drugs for "obesity management" must be "used in conjunction with [a] reduced-calorie diet" in order to be effective.

Diet pills can produce symptoms that range from dizziness to an increased number of bowel movements. Possible side effects include light-headedness, dry mouth, a false feeling of well-being, nausea, irritability, INSOMNIA, trembling, blurred vision, nervousness, increased sweating and urination, and problems with the blood vessels in the lungs.

Sibutramine (Meridia), a prescription diet pill approved by the FDA in 1997, may cause an increase in heart rate and blood pressure. Long-term use of any prescription appetite suppressant can lead to addiction. Taking anorectics can impair a person's ability to drive, operate heavy equipment, or perform other potentially hazardous activities. Sympathomimetics or anorectics should not be prescribed to people with a history of drug abuse.

Taking orlistat, the lipase-inhibiting-type diet pill, can bring on an increased number of bowel movements, gas with discharge, oily or fatty stools, and the inability to control a bowel movement. Because orlistat blocks the absorption of fat in the intestines, the fat is eliminated from the body as part of a bowel movement. Orlistat users may sometimes feel an urgent need to go to the bathroom. These symptoms are often aggravated if the user eats too many high-fat foods.

Women who are pregnant or nursing their babies should consult with their physician about any diet pill use. Most prescription diet pills are not recommended for use by pregnant or nursing women. Diet pills can also affect bone development in children and young adults.

When patients stop taking anorectics, their bodies need to adapt to the lack of drugs in their systems. The amount of WITHDRAWAL time will vary, depending on the strength of the dosage taken and the length of time it was used. Withdrawal symptoms may include insomnia, nightmares, nausea, vomiting, and stomach cramps. The user typically experiences strong hunger pangs as well.

Possible Dopamine Connection

A study conducted by the National Institute on Drug Abuse (NIDA) suggests that the same factors that control excessive behaviors such as drug abuse and gambling may be associated with overeating. The main factor may be an abnormality in the brain involving chemical messengers called NEUROTRANSMITTERS. DOPAMINE is the neurotransmitter that acts on the part of the brain responsible for feeling pleasure, filtering incoming information, making choices, judging behavior, and deciding when and how to act.

NIDA researchers believe that obese people do not have enough receptors on their brains' nerve endings to grab on to dopamine and allow it to do its work. The decrease in dopamine receptors is apparently linked to a high BMI. The greater a person's BMI number, the fewer dopamine receptors they seem to have in their brains. *NIDA Notes* staff writer Robert Mathias quoted Dr. Nora Volkow as saying: "An individual who has low sensitivity to normal stimuli learns behaviors, such as abusing drugs or overeating, that will activate" those areas of the brain that "create a sense of well-being." The next step in this research is to determine if there are ways other than overeating or drug-taking that can stimulate the pleasure centers in the brains of these individuals.

Reactions with Other Drugs or Substances

Before taking diet pills, patients need to inform their health care providers of any other medications they are already taking. Diet pills are often taken in combination with LAXATIVES, DIURETICS, and herbal remedies, which can lead to dangerous drug reactions. Mixing diet pills with alcohol can have serious side effects. In addition, certain antidepressants can interact negatively with prescription diet pills, causing high blood pressure or an irregular heartbeat. Physicians may decide to adjust drug dosages, have patients discontinue certain medications, or counsel the patient not to use prescription diet pills at all.

Treatment for Habitual Users

Since many of the prescription diet pills available to overweight patients are amphetamine-like substances, they tend to have the same effects on users as amphetamines. TOLERANCE to diet pills can

neurotransmitters: substances that help spread nerve impulses from one nerve cell to another

dopamine: pronounced DOPE-uh-meen; a combination of carbon, hydrogen, nitrogen, and oxygen that acts as a neurotransmitter in the brain

laxatives: drugs that help produce bowel movements

diuretics: pronounced die-er-EH-tiks; substances that reduce bodily fluids by increasing the production of urine

tolerance: a condition in which higher and higher doses of a drug are needed to produce the original effect or high experienced

Eating Disorder Facts

Eating disorders are more common than most people realize and lead to a variety of health risks:

- Close to 10 million women and 1 million men suffer from anorexia nervosa or bulimia nervosa.
- Another 25 million people are affected by binge eating disorder.
- Eating disorders can cause osteoporosis (the loss of bone mass).
- Changes in the mouth and teeth are often the first signs of an eating disorder. Lips may look red, cracked, and dry, and teeth often erode (become brittle and weak) due to frequent vomiting and nutritional deficiencies.
- If left untreated, eating disorders can be fatal.

occur if the user takes the drugs in a greater quantity or for a longer time than instructed.

It is very important to remember that prescription weight-loss medications are meant to be used only for a limited time. If diet drug dependence or addiction does occur, experts consider behavioral therapy—sometimes referred to as "talk" therapy—and emotional support essential for treatment and rehabilitation. Treatment must be adapted to the individual. It should include nutritional counseling and advice on lifestyle changes that will help the patient reach and maintain a healthy weight.

Consequences

In a society where "thin is in" and people are often judged by their appearance, diet pill use has skyrocketed. However, diet pills are merely a temporary solution to a long-term problem. Maintaining a healthy weight is an ongoing process that involves adopting a whole new lifestyle of eating healthy meals and exercising regularly.

Diet Pill Abuse

People who use diet pills often put the pounds they have lost right back on as soon as they stop taking the drugs. Not only do they regain the weight they first lost, they sometimes gain even more. This process is called the "yo-yo syndrome" because the affected individual's weight goes up and down like a yo-yo. Common consequences of diet pill abuse include muscle loss, psychological dependency, feelings of failure, and a generally unhealthy physical state. Overuse of pills can affect concentration and performance in school or work. In addition, there is a potential for addiction to some diet pills.

The Struggle to Be Thin

anorexia: pronounced ah-nuh-REK-see-uh; a severe eating disorder characterized by an intense fear of gaining weight, a refusal to eat, a distorted sense of self-image, and excessive weight loss

Although excessive weight and obesity are problems in the United States and other countries, there is also a concern about people who diet to an unhealthy low weight. Individuals suffering from eating disorders have an unrealistic image of themselves and their bodies. The most common eating disorders are ANOREXIA nervosa and BULIMIA nervosa. For someone with an eating disorder, taking diet pills can aggravate an already serious condition. If left untreated, eating disorders can be fatal.

The Law

The Food and Drug Administration (FDA) oversees the regulation of prescription diet pills. The Controlled Substances Act (CSA), a portion of the 1970 Comprehensive Drug Abuse Prevention and Control Act, classified drugs into five categories, or schedules, based on the effect of the drug, its medical use, and potential for abuse. Schedule I drugs, those in the most tightly controlled category, have no medical use and an extremely high potential for abuse.

Among diet drugs, benzphetamine and phendimetrazine are considered Schedule III drugs. Abuse of these drugs may lead to physical or psychological dependence. Diethylpropion, phentermine, and sibutramine diet pills are considered Schedule IV drugs. They have a lower potential for abuse than the Schedule IIIs, but still may lead to physical or psychological dependence in some users. Federal law prohibits the use or distribution of diet pills obtained without a prescription.

People suffering from anorexia and bulimia see themselves as overweight no matter how thin they really are.

© Ariel Skelley/Corbis.

For More Information

Books

Clayton, Lawrence. *Diet Pill Dangers.* Springfield, NJ: Enslow Publishers, 1999.

Mitchell, Deborah R., and David Charles Dodson. *The Diet Pill Guide.* New York: St. Martin's Griffin, 2002.

Schull, Patricia Dwyer. *Nursing Spectrum Drug Handbook.* King of Prussia, PA: Nursing Spectrum, 2005.

Silverman, Harold M. *The Pill Book,* 11th ed. New York: Bantam, 2004.

Yancy, Diane. *Eating Disorders.* Brookfield, CT: Twenty-First Century Medical Library, 1999.

bulimia: pronounced bull-EEM-eeh-yuh; an eating disorder that involves long periods of bingeing on food, followed by self-induced vomiting and abuse of laxatives

Periodicals

Gorman, Christine. "Danger in the Diet Pills?" *Time* (July 21, 1997): p. 58.

Grady, Denise. "History Counsels Caution on Diet Pills." *New York Times* (May 25, 1999).

Proulx, Lawrence G. "Diet Drugs at a Glance." *Buffalo News* (September 23, 1997): p. D3.

"Suppressing Appetites, Burning Calories: Diet Drugs at a Glance." *Seattle Times* (August 6, 1997): p. E2.

Web Sites

"The Autonomic Nervous System." *Neuroscience for Kids.* http://faculty.washington.edu/chudler/auto.html (accessed June 30, 2005).

"Diet Pill Keeps Pounds Off, Study Finds."*MSNBC.com,* March 8, 2005. http://www.msnbc.msn.com/id/7127442/ (accessed June 30, 2005).

"Doctors Fight Fat with Fitness Prescriptions." *MSNBC.com,* February 8, 2005. http://www.msnbc.msn.com/id/6914627/ (accessed June 30, 2005).

"Drugs@FDA." *U.S. Food and Drug Administration, Center for Drug Evaluation and Research.* http://www.accessdata.fda.gov/scripts/cder/drugsatfda/ (accessed June 30, 2005).

"Eating Disorders Information Index." *National Eating Disorders Association.* http://www.NationalEatingDisorders.org (accessed June 30, 2005).

"FDA Drug Complaints Surge." *CNN.com,* March 14, 2005. http://money.cnn.com/2005/03/14/news/economy/drugcomplaints/index.htm (accessed June 30, 2005).

"Girls Are Abusing Steroids Too, Experts Say." *MSNBC.com,* April 25, 2005. http://www.msnbc.msn.com/id/7633384/ (accessed June 30, 2005).

"Glaxo to Tout Roche's Obesity Drug." *CNN.com,* April 12, 2005. http://money.cnn.com (accessed April 25, 2005).

Mathias, Robert. "Pathological Obesity and Drug Addiction Share Common Brain Characteristics." *National Institute on Drug Abuse, NIDA Notes.* http://www.drugabuse.gov/NIDA_Notes/NNVol16N4/pathological.html (accessed June 30, 2005).

"Study: Obesity Death Risk Overstated." *CNN.com,* April 20, 2005. http://www.cnn.com/2005/HEALTH/diet.fitness/04/20/obesity.deaths.ap/index.html (accessed April 20, 2005).

See also: Amphetamines; Caffeine; Dextroamphetamine; Ephedra; Herbal Drugs; Methamphetamine; Steroids

Dimethyltryptamine (DMT)

What Kind of Drug Is It?

Dimethyltryptamine, most commonly known as DMT, is a fast-acting hallucinogen—a substance that brings on HALLUCINATIONS, which alter the user's perception of reality. It is related to LSD (lysergic acid diethylamide) and psilocybin. (An entry for each of these drugs is available in this encyclopedia.) DMT causes a rapid rush of mind-altering states that end fairly quickly, usually within an hour. For this reason, DMT has been nicknamed the "businessman's special."

The compound can be found in many kinds of plants. It is even found in the poisonous venom of certain toads. (Venom is a liquid poison created by an animal for defense against predators or for killing smaller prey.) DMT is also created synthetically in laboratories.

Although the hallucinations brought on by DMT use are brief in duration, they are extremely powerful. Unlike LSD, which works over a period of hours, DMT alters the brain's chemistry in a matter of minutes. Ancient cultures brewed teas from plants containing DMT for use in religious ceremonies. More modern users often find themselves bewildered by the way the drug changes perceptions. Because people under the influence of DMT often lose contact with reality, they can behave in ways dangerous to themselves or others. For this and many other reasons, the compound is classified as a Schedule I controlled substance.

Overview

The use of hallucinogenic mushrooms, snuffs, and brews dates back thousands of years and has occurred all over the world. In his book *Illegal Drugs: A Complete Guide to Their History, Chemistry, Use and Abuse*, Paul M. Gahlinger discusses early reports of drug use. He explains that the naturalist hired by explorer Christopher Columbus (1451–1506) for his second voyage (1493–1496) described a strange behavior of the Tairo Indians. The naturalist observed the native peoples using a snuff derived from seeds of the yopo tree (*Anadenatherea peregrine*).

Official Drug Name: N,N-dimethyltryptamine (dy-meth-ull-TRIP-tuh-meen), Nigerine, desoxybufotenine (dess-OKS-ee-byoo-foh-tenn-inn), 3-(2-dimethylaminoethyl)-indole; 5-MeO-DMT; (related compounds) 5-MeO-DIPT, alpha-methyltryptamine (AMT)

Also Known As: 45-minute psychosis, businessman's special, DET, fantasia, foxy, foxy methoxy

Drug Classifications: Schedule I, hallucinogen

hallucinations: visions or other perceptions of things that are not really present

Using a double-stemmed tube and coffee powder, a boy shows visitors at the Bogota Gold Museum in Colombia how his ancestors inhaled the narcotic *yopo*. Explorer Christopher Columbus and his men observed the native peoples inhaling the narcotic powder. © *Adam Woolfitt/Corbis.*

The Mayan, Olmec, and Cherokee Indians all left behind archeological evidence that they worshiped toads and used toad venom in their religious ceremonies. Even in modern times, native cultures in Colombia, Ecuador, Peru, and Brazil prepare a brew from jungle plants that is variously called *yagé, caapi,* and AYAHUASCA ("vine of souls"). One of the active ingredients in this brew is DMT.

Chemists began to synthesize, or manufacture, DMT in the 1930s. By the 1950s, they understood the chemical composition of *ayahuasca* tea and BUFOTENINE. In the late 1950s and early 1960s, hallucinogens were not illegal. Thus, some experimental chemists used themselves and their friends as subjects, taking various strengths of hallucinogenic compounds and recording their reactions. These scientists determined that DMT did not produce any mental effects if taken by mouth. (*Ayahuasca* tea, however, has an added ingredient that allows the body to metabolize, or break down, DMT.)

DMT, bufotenine, and other similar compounds are snorted or injected to produce hallucinations. DMT has never been as widely abused as LSD, but it is named in the U.S. Controlled Substances Act of 1970. At that time, dimethyltryptamine (DMT) was named a Schedule I hallucinogen, making its possession, distribution, and creation a crime.

What Is It Made Of?

ayahuasca: one of several teas of South American origin, used in religious ceremonies, known to contain DMT; also a plant

bufotenine: the component of venom from the toad genus *Bufo* that contains DMT

SYNTHETIC dimethyltryptamine is a white or sometimes light brown crystalline solid, like a small, strong-smelling chunk of salt. Some people have compared its odor to mothballs. Others have said that it smells like plastic being burned. As its name suggests, its chemical composition is complicated. Once crystallized, it cannot be dissolved in water. Instead it must be dissolved either in an ORGANIC SOLVENT like alcohol or in an acid.

An Inga Indian shaman in Colombia prepares a drink called *yagé*,
a hallucinogenic brew said to have healing powers. *AP/Wide World Photos.*

DMT occurs widely in nature, in the leaves, seeds, and roots of certain plants, and in the milky venom of toads in the genus *Bufo.* Its synthetic, or laboratory-made form, mimics the chemical composition of its natural form.

DMT is unique in its hallucinogenic family in two ways. First, when snorted, injected, or smoked, it acts much more quickly than LSD or psilocybin. This is because fat cells in the human body absorb LSD and psilocybin and release them more slowly to the brain. DMT is not absorbed by fat cells. The entire dose races to the brain as soon as it is taken. Second, pure DMT loses its hallucinogenic qualities if eaten. It is destroyed by monoamine oxidase in the stomach. Monoamine oxidase is a naturally occurring enzyme that detoxifies amino

synthetic: (on opposite page) made in a laboratory

organic: (on opposite page) a term used to describe chemical compounds that contain carbon

solvent: (on opposite page) a substance, usually liquid, that dissolves another substance

The tea made from the *ayahuasca* plant is one of several teas of South American origin, used in religious ceremonies, known to contain DMT.
© *Alison Wright/Corbis.*

compounds in ingested foods. The tea preparations used in South America contain ingredients that inhibit monoamine oxidase action. That is why they can be consumed orally. Still, those who have tasted *ayahuasca* and other similar herbal brews find them quite foul on the tongue.

How Is It Taken?

In some religious rituals, participants drink brews concocted from plants containing DMT and other ingredients. RECREATIONAL USERS smoke plant matter soaked in dissolved DMT, snort ground-up DMT crystals, or inject DMT that has been dissolved in a non-water solvent. Users experience nearly immediate—and sometimes very bizarre—mental effects, often including loss of touch with reality.

Even the most hard-core hallucinogen users have reported that DMT is strong, unpredictable, and can produce frightening effects. A report in the *Journal of Toxicology: Clinical Toxicology* detailed the case of a seventeen-year-old college student who nearly died of heart failure after taking DMT. The student had to be restrained at the hospital and was sent by helicopter to a regional poison center. His temperature at the time he was admitted to the hospital was 105°F.

recreational users: people who use drugs solely to achieve a high, not to treat a medical condition

Are There Any Medical Reasons for Taking This Substance?

Medical researchers have been granted limited opportunities to study the use of hallucinogens for treating anxiety in terminally ill patients, SCHIZOPHRENIA, and opiate addiction. Because DMT moves through the brain so quickly, it is not likely to be used for medical research. The substance's Schedule I classification reveals that the U.S. government sees it as having no value for the treatment of illness.

Usage Trends

DMT has never been as popular among drug abusers as LSD and other hallucinogens. Its delivery system is more complicated. Its effects usually last less than an hour, although the abuser can experience longer periods of confusion afterward.

Chemists constantly tinker with the compound, however. In October of 2002, the DEA announced the seizure of two new compounds: 5-MeO-DIPT, known on the street as "foxy" or "foxy methoxy," and alpha-methyltryptamine (AMT). Both of these compounds are closely related to DMT, but they can be used in tablet form.

Tablets or the chemicals used to create the tablets have been found in Arizona, Delaware, Florida, Idaho, Illinois, New Jersey, Oregon, Virginia, Washington, and the District of Columbia. Some of the drug seizures by law enforcement officials have occurred at all-night clubs or at raves, wild overnight dance parties that typically involve huge crowds of people, loud techno music, and illegal drug use.

People creating foxy or AMT may believe they are not breaking the law because these hallucinogens are not specifically covered by the Controlled Substances Act. However, it is against the law to manufacture or sell a "CONTROLLED SUBSTANCE ANALOG." Anyone buying, selling, or using foxy and AMT may face the same penalties as someone buying, selling, or using DMT.

About the Toads. . . .

The *Bufo marinus* toad is a native of the Americas and one of the toads that secretes DMT in its venom. When interest in hallucinogens was at its height in the 1960s and early 1970s, some people in Australia (where the toads had been imported) and America actually *licked* the toads in an effort to get high. What the toad-lickers quickly discovered was that *Bufo marinus* venom

schizophrenia: a mental disease characterized by a withdrawal from reality and other intellectual and emotional disturbances

controlled substance analog: any chemical compound that acts on the body the same way a controlled substance does

Foxy and AMT

Pure DMT is relatively rare on the illegal drug market. But a new generation of hallucinogens has been created that can be taken in tablet form. Two of these, "foxy" or "foxy methoxy" and AMT, mimic the actions of DMT. Tablets of foxy and AMT have been seized at raves and clubs in more than a half dozen states in the United States.

These two hallucinogens may at first appear to be legal because their specific chemical compounds are not listed as controlled substances. But since they act like DMT in the body, they are known as "controlled substance analogs," and they are indeed illegal. Anyone caught selling or making foxy and AMT faces prosecution under state and federal laws.

contains many ingredients *besides* DMT. People became violently ill with heart palpitations, drooling, and intense, long-lasting headaches.

Others tried drying and smoking the venom of *Bufo alvarius,* a desert toad found in California, Arizona, and parts of Mexico. To quote Paul M. Gahlinger in *Illegal Drugs:* "Smoking toad . . . proved to be too powerful an experience for most people. Besides the obvious difficulty of getting and handling the toad, the intoxication was too intense, with too many physical side effects, to achieve any real popularity." Nevertheless, the U.S. government added bufotenine, the hallucinogenic ingredient in toad venom, to the list of illegal drugs.

Effects on the Body

Dimethyltryptamine is called a "serotonin agonist." When the chemical enters the brain, it interferes with the normally occurring NEUROTRANSMITTER called SEROTONIN. Serotonin serves many functions in the brain, from regulating moods to assisting the brain in the way it processes information. According to David Porush in *Omni* magazine, serotonin plays a role in how people sense reality.

Altering Reality

DMT has been shown to alter the way the brain perceives reality. Users experience visual hallucinations, both with eyes closed and open. They may feel detached from themselves or have an "out of body" experience. And because serotonin affects reasoning, DMT may cause an abuser to think that he or she is having a moment of religious ecstasy, of communion with the divine. Repeat users of hallucinogens have reported "seeing" fairies, elves, and angels. Some users have had the feeling of being in the presence of God. It is this aspect of the drug's behavior that has tied it to certain religious practices.

Some DMT abusers also experience intense fear, anxiety, and paranoia—the feeling that other people and ordinary, inanimate objects have become agents of evil. Human faces become like masks. Furniture can seem to have human characteristics. Once the drug has produced this kind of anxiety, no antidote exists to stop it.

neurotransmitter: a substance that helps spread nerve impulses from one nerve cell to another

serotonin: a combination of carbon, hydrogen, nitrogen, and oxygen; it is found in the brain, blood, and stomach lining and acts as a neurotransmitter and blood vessel regulator

DMT occurs in the milky venom of toads in the genus *Bufo marinus*. People have actually licked toads trying to get high. *© Wayne Lawler; Esoscene/Corbis.*

The user must "ride out" the experience until the DMT exits the brain and the normal levels of serotonin return. In the case of DMT, the "TRIP" is of short duration, but users report that the drug alters one's sense of time. Minutes may seem like hours, and the user may have a difficult time communicating during those minutes.

Other side effects of DMT include dizziness, nausea, sweating, runny nose, and drooling. In certain extreme cases, users may experience a racing heartbeat, elevated body temperature, and convulsions. Heavy users risk brain damage and a condition called "serotonin syndrome" that can cause muscle tremors or rigidity, confusion, and changes in blood pressure.

People with mental illness who experiment with DMT run significantly greater risks of having "bad trips" or other lasting emotional side effects. As with other hallucinogens, DMT tends to magnify the levels of emotion in the brain. Thus, if depression or anxiety already

trip: an intense and usually very visual experience produced by an hallucinogenic drug

Historical Accounts

Use of hallucinogens has been documented in many ancient cultures. DMT use has been more common in the Americas because the toads and plants containing it are widespread in North and South America. Here is a look at some examples from the historical record, both long ago and recent.

- The skeletons of 10,000 toads were found in an ancient Cherokee Indian burial site in North America.
- During Christopher Columbus's second voyage to the New World (1493–1496), his naturalist, Friar Ramón Paul, wrote about the Tairo Indians of Haiti. As noted in Paul M. Gahlinger's book *Illegal Drugs,* the friar observed: "This powder they draw up through the nose and it intoxicates them to such an extent that when they are under its influence, they know not what they do."

- In 2000, members of the O Centro Espirita Beneficiente Uniao do Vegetal religious sect claimed that the seizure of thirty gallons of *hoasca* tea by the U.S. Drug Enforcement Administration (DEA) violated their right to freedom of religion. As reported by Scott Sandlin in the *Albuquerque Journal,* their case reached the Tenth Circuit Court of Appeals late in 2004, where judges ruled in favor of the church. The tea is considered a sacrament, but its use will be closely monitored by church members and the DEA so that it does not invite abuse by outsiders.

exist, the drug will make these conditions worse. Depression is a mood disorder that causes people to have feelings of hopelessness, loss of pleasure, self-blame, and sometimes suicidal thoughts. Anxiety is a feeling of being extremely overwhelmed, restless, fearful, and worried.

Reactions with Other Drugs or Substances

DMT is extremely dangerous when combined with some drugs prescribed for depression. DMT also reacts badly with AMPHETAMINES, SEDATIVES, ANTIHISTAMINES, and strong ANALGESICS. (An entry on amphetamines is available in this encyclopedia.) It can increase or intensify the side effects of any of these substances. Mixing DMT with drugs from poisonous plants (strychnine or belladonna alkaloids, for example) can be fatal.

On its own, DMT renders the user unable to judge ordinary situations. For instance, a person high on DMT runs a much greater risk of being involved in an automobile crash (either by driving or walking into traffic) or other injury. The combination of alcohol and DMT further increases the risk of accident or injury.

amphetamines: pronounced am-FETT-uh-meens; stimulant drugs that increase mental alertness, reduce appetite, and help keep users awake

sedatives: drugs used to treat anxiety and calm people down

antihistamines: drugs that block *histamine,* a chemical that causes nasal congestion related to allergies

analgesics: pain relievers or the qualities of pain relief

DMT use has been linked to hyperthermia, or an elevated body temperature. It is dangerous to use the drug in rave situations where a great number of people are crowded into a small space, dancing or milling about. The use of a strong, quick-acting hallucinogen like DMT might also lead to panic or paranoia in a dance club environment. Those who use the drug as part of religious rituals take extreme care to create the most soothing surrounding environment.

Treatment for Habitual Users

Over time the human body develops a tolerance to DMT. Users must take higher and higher doses to achieve the same effect. Although the drug is not habit-forming, it can encourage risk-taking behavior, including the use of other drugs. Long-term use can lead to brain damage.

Self-help groups such as Narcotics Anonymous (NA) welcome anyone who wishes to quit using any kind of mind-altering substance, including hallucinogens. Most communities have at least one chapter of Narcotics Anonymous, an international organization that connects drug abusers with others who have experienced the same difficulties. NA meetings encourage drug abusers to share their stories, and they offer the support of group acceptance.

Abusers of hallucinogens should also seek the guidance of a licensed professional psychiatrist or psychologist who can help determine the root feelings that led to drug experimentation. Licensed doctors treating hallucinogen abusers may prescribe anti-anxiety medications or anti-psychotic drugs if the abuser has a history of mental problems related to drug use. There are no specific WITHDRAWAL symptoms associated with DMT, although users will experience fatigue and occasionally confusion that lasts several hours after a dose.

The Other DMT

DMT the *hallucinogen* should not be confused with desoxy-methyl-testosterone, or DMT, a *"designer steroid."* This latter DMT was developed in the twenty-first century to fool drug testers at athletic events. It is in the steroid family and is related to testosterone, a hormone found in greater quantities in males than in females. According to Lynn Zinser in a 2005 article for the *International Herald Tribune*, scientists working for the World Anti-Doping Agency vowed to develop urine tests that show the presence of desoxy-methyl-testosterone, the "other" DMT.

Consequences

As with other hallucinogens, DMT can cause "flashbacks." Days, weeks, or months after use, an abuser can suddenly relive an entire hallucinogenic experience, or parts of it. The loss of judgment that occurs with DMT use sometimes causes abusers to become violent, to strike out at those trying to help, or to behave in

withdrawal: the process of gradually cutting back on the amount of a drug being taken until it is discontinued entirely; also the accompanying physiological effects of terminating use of an addictive drug

other self-destructive ways. The *Journal of Toxicology: Clinical Toxicology* cited a case of a young man who fought with paramedics as they tried to save his life. The patient ended up with "multiple abrasions on his arms and chest" from his struggle with health care providers.

In a federal court case that ended in 2004, the O Centro Espirita Beneficiente Uniao do Vegetal religious sect won the right to use an hallucinogenic tea in its religious services. The sect cited the U.S. Constitution's right to freedom of religion in its winning court case. It is important to note that religious use of hallucinogenic teas differs greatly from recreational drug use. Religious rites featuring DMT-laced teas are presided over by experienced leaders who create a proper atmosphere for use. They help their followers to understand the experience. Abuse or overdose of the substance is not tolerated. In contrast, street DMT users often encounter preparations that might contain other ingredients, or higher doses, than expected. The resulting hallucinatory experience, while lasting only a short time, may be terrifying or life-threatening.

The Risks Are High

In an effort to bypass laws against DMT, certain companies have been selling "research chemicals" through the Internet. The legality of these chemicals is open to debate. However, these substances have not been tested for safety even through illegal experimentation. The United Kingdom's *Guardian* newspaper reported on two deaths, both young men under the age of twenty-one, both from a "research chemical" called 2-CT-7 they had bought over the Internet. Responding to the deaths, the DEA scheduled 2-CT-7 as a controlled substance, and its sale on the Internet ceased. Ingesting "research chemicals" bought online is as risky as any other form of drug abuse.

Anyone who shares a needle to inject street drugs runs the risk of contracting the human immunodeficiency virus (HIV). This virus leads to acquired immunodeficiency syndrome (AIDS), an as-yet-incurable disease that destroys the human immune system. So while DMT may not be habit-forming, it can lead to deadly complications when delivered by injection.

The Law

The Controlled Substances Act of 1970 created five schedules based on a drug's value as a medicine, its chances of causing addiction, and its possibilities for abuse. DMT is a Schedule

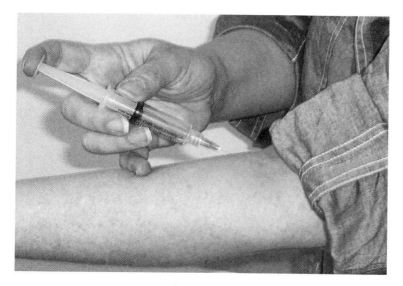

One of the ways that DMT is taken is by injection. Anyone who shares a needle to inject street drugs runs the risk of contracting the human immunodeficiency virus (HIV), hepatitis, and other diseases. *Photograph by Leitha Etheridge-Sims.*

I drug, meaning that U.S. government authorities consider it one of the most dangerous drugs. Possession of DMT is illegal in the United States, Canada, and the United Kingdom, among other countries. It cannot be prescribed by a doctor for any illness. As a Schedule I drug, DMT possession carries stiff fines and imprisonment. The penalties increase significantly for repeat offenders.

DMT-Like Substances

DMT can be extracted from plants that are legal to buy. However, people can be arrested for creating DMT from those plants, even if they only plan to use it themselves.

Any substance that behaves like DMT—for instance, the hallucinogens foxy and AMT—are considered "controlled substance analogs." Although their names and chemical compositions may not be specifically listed in controlled substance legislation, they are still illegal because they mimic the behavior of other illegal drugs. The same holds true for many of the "research chemicals" sold over the Internet. If the effects of the chemicals mimic DMT—or if the chemicals are used to create DMT—the user/creator violates the law.

For More Information

Books

Clayman, Charles B., editor. *The American Medical Association Encyclopedia of Medicine.* New York: Random House, 1989.

Gahlinger, Paul M. *Illegal Drugs: A Complete Guide to Their History, Chemistry, Use and Abuse.* Las Vegas, NV: Sagebrush Press, 2001.

Kuhn, Cynthia, Scott Swartzwelder, and Wilkie Wilson. *Buzzed: The Straight Facts about the Most Used and Abused Drugs from Alcohol to Ecstasy,* 2nd ed. New York: W.W. Norton, 2003.

Periodicals

Brush, D. Eric, Steven B. Bird, and Edward W. Boyer. "Monoamine Oxidase Inhibitor Poisoning Resulting from Internet Misinformation on Illicit Substances." *Journal of Toxicology: Clinical Toxicology* (March, 2004): p. 191.

McCandless, David. "Goodbye Ecstasy, Hello 5-MeO-DMT: New Designer Drugs Are Just a Click Away." *Guardian* (February 16, 2004): p. 3.

Miller, Sukie. "Terence McKenna." *Omni* (May, 1993): p. 69.

Nyman, T., K. Hoppu, R. Koskinene, V. Harjola, and M. Kuisma. "A Case of Severe Poisoning Caused by 5-MeO-DMT." *Journal of Toxicology: Clinical Toxicology* (April, 2002): p. 324.

Porush, David. "Finding God." *Omni* (October, 1993): p. 60.

Sandlin, Scott. "Santa Fe Church Gets Permit for Tea." *Albuquerque Journal* (December 11, 2004): p. 1.

Sharpe, Tom. "Hallucinogenic Tea Case Starts in Albuquerque." *New Mexican* (October 28, 2001).

Zinser, Lynn. "Scientists Find New Designer Steroid: Drugs." *International Herald Tribune* (February 3, 2005): p. 18.

Web Sites

Comprehensive Drug Abuse Prevention and Control Act of 1970. http://www.usdoj.gov/dea/ (accessed June 30, 2005).

Drug Intelligence Brief: Trippin' on Tryptamines, October 2002. http://www.usdoj.gov/dea/pubs/intel/02052/02052.html (accessed June 30, 2005).

Narcotics Anonymous. http://www.na.org (accessed June 30, 2005).

"Psilocybin & Psilocyn and Other Tryptamines." *DEA Briefs & Background.* http://www.dea.gov/concern/psilocybinp.html (accessed June 30, 2005).

See also: LSD (Lysergic Acid Diethylamide); Psilocybin

Diuretics

What Kind of Drug Is It?

The main goal of diuretic therapy is to get rid of extra fluids in the body. Diuretics reduce bodily fluids by increasing the production of urine. Diuretic drugs are used to treat high blood pressure, congestive heart failure (CHF), and various other conditions that cause the body to retain, or hold in, water. CHF occurs when the heart is unable to circulate, or pump, the blood throughout the body with sufficient force.

Overview

Diuretics are a class of drugs that increase urine output. That means that users not only urinate more often, they urinate in greater amounts than usual. The main medical uses for diuretics are the treatment of high blood pressure and congestive heart failure.

Because diuretics cause an overall water weight loss, they are often abused by individuals with eating disorders such as anorexia (pronounced ah-nuh-REK-see-uh) and bulimia (pronounced bull-EEM-eeh-yuh). Anorexia is a severe disorder characterized by an intense fear of gaining weight, a refusal to eat, a distorted sense of self-image, and excessive weight loss. Bulimia is a disorder that involves long periods of bingeing on food, followed by self-induced vomiting and abuse of laxatives. The words anorexia and bulimia are both taken from the Greek language. Anorexia means "no appetite" and bulimia means "great hunger."

Diuretics are also abused by athletes who are trying to "make weight" for certain classes of competition. Oftentimes, the use of diuretics can help athletes, such as weightlifters, lose just enough—perhaps an extra pound or so—to remain in their chosen weight class. This practice is illegal in sporting competition, however. Diuretics are considered banned substances according to the International Olympic Committee (IOC), the United States Anti-Doping Agency (USADA), the World Anti-Doping Agency (WADA), the National Collegiate Athletic Association (NCAA), and a number of other national and international sporting authorities.

Official Drug Name: The three main groups of diuretics (die-er-EH-tiks) discussed in this entry are: 1) the loop diuretics, 2) the potassium-sparing diuretics, and 3) the thiazide (THY-uh-zide) diuretics. Loop diuretics include bumetanide (byoo-MEH-tuh-nide; Bumex), furosemide (fur-OH-seh-mide; Lasix), and torsemide (TORE-seh-mide; Demadex). Potassium-sparing diuretics include amiloride hydrochloride (am-ILL-ohr-ide high-droh-KLOR-ide; Midamor), spironolactone (speer-oh-noh-LACK-tone; Aldactone), and triamterene (try-AM-tuh-reen; Dyrenium). Thiazide (and thiazide-like) diuretics include chlorothiazide (KLOR-oh-THY-uh-zide; Diurigen, Diuril), chlorthalidone (klor-THAL-ih-doan; Hygroton, Thalitone), hydrochlorothiazide (HIGH-droh-KLOR-oh-THY-uh-zide; Dichlotride, Esidrix, Ezide, Hydrochlor, Hydro-D, Hydro-DIURIL, Hydro-Par, and Microzide), indapamide (inn-DAH-puh-mide; Lozol), and metolazone (meh-TOE-luh-zone; Diulo, Mykrox, Zaroxolyn).
Also Known As: Water pills
Drug Classifications: Not scheduled

283

Digitalis is derived from the dried leaves of the foxglove plant. The drug gives the heart muscle a boost, making its contractions stronger and faster. © *Eric Crichton/Corbis.*

edema: pronounced ih-DEEM-uh; water buildup in the body's tissues that causes swelling

kidney: the body's urine-producing organ

loop of Henle: the U-shaped part of the nephron (tiny filtering unit of the kidney) where reabsorption processes take place

William Withering's Work on Diuretics

The name *diuretic* comes from a Greek term meaning "to urinate." This type of drug first gained acceptance in the medical community when eighteenth-century British physician William Withering (1741–1799) created digitalis (dij-ih-TAL-us) from the dried leaves of the foxglove plant (*Digitalis purpurea*). Digitalis gives the heart muscle a boost, making its contractions stronger and faster.

Digitalis also acts as a diuretic. In Withering's time, it became a popular treatment for dropsy (DROP-see), an old-fashioned term for EDEMA. People with edema often have swollen feet, ankles, and lower legs due to water buildup in their tissues. Fluid retention in the tissues of the body can be very dangerous. It is frequently related to congestive heart failure, which can be deadly. As of 2005, digitalis-type drugs were still being used in the treatment of heart failure. By strengthening the contractions of the heart muscle, digitalis helps pump excess fluids throughout the body. When the heart works more efficiently, fluids are less likely to pool, or accumulate, in the feet and legs.

Breakthroughs in Diuretic Research

In 1957, researchers John Baer, Karl Beyer, James Sprague, and Frederick Novello formulated the drug chlorothiazide (KLOR-oh-THY-uh-zide), the first of the thiazide diuretics. It was a pioneering achievement in medicine. Chlorothiazide was the first safe and effective long-term treatment for patients with high blood pressure and heart failure. All four scientists received the Albert and Mary Lasker Foundation Special Public Health Award for 1975 for their work on diuretic drug compounds. According to the *Lasker Foundation* Web site, "Such compounds are now universally accepted as a primary treatment for these conditions."

The next class of diuretic drugs to be developed were the so-called "loop diuretics." They take their name from the fact that they work on a specific part of the KIDNEY known as the LOOP OF HENLE. Loop diuretics are the most powerful of all diuretics. The first one to appear on the market was furosemide (Lasix) in 1965. Loop diuretics were hailed as a major advance in the treatment of congestive heart failure.

It was around this time that over-the-counter diuretics first became available. Pamabrom (Pamprin), a medication that relieves the fluid retention and bloating associated with a woman's MENSTRUAL CYCLE, is still available without a prescription. There are also certain dietary supplements that may have diuretic action as a side effect, but have a different primary purpose. For example, the supplement creatine promotes fluid loss with regular use. (A separate entry on creatine is available in this encyclopedia.)

What Is It Made Of?

Diuretics are medicines with complex chemical structures. For example, the chemical formula for chlorothiazide, the best known of the thiazide diuretics, is $C_7H_6ClN_3O_4S_2$.

How Is It Taken?

Diuretics are most commonly available in pill form. In a hospital setting, they may be injected directly into a patient's veins. Certain diuretics used to control pressure on the eyeball may be administered in eye drop form. Some diuretics are consumed naturally in foods, including various fruits, vegetables, and herbs.

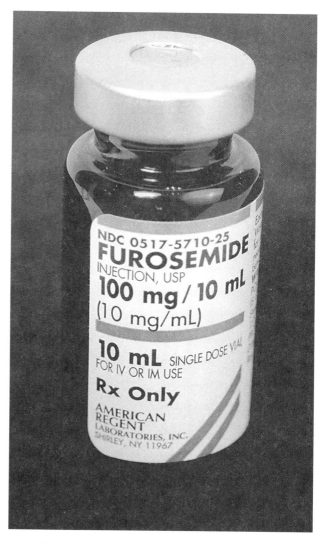

Loop diuretics are the most powerful of all diuretics. The first to appear on the market was furosemide, which is used to treat congestive heart failure. *Scott Camazine/Photo Researchers, Inc.*

Are There Any Medical Reasons for Taking This Substance?

Diuretics are typically used to treat high blood pressure, congestive heart failure, edema, and other conditions that cause the body to retain excess fluids. In addition to their traditional uses, diuretics show promise in the treatment of several other

menstrual cycle: commonly referred to as a woman's "period"; the monthly discharge of blood and other secretions from the uterus of nonpregnant females

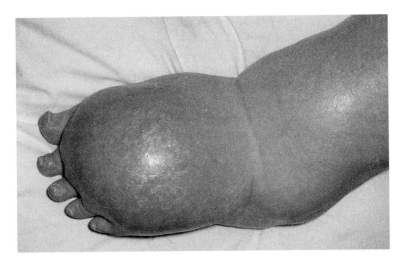

One of the medical uses of diuretics is in the treatment of edema. People suffering from edema retain excess fluids in their bodies, often in their feet.
© Mediscan/Visuals Unlimited.

medical conditions, including OSTEOPOROSIS, heart attack, and STROKE.

Usage Trends

The 2004 edition of *The Pill Book* and the 2005 edition of the *Nursing Spectrum Drug Handbook* list the loop diuretic furosemide (Lasix) among the top ten most commonly prescribed drugs in the United States. Not far behind were the thiazide diuretic hydrochlorothiazide and the potassium-sparing diuretic triamterene, both of which landed in the top twenty.

Cheap but Effective Prescription Drugs

Lawrence K. Altman reported in the *New York Times* that "traditional water pills, or diuretics, are superior to newer, more expensive drugs in lowering high blood pressure and preventing its serious and often fatal complications." In 2002, a New Jersey-based study was conducted involving more than 42,000 men and women of varied ethnic backgrounds age fifty-five and older. The results showed that diuretics were found more effective in lowering the participants' blood pressure than the trendier—and extremely costly—new classes of blood pressure drugs. In follow-up reports published in 2005, researchers suggested that thiazide diuretics, in particular, are also helpful in preventing heart attacks and strokes.

osteoporosis: a loss in bone density resulting in thinned and fragile bones

stroke: a loss of feeling, consciousness, or movement caused by the breaking or blocking of a blood vessel in the brain

In addition, several sources, including the 2003 Rotterdam Study, have shown that thiazide diuretics "may reduce bone loss by reducing the amount of calcium excreted in the urine," reported Eric Nagourney in the *New York Times*. Thiazide diuretics seem to protect the elderly against hip fractures, a common and potentially life-threatening ailment among older people. "The benefit was most pronounced in people over eighty," noted Nagourney.

Abusing Diuretics to Lose Weight

Although diuretics have legitimate uses, some people abuse the drugs. The most widespread abuses of diuretics appear among: 1) individuals suffering from eating disorders; and 2) athletes attempting to keep their weight down for sporting competitions.

According to the National Institute of Mental Health (NIMH), up to 3.7 percent of females suffer from anorexia, and up to 4.2 percent of females suffer from bulimia at some point in their lives. Anorexia involves self-starvation in an effort to keep off weight. Bulimia involves a cycle of bingeing and purging, meaning people eat massive amounts of food in a single sitting and then attempt to rid themselves of the huge caloric intake before it can be digested. Bulimics purge the food through self-induced vomiting, laxative use, and diuretics.

Males generally develop eating disorders less frequently than females. However, as of 2005, the percentage of males with eating disorders was on the rise. In addition, the National Eating Disorders Association (NEDA) reported that patients with either anorexia or bulimia frequently "develop the other eating disorder" within five to fifteen years of developing the first. In other words, a person with anorexia may end up with bulimia and a person with bulimia may end up with anorexia. This shift in disorders, according to NEDA president Doug Bunnell, helps "remind clinicians, patients, and families that these disorders are complicated."

The Sports Connection

Diuretic use and eating disorders in sports and professional athletics are growing concerns both in the United States and abroad. Jockeys, swimmers, and gymnasts, for instance, compete under

---

Blood Pressure Facts

The following statistics were cited in reports on a study of diuretics funded by the National Heart, Lung and Blood Institute, the National Institute on Aging, and the Robert Wood Johnson Foundation.

- High blood pressure affects about 50 million people in the United States, and the risk increases with age.
- Half of all Americans over the age of sixty have high blood pressure.
- One-third of Americans over the age of sixty have both high blood pressure and diabetes, a serious disorder affecting the level of sugars in the blood.

Many sporting organizations test athletes for diuretic use. Some athletes use diuretics to lose weight or cover up steroid use. In 2003 Australian cricket player Shane Warne received a one-year suspension after testing positive for a banned diuretic. *AP/Wide World Photos.*

conditions where "smaller" is considered "better." Weight loss among these and other athletes may be encouraged by coaches. Female athletes, in particular, often develop eating disorders and unhealthy weight-loss practices, including diuretic abuse. This puts them at a higher risk for osteoporosis and interrupting their menstrual cycle.

Sports such as weightlifting, wrestling, and boxing require regular weigh-ins. Diuretics are sometimes used by athletes to lose weight quickly in order to compete in lower-weight classes. The pressure to keep their weight down may extend beyond the use of diuretics, leading to starvation diets and attempts to sweat off pounds in rubber suits or saunas. These and other unsafe practices can put athletes at risk for severe DEHYDRATION, seizures, and even death.

Diuretics in the sports world have another documented use. Called "masking," it is when diuretics are used to speed the elimination of banned performance-enhancing substances from the body. This practice increases the users' chances of passing mandatory drug tests. Athletes using steroids, for instance, might attempt to rid their bodies of trace amounts of the banned drug by taking diuretics.

Many sports organizations have added diuretics and other masking agents to their list of banned substances. For example, the National Football League Players Association (NFLPA) mentions diuretic use in its steroid policy. The organization notes that "masking agents or diuretics used to hide [the presence of steroids and other performance-enhancing substances]" are considered "Prohibited Substances." Steroids, masking agents, diuretics, and other banned substances "have no legitimate place in professional football."

Effects on the Body

There are three main classes of diuretics: loop diuretics, potassium-sparing diuretics, and thiazide diuretics. The main function of diuretics is to increase the amount of sodium and fluids excreted by the kidneys.

dehydration: an abnormally low amount of fluid in the body

Kidneys and Electrolytes

The kidneys are the urine-producing organs of the body. They act as filters for body fluids, sifting out waste products and keeping important body chemicals called ELECTROLYTES at steady levels. As the *Kidney Learning System* Web site points out, another key function of these "powerful chemical factories" is to "remove drugs from the body."

Sodium, potassium, chloride, calcium, and magnesium are all examples of electrolytes. These chemicals are present in the body's fluids and help move nutrients into cells and wastes out of them. Nerve, muscle, and heart functions depend on proper levels of electrolytes in the body. The use of diuretics, however, can trigger electrolyte imbalances. This occurs because diuretics increase the amount of urine the body releases. Sodium, potassium, and other electrolytes can be removed from the body along with the urine.

The kidneys work to keep electrolyte concentrations in the blood at an even level. However, swings in body fluid chemicals do occur. Improper levels of electrolytes can cause a variety of symptoms, including confusion, fainting, dizziness, and headache.

Reducing Fluid Levels

In general, diuretics work by encouraging the loss of sodium and fluid from the body. This is the key to their effectiveness in treating high blood pressure and congestive heart failure.

People who suffer from long-term high blood pressure are said to have hypertension. Hypertension occurs when the force of blood against the blood vessel walls increases. This condition may be treated with diuretics from all three classes. Those used most often include thiazides such as chlorothiazide and hydrochlorothiazide; the potassium-sparing diuretic spironolactone; and the loop diuretic furosemide. Diuretics relieve hypertension by flushing excess water and sodium from the body. Lower fluid levels decrease the pressure on blood vessels and help improve blood circulation, resulting in lower blood pressure.

Congestive heart failure occurs when the pumping ability of the heart is impaired. Loop diuretics such as furosemide are most frequently prescribed to reduce the edema that results from congestive heart failure. Thiazide and potassium-sparing diuretics may also be prescribed.

Doctors also prescribe diuretics for other conditions that cause fluid retention, including certain types of DIABETES and various

electrolytes: charged atoms such as sodium, potassium, chloride, calcium, and magnesium that conduct electrical impulses in the body, and therefore are essential in nerve, muscle, and heart function

diabetes: a serious disorder that causes problems with the normal breakdown of sugars in the body

The All-Important Kidney

Just how important are the kidneys? The National Kidney Foundation's *Kidney Learning System* Web site reveals some interesting facts about the kidneys and their function.

- Humans have two kidneys, one on either side of the spinal column near the middle of the back.
- The kidneys are shaped like beans. They get their name from the "kidney bean."
- On average, each kidney weighs about 5 ounces.
- The kidneys filter about 200 quarts of fluid in a 24-hour period.

- Of those 200 quarts of fluid, about 2 quarts are made into urine and excreted from the body.
- The other 198 quarts of fluid are "cleaned up" and returned to the bloodstream.
- Urine is usually stored in the bladder anywhere from one hour to eight hours before it is excreted.
- Diabetes and high blood pressure are the most common causes of kidney disease.
- Over-the-counter pain relievers taken in large doses or for more than several weeks at a time can cause serious damage to the kidneys.

diseases of the kidneys and the liver. Water retention related to menstruation is usually relieved with over-the-counter diuretics containing Pamabrom (Pamprin).

Among the more common side effects of diuretic use are nausea, dizziness, skin rashes, sensitivity to sunlight, high blood sugar levels, and an inability to control urination. Less common side effects associated with diuretic use include hearing loss, lowered red blood cell or white blood cell levels, and inflammation of the pancreas, a gland vital to digestion.

The Loop Diuretics and Their Action on the Kidneys

Each kidney consists of about 1 million NEPHRONS held in place by supporting tissue. Nephrons are the tiny filtering units of the kidney. These structures are responsible for moving fluids and waste out of the bloodstream, resulting in urine formation. Loop diuretics take their name from the part of the kidney upon which they work—the loop of Henle. The loop of Henle is a branch within each nephron where sodium and potassium are reabsorbed back into the bloodstream instead of being filtered into the urine. Loop diuretics inhibit this action and promote excretion of the sodium and potassium instead, along with calcium, magnesium, and, of course, water. Loop diuretics are considered the most powerful of all diuretics. Bumetanide (Bumex), furosemide (Lasix), and torsemide (Demadex) are all loop diuretics.

nephrons: tiny working units of the kidney; each kidney has more than a million nephrons

The Potassium Balancing Act and Other Things to Know about Diuretics

Two other classes of diuretics are the thiazides and the potassium-sparing diuretics. Thiazide diuretics such as chlorothiazide and hydrochlorothiazide work by blocking sodium reabsorption by the kidneys. They are "potassium-depleting" diuretics, meaning that they cause a loss of potassium from the body. This condition is known as HYPOKALEMIA. This loss may be reversed by eating potassium-rich foods, such as bananas, or by taking potassium supplements. Signs of hypokalemia include a rapid or irregular heartbeat, fatigue, weakness, mood swings, muscle cramps, nausea, vomiting, a dry mouth, and persistent thirst.

The diuretics amiloride, spironolactone, and triamterene are known as "potassium-sparing" diuretics. This type of diuretic is used commonly in the treatment of congestive heart failure. Their use may cause HYPERKALEMIA, a condition where there is too much potassium in the body. Signs of hyperkalemia include an irregular heartbeat, tiredness, weakness, difficulty breathing, numbness, a tingling sensation in the hands or feet, anxiety, and difficulty concentrating.

Sometimes, potassium-sparing diuretics are used in conjunction with thiazide diuretics to keep potassium levels in the user's body stable. One drug known by the brand name Dyazide is a good example of a combination-type diuretic. It contains hydrochlorothiazide (a thiazide diuretic that causes a loss of potassium in the body) *and* triamterene (a diuretic that helps the body retain potassium).

Other Risks: The use of diuretics can be especially risky among pregnant women, people with compromised immune systems, and individuals with certain drug allergies. Physicians must be made aware of a patient's complete medical history before they can prescribe diuretics safely. Individuals who take diuretics for more than six months at a time run the risk of developing chemical imbalances that can result in serious side effects.

Magnesium deficiency may occur with long-term use of the loop and thiazide diuretics. Symptoms include nausea and vomiting, muscle cramps, weakness (especially when exercising), INSOMNIA, an irregular heartbeat, and difficulty sleeping. Calcium deficiency is a possible side effect of both loop and potassium-sparing diuretics.

Natural Diuretics

In his book *The Healing Power of Foods,* nutritional expert Michael T. Murray details the natural medicinal properties of common foods. The following foods and spices are considered natural diuretics:

- watermelon
- horseradish
- pepper
- celery
- herbal salads that include ingredients such as dandelion leaves

hypokalemia: a loss of potassium in the body

hyperkalemia: a dangerous build-up of excess potassium in the body

insomnia: difficulty falling asleep or an inability to sleep

Signs of insufficient calcium in the body include a rapid heartbeat, muscle cramps, bone thinning, tooth decay, and difficulty sleeping.

Dehydration

Diuretic use in sports is usually prompted by the belief that a lower weight will improve athletic performance. However, the side effects experienced from long-term diuretic abuse typically offset any temporary gains in ability.

The main risk of diuretic abuse is severe dehydration. This is of special concern to athletes who might take the drug to "make weight" for sporting events or to improve performance. People exercising or participating in athletic competition are already at risk for dehydration because they are losing large amounts of fluids and electrolytes in their sweat. Diuretics can speed up this process.

Patients on doctor-prescribed diuretics must take extra precautions when exercising. These include: 1) drinking adequate amounts of water, sports drinks, or other non-caffeinated fluids; 2) wearing loose and comfortable clothing; 3) setting aside time for regular rest periods; and 4) watching for signs of HEAT EXHAUSTION.

It is absolutely essential that a patient remain in regular touch with the prescribing doctor throughout the course of diuretic therapy.

Reactions with Other Drugs or Substances

Over-the-counter diuretic preparations are available in any drug store. Even though some diuretics are available without a prescription, the risk for serious side effects remains. Diuretics should always be taken under the recommendation and guidance of a trained healthcare professional.

Diuretics affect potassium levels. Drugs that are known to decrease potassium levels (certain anti-inflammatory steroids and heart drugs, for instance) should be avoided by anyone taking potassium-depleting diuretics. Potassium deficiencies can cause potentially dangerous side effects. In contrast, patients taking potassium-sparing diuretics such as amiloride, spironolactone, or triamterene should not eat foods high in potassium. The action of these diuretics raises the amount of potassium in their bodies. Thus, food rich in potassium—bananas, tomatoes, sweet potatoes, and oranges, to name a few—would only add to the problem and should be avoided.

Individuals taking prescription diuretics should always check with their doctors before adding herbal supplements

heat exhaustion: a condition that results from physical exertion in extreme heat; symptoms range from clammy and cool skin, tiredness, nausea, weakness, confusion, and vision problems to a possible loss of consciousness

St. John's wort, available as an herbal remedy, acts as a natural diuretic.
© *Clay Perry/Corbis.*

to their drug regimen. Herbal diuretics can actually increase the effect of prescription diuretics, so the two should not be combined. Some of the more well-known diuretic herbs include bilberry, celery seed, dandelion leaf, goldenrod, horse chestnut seeds, juniper, parsley, and St. John's wort. Foods and beverages rich in caffeine—such as chocolate, coffee, and tea—can also have a diuretic effect at high doses. They should not be consumed in excess with prescription diuretics. Alcohol has a diuretic effect as well and should be avoided by patients taking doctor-prescribed diuretics.

Treatment for Habitual Users

Treatment for diuretic abuse starts with examining an individual's reasons for taking the drugs. People mainly abuse diuretics in order to lose weight. These individuals include

What is an eating disorder? Some basic facts

Eating Disorders—such as anorexia, bulimia, and binge eating disorder—include extreme emotions, attitudes, and behaviors surrounding weight and food issues. Eating disorders are serious emotional and physical problems that can have life-threatening consequences for females and males.

Anorexia nervosa is characterized by self-starvation and excessive weight loss.

Symptoms include:
- Refusal to maintain body weight at or above a minimally normal weight for height, body type, age, and activity level
- Intense fear of weight gain or being "fat"
- Feeling "fat" or overweight despite dramatic weight loss
- Loss of menstrual periods
- Extreme concern with body weight and shape

Bulimia nervosa is characterized by a secretive cycle of binge eating followed by purging. Bulimia includes eating large amounts of food—more than most people would eat in one meal—in short periods of time, then getting rid of the food and calories through vomiting, laxative abuse, or over-exercising.

Symptoms include:
- Repeated episodes of bingeing and purging
- Feeling out of control during a binge and eating beyond the point of comfortable fullness
- Purging after a binge (typically by self-induced vomiting, abuse of laxatives, diet pills and/or diuretics, excessive exercise, or fasting)
- Frequent dieting
- Extreme concern with body weight and shape

Binge eating disorder (also known as **compulsive overeating**) is characterized primarily by periods of uncontrolled, impulsive, or continuous eating beyond the point of feeling comfortably full. While there is no purging, there may be sporadic fasts or repetitive diets and often feelings of shame or self-hatred after a binge. People who overeat compulsively may struggle with anxiety, depression, and loneliness, which can contribute to their unhealthy episodes of binge eating. Body weight may vary from normal to mild, moderate, or severe obesity.

Other eating disorders can include some combination of the signs and symptoms of anorexia, bulimia, and/or binge eating disorder. While these behaviors may not be clinically considered a full syndrome eating disorder, they can still be physically dangerous and emotionally draining. All eating disorders require professional help.

SOURCE: "What Is an Eating Disorder? Some Basic Facts," National Eating Disorders Association, Seattle, WA, 2003. www.NationalEatingDisorders.org

people with eating disorders as well as athletes trying to make a certain weight class.

Help for Disordered Eaters and Athletic Abusers

The *National Eating Disorders Association* Web site suggests that "the most effective and long-lasting treatment for an eating disorder is some form of psychotherapy or counseling, coupled with careful attention to medical and nutritional needs." Experts consider emotional support and behavioral therapy—sometimes referred to as "talk" therapy—essential for treatment and rehabilitation. It is vital to address the emotional motives and distorted thinking behind the behavior of a patient with an eating disorder.

The main goals of treatment are: 1) to stabilize the patient's weight; 2) to put an end to self-destructive behaviors, such as diuretic abuse, binge eating, and self-starvation; and 3) to help the patient relearn healthy nutritional practices. Patients with anorexia may be so severely malnourished that they require intravenous feeding in a hospital setting. Nutritional counseling and advice on lifestyle changes can help the patient reach and maintain a healthy weight.

Athletes who abuse or misuse diuretics for purposes of performance enhancement or "making weight" face special treatment challenges. Coaches, trainers, and teammates may praise weight loss and an excessively low percentage of body fat, making it harder to change one's behavior. In addition, obsessive exercise and workout routines are often rewarded in sports and competition rather than questioned. In these cases, a treatment strategy must include educational training for the coaching and training staff as well as the athlete.

Consequences

Diuretics are not a PSYCHOACTIVE DRUG and have no direct mental effects on the user. However, abuse and misuse of this medication can lead to severe dehydration, which may bring on headaches, mental confusion, and even seizures.

Patients using diuretics for a specific medical reason under a doctor's supervision rarely experience problems. The misuse of diuretics, however, can result in serious consequences for the user. Diuretic use among people suffering from eating disorders can cause their health to worsen even further. Competitive athletes who misuse diuretics, either due to an eating disorder or for performance-enhancing purposes, usually find that their athletic performance suffers in the long run.

The Law

Diuretics are not controlled substances. Federal law does not regulate their possession and use. Some diuretic drugs are even available without a prescription. For those that do require a doctor's prescription, several rules apply to their use. The U.S. Food and Drug Administration (FDA) oversees the regulation of non-controlled drugs such as diuretics. Illegally selling or distributing prescription diuretics is against the law.

Professional athletes who test positive for diuretics in Olympic competition are suspended from participation in the games. They may also be stripped of any medals they have won. At the Summer Olympic Games in Athens, Greece, in 2004, Sanamachu Chanu of India was disqualified from competition after she tested positive for a banned diuretic. Her fourth-place finish in the weightlifting competition was tossed out.

Another incident occurred at the 2000 Olympics, when three Bulgarian weightlifters tested positive for the diuretic furosemide. The athletes involved were Izabela Dragneva, winner of the gold medal; Ivan Ivanov, winner of the silver medal; and Sevdalin Minchev, winner of the bronze medal. The International Olympic Committee took back the athletes' medals after they failed their mandatory drug tests. Alan Tsagaev, another Bulgarian weightlifter whose drug test was clean, went on to win the silver in his weight class. The coach of the Bulgarian team later took responsibility for the disqualification of his players. He claimed that he did not realize furosemide was one of the ingredients in a Bulgarian medicine named Orotsetam, which he had distributed to his team.

psychoactive drug: a drug that alters the user's mental state or changes behavior

Sanamacha Chanu of India tested positive for a banned diuretic at the Olympic Games in 2004. She was disqualified from the competition.
AP/Wide World Photos.

Diuretics appear on the World Anti-Doping Agency's "2005 Prohibited List" of drugs. Since 2000, the United States has stepped up its own investigation of performance-enhancing drugs in sports by forming the U.S. Anti-Doping Agency (USADA). The agency's main goal is "to provide clean athletes with a level playing field." According to the USADA's 2004 Testing and Results Management Numbers, the diuretic hydrochlorothiazide was one of nearly twenty "adverse findings" connected with doping violations for the year.

For More Information

Books

Murray, Michael T. *The Healing Power of Foods: Nutrition Secrets for Vibrant Health and Long Life.* Rocklin, CA: Prima Publishing, 1993.

Physicians' Desk Reference, 59th ed. Montvale, NJ: Thomson PDR, 2004.

Schull, Patricia Dwyer. *Nursing Spectrum Drug Handbook.* King of Prussia, PA: Nursing Spectrum, 2005.

Silverman, Harold M. *The Pill Book,* 11th ed. New York: Bantam, 2004.

Periodicals

Altman, Lawrence K. "Older Way to Treat Hypertension Found Best." *New York Times* (December 18, 2002): p. 1A.

Anderson, Kelli. "Losing to Win." *Sports Illustrated for Women* (May-June, 2001): p. 88.

"Diuretics Cut Heart Attack Risk." *St. Louis Post-Dispatch* (January 4, 2005): p. A5.

Krauskopf, Lewis. "Spreading the Word: Doctors Tout Value of Diuretics." *The Record* (March 2, 2005): p. L9.

Nagourney, Eric. "Healthier Hips, with Diuretics." *New York Times* (September 16, 2003): p. F6.

Nagourney, Eric. "More Bananas, Fewer Strokes?" *New York Times* (August 13, 2002): p. F6.

Stewart, Angela. "Water Pills Lower Risk of Stroke, Study Finds." *Star-Ledger* (January 4, 2005): p. 5.

Web Sites

"Coach Takes Responsibility for Failed Tests." *ESPN.com,* September 24, 2000. http://espn.go.com/oly/summer00/news/2000/0924/774153.html (accessed July 1, 2005).

"Eating Disorders: Facts about Eating Disorders and the Search for Solutions." *National Institute of Mental Health.* http://www.nimh.nih.gov/publicat/eatingdisorders.cfm (accessed July 1, 2005).

"Eating Disorders Information Index." *National Eating Disorders Association.* http://www.nationaleatingdisorders.org (accessed July 1, 2005).

Freudenrich, Craig C. "How Your Kidneys Work." *How Stuff Works.* http://science.howstuffworks.com/kidney.htm/printable (accessed July 1, 2005).

"How Your Kidneys Work." *Kidney Learning System.* http://www.kidney.org/kls/public/howkidneyswrk.cfm (accessed July 1, 2005).

"Lasker Awards: Former Awards." *Lasker Foundation.* http://www.laskerfoundation.org/awards/other.html (accessed July 1, 2005).

"News Release: The Changing Face of Eating Disorders." *National Eating Disorders Association.* http://www.nationaleatingdisorders.org/p.asp?WebPage_ID=805 (accessed July 1, 2005).

"Steroid Policy—Full." *National Football League Players Association.* http://www.nflpa.org/agents/main.asp?subpage=Steroid+Policy+-+Full&section=ALL (accessed July 5, 2005).

"United States Anti-Doping Agency's 2004 Annual Report." *United States Anti-Doping Agency.* http://www.usantidoping.org/files/active/resources/press_releases/2004%20USADA%20Annual%20Report.pdf (accessed July 1, 2005).

"What Are Electrolytes?" *How Stuff Works.* http://science.howstuffworks.com/question565.htm (accessed July 1, 2005).

"William Withering." *BBC Historical Figures.* http://www.bbc.co.uk/history/historic_figures/withering_william.shtml (accessed July 1, 2005).

"The World Anti-Doping Code: The 2005 Prohibited List." *World Anti-Doping Agency.* http://www.wada-ama.org/rtecontent/document/list_2005.pdf (accessed July 1, 2005).

See also: Caffeine; Creatine; Diet Pills; Herbal Drugs; Over-the-Counter Drugs

Highlights of the U.S. Controlled Substances Act (CSA) of 1970

The Controlled Substances Act (CSA) is part of a larger piece of legislation called the Comprehensive Drug Abuse Prevention and Control Act of 1970. It provides the legal basis for the U.S. government to fight the ongoing war against drugs.

Under the CSA, all drugs are categorized into one of five "schedules." A substance's scheduling is based on three factors: 1) its medicinal value; 2) its possible harmfulness to human health; and 3) its potential for abuse or addiction. Schedule I is reserved for the most dangerous drugs that have no recognized medical use, while Schedule V is the classification used for the least dangerous drugs.

Schedule I Drugs

- have no known medical use in the United States
- have a very high potential for abuse
- are too dangerous to be used even under medical supervision

Drugs classified as Schedule I include 2C-B (Nexus), dimethyl-tryptamine (DMT), ecstasy (MDMA), GHB, heroin, LSD, mescaline, PMA, and psilocybin.

Schedule II Drugs

- are accepted for medical use in the United States
- may cause severe psychological and/or physical dependence
- have a high potential for abuse

Drugs classified as Schedule II include Adderall, cocaine, hydro-morphone, methylphenidates such as Concerta and Ritalin, morphine, and oxycodone.

Schedule III Drugs

- are accepted for medical use in the United States
- may lead to moderate psychological and/or physical dependence
- are less likely to be abused than drugs categorized as Schedule I or Schedule II

Drugs classified as Schedule III include certain barbiturates such as aprobarbital (Alurate), butabarbital (Butisol), and butalbital

(Fiorinal and Fioricet), as well as muscle-building steroids and testosterone.

Schedule IV Drugs

- are accepted for medical use in the United States
- may lead to limited psychological and/or physical dependence
- have a relatively low potential for abuse

Drugs classified as Schedule IV include various benzodiazepines, including alprazolam (Xanax) and diazepam (Valium).

Schedule V Drugs

- are accepted for medical use in the United States
- are less likely to cause psychological and/or physical dependence than drugs in any other Schedule
- have a low potential for abuse

Drugs classified as Schedule V include various over-the-counter medicines that contain codeine.

Source: Compiled by Thomson Gale staff from data reported in "Controlled Substances Act," U.S. Drug Enforcement Administration (DEA), http://www.usdoj.gov/dea/agency/csa.htm (accessed September 4, 2005); and "Controlled Substance Schedules," U.S. Department of Justice, Drug Enforcement Administration (DEA) Office of Diversion Control, http://www.deadiversion.usdoj.gov/schedules/alpha/alphabetical.htm (accessed September 4, 2005).

Where to Learn More

Books

Balkin, Karen F. *Tobacco and Smoking.* San Diego, CA: Greenhaven Press, 2005.

Beers, Mark H., and others. *The Merck Manual of Medical Information,* 2nd ed. New York: Pocket Books, 2003.

Brecher, Edward M., and others. *The Consumers Union Report on Licit and Illicit Drugs.* Boston: Little Brown & Co., 1972. http://www.druglibrary.org/schaffer/library/studies/cu/cumenu.htm (accessed September 12, 2005).

Connelly, Elizabeth Russell. *Psychological Disorders Related to Designer Drugs.* Philadelphia, PA: Chelsea House, 2000.

Drug Enforcement Administration, U.S. Department of Justice. *Drugs of Abuse: 2005 Edition.* Washington, DC: Government Printing Office, 2005. http://www.usdoj.gov/dea/pubs/abuse/index.htm (accessed September 12, 2005).

Drummond, Edward H. *The Complete Guide to Psychiatric Drugs: Straight Talk for Best Results.* New York: Wiley, 2000.

Fenster, Julie M. *Ether Day: The Strange Tale of America's Greatest Medical Discovery and the Haunted Men Who Made It.* New York: HarperCollins, 2001.

Gahlinger, Paul M. *Illegal Drugs: A Complete Guide to Their History, Chemistry, Use and Abuse.* Las Vegas, NV: Sagebrush Press, 2001.

Gorman, Jack M. *The Essential Guide to Psychiatric Drugs,* 3rd ed. New York: St. Martin's Griffin, 1997.

Hyde, Margaret O., and John F. Setaro. *Drugs 101: An Overview for Teens.* Brookfield, CT: Twenty-first Century Books, 2003.

Keltner, Norman L., and David G. Folks. *Psychotropic Drugs.* Philadelphia: Mosby, 2001.

Kuhn, Cynthia, Scott Swartzwelder, and Wilkie Wilson. *Buzzed: The Straight Facts about the Most Used and Abused Drugs from Alcohol to Ecstasy,* 2nd ed. New York: W.W. Norton, 2003.

McCay, William. *The Truth about Smoking.* New York: Facts on File, 2005.

Olive, M. Foster. *Designer Drugs.* Philadelphia: Chelsea House, 2004.

Physicians' Desk Reference, 59th ed. Montvale, NJ: Thomson PDR, 2004.

Physicians' Desk Reference for Nonprescription Drugs and Dietary Supplements, 25th ed. Montvale, NJ: Thomson Healthcare, 2004.

Preston, John D., John H. O'Neal, and Mary C. Talaga. *Consumer's Guide to Psychiatric Drugs.* Oakland, CA: New Harbinger Publications, 1998.

Silverman, Harold M. *The Pill Book,* 11th ed. New York: Bantam Books, 2004.

Sonder, Ben. *All about Heroin.* New York: Franklin Watts, 2002.

Wagner, Heather Lehr. *Cocaine.* Philadelphia: Chelsea House, 2003.

Weatherly, Myra. *Ecstasy and Other Designer Drug Dangers.* Berkeley Heights, NJ: Enslow Publishers, 2000.

Weil, Andrew, and Winifred Rosen. *From Chocolate to Morphine.* Boston: Houghton Mifflin, 1993, rev. 2004.

Wolfe, Sidney M. *Worst Pills, Best Pills: A Consumer's Guide to Avoiding Drug-Induced Death or Illness.* New York: Pocket Books, 2005.

Periodicals

Hargreaves, Guy. "Clandestine Drug Labs: Chemical Time Bombs." *FBI Law Enforcement Bulletin* (April, 2000): pp. 1-9. http://www.fbi.gov/publications/leb/2000/apr00leb.pdf (accessed September 13, 2005).

Jefferson, David J. "America's Most Dangerous Drug." *Newsweek* (August 8, 2005).

Reid, T.R. "Caffeine." *National Geographic* (January, 2005): pp. 3-33.

Web Sites

"2003 National Survey on Drug Use and Health (NSDUH)." *Substance Abuse and Mental Health Services Administration (SAMHSA).* http://www.drugabusestatistics.samhsa.gov (accessed September 13, 2005).

"A to Z of Drugs." *British Broadcasting Corporation (BBC).* http://www.bbc.co.uk/crime/drugs (accessed September 13, 2005).

"Cigarette Smoking among American Teens Continues to Decline, but More Slowly than in the Past." *National Institute of Drug Abuse.* http://www.nida.nih.gov/Newsroom/04/2004MTFTobacco.pdf (accessed September 13, 2005).

"Club Drugs—An Update: Drug Intelligence Brief" (September 2001). *U.S. Department of Justice, Drug Enforcement Administration, Intelligence Division.* http://www.usdoj.gov/dea/pubs/intel/01026 (accessed September 13, 2005).

"Consumer Education: Over-the-Counter Medicine." *Center for Drug Evaluation and Research, U.S. Food and Drug Administration.* http://www.fda.gov/cder/consumerinfo/otc_text.htm (accessed September 13, 2005).

"DEA Briefs & Background: Drug Descriptions." *U.S. Drug Enforcement Administration.* http://www.dea.gov/concern/concern.htm (accessed September 13, 2005).

"Drug Abuse Warning Network, 2003: Interim National Estimates of Drug-Related Emergency Department Visits." *U.S. Department of Health and Human Services, Substance Abuse and Mental Health Services Administration.* http://dawninfo.samhsa.gov/files/DAWN_ED_Interim2003.pdf (accessed September 13, 2005).

"Drug Facts." *Office of National Drug Control Policy.* http://www.whitehousedrugpolicy.gov/drugfact/ (accessed September 13, 2005).

Drug Free AZ. http://www.drugfreeaz.com/ (accessed September 13, 2005).

"Drug Guide by Name." *Partnership for a Drug-Free America.* http://www.drugfree.org/Portal/Drug_Guide (accessed September 13, 2005).

"Drug Information." *CESAR: Center for Substance Abuse Research at the University of Maryland.* http://www.cesar.umd.edu/cesar/drug_info.asp (accessed September 13, 2005).

"Drug Information." *MedlinePlus.* http://www.nlm.nih.gov/medlineplus/druginformation.html (accessed September 13, 2005).

"Drugs and Chemicals of Concern." *U.S. Department of Justice, Drug Enforcement Administration, Office of Diversion Control.* http://www.deadiversion.usdoj.gov/drugs_concern (accessed September 13, 2005).

"Drugs and Human Performance Fact Sheets." *National Highway Traffic Safety Administration.* http://www.nhtsa.dot.gov/people/injury/research/job185drugs/technical-page.htm (accessed September 13, 2005).

"Drugs of Abuse: Uses and Effects Chart." *U.S. Department of Justice, Drug Enforcement Administration.* http://www.usdoj.gov/dea/pubs/abuse/chart.htm (accessed September 13, 2005).

"Eating Disorders Information Index." *National Eating Disorders Association.* http://www.nationaleatingdisorders.org/p.asp?WebPage_ID=294. (accessed September 13, 2005).

"Educating Students about Drug Use and Mental Health." *Centre for Addiction and Mental Health.* http://www.camh.net/education/curriculum_gr1to8intro.html (accessed September 13, 2005).

"The Faces of Meth." *Multnomah County Sheriff's Office.* http://www.facesofmeth.us/main.htm (accessed September 13, 2005).

"Generation Rx: National Study Reveals New Category of Substance Abuse Emerging: Teens Abusing Rx and OTC Medications Intentionally to Get High" (April 21, 2005). *Partnership for a Drug-Free America.* http://www.drugfree.org/Portal/About/NewsReleases/Generation_Rx_Teens_Abusing_Rx_and_OTC_Medications (accessed September 13, 2005).

"Health Channel—Drugs." *How Stuff Works.* http://health.howstuffworks.com/drugs-channel.htm (accessed September 13, 2005).

"Health Information from the Office of Dietary Supplements." *National Institutes of Health, Office of Dietary Supplements.* http://ods.od.nih.gov/Health_Information/Health_Information.aspx (accessed September 13, 2005).

"Herbal Supplements: Consider Safety, Too." *National Institutes of Health, National Center for Complementary and Alternative Medicine.* http://nccam.nih.gov/health/supplement-safety/ (accessed September 13, 2005).

"In the Spotlight: Club Drugs" (updated September 1, 2005). *National Criminal Justice Reference Service.* http://www.ncjrs.gov/spotlight/club_drugs/summary.html (accessed September 13, 2005).

"Index to Drug-Specific Information." *Center for Drug Evaluation and Research, U.S. Food and Drug Administration.* http://www.fda.gov/cder/drug/DrugSafety/DrugIndex.htm (accessed September 13, 2005).

Kyle, Angelo D., and Bill Hansell. "The Meth Epidemic in America—Two Surveys of U.S. Counties: The Criminal Effect of Meth on Communities and The Impact of Meth on Children" (July 5, 2005). *National Association of Counties (NACo).* http://www.naco.org/Content/ContentGroups/Publications1/Press_Releases/Documents/NACoMethSurvey.pdf (accessed September 13, 2005).

Monitoring the Future. http://www.monitoringthefuture.org/ and http://www.nida.nih.gov/Newsroom/04/2004MTFDrug.pdf (both accessed September 13, 2005).

"National Drug Intelligence Center (NDIC) Fast Facts Page." *National Drug Intelligence Center.* http://www.usdoj.gov/ndic/topics/ffacts.htm (accessed September 13, 2005).

"National Drug Threat Assessment: 2005" (February 2005). *U.S. Department of Justice, National Drug Intelligence Center.* http://www.usdoj.gov/ndic/pubs11/12620/index.htm (accessed September 13, 2005).

National Institute on Drug Abuse. http://www.nida.nih.gov/ and http://www.drugabuse.gov/ (both accessed September 13, 2005).

Neuroscience for Kids. http://faculty.washington.edu/chudler/neurok.html (accessed September 13, 2005).

"NIDA for Teens: The Science behind Drug Abuse: Mind over Matter." *National Institute on Drug Abuse.* http://teens.drugabuse.gov/mom/ (accessed September 13, 2005).

"NIDA InfoFacts: Science-Based Facts on Drug Abuse and Addiction." *National Institutes of Health, National Institute on Drug Abuse.* http://www.nida.nih.gov/infofacts/ (accessed September 13, 2005).

"NIDA Research Reports Index." *National Institutes of Health, National Institute on Drug Abuse.* http://www.nida.nih.gov/ResearchReports (accessed September 13, 2005).

"Partnership Attitude Tracking Study (PATS): Teens, 2004." *Partnership for a Drug-Free America.* http://www.drugfree.org/Files/Full_Report_

PATS_TEENS_7th-12th_grades_2004 (accessed September 13, 2005).

"Pulse Check: Drug Markets and Chronic Users in 25 of America's Largest Cities." *Executive Office of the President, Office of National Drug Control Policy.* http://www.whitehousedrugpolicy.gov/publications/drugfact/pulsechk/january04/january2004.pdf (accessed on September 13, 2005).

"Tobacco Information and Prevention Source (TIPS)." *Centers for Disease Control, National Center for Chronic Disease Prevention and Health Promotion.* http://www.cdc.gov/tobacco/issue.htm (accessed September 13, 2005).

"Under the Counter: The Diversion and Abuse of Controlled Prescription Drugs in the U.S." (July 2005). *National Center on Addiction and Substance Abuse at Columbia University.* http://www.casacolumbia.org/Absolutenm/articlefiles/380-final_report.pdf (accessed September 13, 2005).

Organizations

Al-Anon/Alateen (Canada)
Capital Corporate Centre, 9 Antares Dr., Suite 245
Ottawa, ON K2E 7V5
Canada
(613) 723-8484
(613) 723-0151 (fax)
wso@al-anon.org
http://www.al-anon.alateen.org/

Al-Anon/Alateen (United States)
1600 Corporate Landing Pkwy.
Virginia Beach, VA 23454-5617
USA
(757) 563-1600
(757) 563-1655 (fax)
wso@al-anon.org
http://www.al-anon.alateen.org/

Alcoholics Anonymous (AA)
475 Riverside Dr., 11th Floor
New York, NY 10115
USA
In the U.S./Canada: Look for "Alcoholics Anonymous" in any telephone directory.
http://www.aa.org/

American Botanical Council
6200 Manor Rd.
Austin, TX 78723
USA

(512) 926-4900
(800) 373-7105
(512) 926-2345 (fax)
abc@herbalgram.org
http://www.herbalgram.org

American Council for Drug Education (ACDE; a Phoenix House agency)
164 West 74th St.
New York, NY 10023
USA
(800) 488-DRUG
acde@phoenixhouse.org
http://www.acde.org

American Society of Addiction Medicine (ASAM)
4601 N. Park Ave., Upper Arcade #101
Chevy Chase, MD 20815
USA
(301) 656-3920
(301) 656-3815 (fax)
email@asam.org
http://www.asam.org/

Attention Deficit Disorder Association (ADDA)
P.O. Box 543
Pottstown, PA 19464
USA
(484) 945-2101
(610) 970-7520 (fax)
http://www.add.org/

Canadian Centre on Substance Abuse (CCSA)
75 Albert St., Suite 300
Ottawa, ON K1P 5E7
Canada
(613) 235-4048
(613) 235-8101 (fax)
info@ccsa.ca
www.ccsa.ca

Center for Substance Abuse Research (CESAR)
4321 Hartwick Rd., Suite 501
College Park, MD 20740
USA
(301) 405-9770
(301) 403-8342 (fax)
CESAR@cesar.umd.edu
www.cesar.umd.edu

Center for Substance Abuse Treatment (CSAT; a division of the Substance
Abuse and Mental Health Services Administration)
1 Choke Cherry Rd., Room 8-1036
Rockville, MD 20857
USA
(800) 662-HELP(4357) or (877) 767-8432 (Spanish)
http://csat.samhsa.gov or http://findtreatment.samhsa.gov

Centers for Disease Control and Prevention (CDC; a division of the U.S.
Department of Health and Human Services)
1600 Clifton Rd.
Atlanta, GA 30333
USA
(404) 639-3311
(800) 311-3435
http://www.cdc.gov/

Cocaine Anonymous World Services (CAWS)
3740 Overland Ave., Suite C
Los Angeles, CA 90034
USA
(310) 559-5833
(310) 559-2554 (fax)
cawso@ca.org
http://www.ca.org/

DARE America
P.O. Box 512090
Los Angeles, CA 90051-0090
USA
(800) 223-DARE
webmaster@dare.com
http://www.dare.com

Do It Now Foundation
Box 27568
Tempe, AZ 85285-7568
USA
(480) 736-0599
(480) 736-0771 (fax)
e-mail@doitnow
http://www.doitnow.org

Europe Against Drugs (EURAD)
8 Waltersland Rd.
Stillorgan, Dublin
Ireland
01-2756766/7
01-2756768 (fax)

eurad@iol.ie
www.eurad.net

Institute for Traditional Medicine (ITM)
2017 SE Hawthorne Blvd.
Portland, OR 97214
USA
(503) 233-4907
(503) 233-1017 (fax)
itm@itmonline.org
http://www.itmonline.org

Join Together (a project of the Boston University School of Public Health)
One Appleton St., 4th Floor
Boston, MA 02116-5223
USA
(617) 437-1500
(617) 437-9394 (fax)
info@jointogether.org
http://www.jointogether.org

Marijuana Anonymous World Services
P.O. Box 2912
Van Nuys, CA 91404
USA
(800) 766-6779
office@marijuana-anonymous.org
http://www.marijuana-anonymous.org

Methamphetamine Treatment Project, University of California at
Los Angeles, Integrated Substance Abuse Programs (ISAP)
11050 Santa Monica Blvd., Suite 100
Los Angeles, CA 90025
USA
(310) 312-0500
(310) 312-0538 (fax)
http://www.methamphetamine.org/mtcc.htm or www.uclaisap.org

Narconon International
7060 Hollywood Blvd., Suite 220
Hollywood, CA 90028
USA
(323) 962-2404
(323) 962-6872 (fax)
info@narconon.org or rehab@narconon.org
http://www.narconon.org

Narcotics Anonymous (NA)
P.O. Box 9999
Van Nuys, CA 91409

USA
(818) 773-9999
(818) 700-0700 (fax)
www.na.org

Narcotics Anonymous World Services Office (WSO)—Europe
48 Rue de l'Été/Zomerstraat
B-1050 Brussels
Belgium
32-2-646-6012
32-2-649-9239 (fax)
http://www.na.org

National Association for Children of Alcoholics (NACoA)
11426 Rockville Pike, Suite 100
Rockville, MD 20852
USA
(301) 468-0985
(888) 55-4COAS
(301) 468-0987 (fax)
nacoa@nacoa.org
http://www.nacoa.org/

National Cancer Institute, Tobacco Control Research Branch (TCRB)
Executive Plaza North, Room 4039B
6130 Executive Blvd. MSC 7337
Rockville, MD 20852
USA
(301) 594-6776
(301) 594-6787 (fax)
blakek@mail.nih.gov
www.tobaccocontrol.cancer.gov or http://dccps.nci.nih.gov/tcrb

National Capital Poison Center—Poison Help
3201 New Mexico Ave., NW Suite 310
Washington, DC 20016
USA
(202) 362-3867
(800) 222-1222
(202) 362-8377 (fax)
pc@poison.org
www.poison.org or www.1-800-222-1222.info

National Center for Complementary and Alternative Medicine Clearing-house (NCCAM; a division of the National Institutes of Health)
P.O. Box 7923
Gaithersburg, MD 20898
USA
(888) 644-6226

info@nccam.nih.gov
http://nccam.nih.gov/

National Center for Drug Free Sport, Inc.
810 Baltimore
Kansas City, MO 64105
USA
(816) 474-8655
(816) 474-7329 (fax)
info@drugfreesport.com
http://www.drugfreesport.com

National Center on Addiction and Substance Abuse at Columbia
University (CASA)
633 Third Ave., 19th Floor
New York, NY 10017-6706
USA
(212) 841-5200
(212) 956-8020 (fax)
www.casacolumbia.org

National Council on Alcohol and Drug Dependence, Inc. (NCADD)
22 Cortlandt St., Suite 801
New York, NY 10007-3128
USA
(212) 269-7797
(800) 622-2255
(212) 269-7510 (fax)
national@ncadd.org
http://www.ncadd.org

National Eating Disorders Association
603 Stewart St., Suite 803
Seattle, WA 98101
USA
(206) 382-3587
(800) 931-2237
info@NationalEatingDisorders.org
http://www.nationaleatingdisorders.org

National Families in Action
2957 Clairmont Road NE, Suite 150
Atlanta, GA 30329
USA
(404) 248-9676
(404) 248-1312 (fax)
nfia@nationalfamilies.org
http://www.nationalfamilies.org/

National Inhalant Prevention Coalition (NIPC)
332 - A Thompson St.
Chattanooga, TN 37405
USA
(423) 265-4662
(800) 269-4237
nipc@io.com
http://www.inhalants.org

National Institute of Mental Health (NIMH; a division of the National Institutes of Health)
6001 Executive Boulevard, Room 8184, MSC 9663
Bethesda, MD 20892-9663
USA
(301) 443-4513
(866) 615-6464
(301) 443-4279 (fax)
nimhinfo@nih.gov
http://www.nimh.nih.gov/

National Institute on Drug Abuse (NIDA; a division of the National Institutes of Health)
6001 Executive Blvd., Room 5213
Bethesda, MD 20892-9561
USA
(301) 443-1124
(888) 644-6432
information@nida.nih.gov
http://www.drugabuse.gov or http://www.nida.nih.gov

National Institutes of Health (NIH)
9000 Rockville Pike
Bethesda, MD 20892
USA
(301) 496-4000
NIHinfo@od.nih.gov
http://www.nih.gov/

Nicotine Anonymous
419 Main St., PMB #370
Huntington Beach, CA 92648
USA
(415) 750-0328
info@nicotine-anonymous.org
http://www.nicotine-anonymous.org

Office of Dietary Supplements (ODS; a division of the National Institutes of Health)
6100 Executive Blvd., Room 3B01, MSC 7517
Bethesda, MD 20892-7517

USA
(301) 435-2920
(301) 480-1845 (fax)
ods@nih.gov
http://ods.od.nih.gov/

Office of National Drug Control Policy (ONDCP; a division of the Executive Office of the President of the United States)
c/o Drug Policy Information Clearinghouse
P.O. Box 6000
Rockville, MD 20849-6000
USA
(800) 666-3332
(301) 519-5212 (fax)
ondcp@ncjrs.gov
http://www.whitehousedrugpolicy.gov/

Oregon Health & Science University, Department of Medicine, Division of Health Promotion and Sports Medicine
3181 S.W. Sam Jackson Park Rd., CR110
Portland, OR 97239-3098
USA
(503) 494-8051
(503) 494-1310 (fax)
hpsm@ohsu.edu
http://www.ohsu.edu/hpsm

SAMHSA's National Clearinghouse for Alcohol and Drug Information (NCADI)
P.O. Box 2345
Rockville, MD 20847-2345
USA
(301) 468-2600
(800) 729-6686
http://www.health.org

Students Against Destructive Decisions (SADD) National
Box 800
Marlborough, MA 01752
USA
(877) SADD-INC
(508) 481-5759 (fax)
info@sadd.org
http://www.sadd.org/

Substance Abuse and Mental Health Services Administration (SAMHSA; a division of the U.S. Department of Health and Human Services)
1 Choke Cherry Rd., Room 8-1036
Rockville, MD 20857

USA
(301) 443-8956
info@samsha.hhs.gov
http://www.samhsa.gov

U.S. Anti-Doping Agency
1330 Quail Lake Loop., Suite 260
Colorado Springs, CO 80906-4651
USA
(719) 785-2000
(866) 601-2632; (800) 233-0393 (drug reference line);
or (877) PLAY-CLEAN (877-752-9253)
(719) 785-2001 (fax)
drugreference@usantidoping.org
http://www.usantidoping.org/

U.S. Drug Enforcement Administration (DEA)
Mailstop: AXS, 2401 Jefferson Davis Hwy.
Alexandria, VA 22301
USA
(202) 307-1000
http://www.dea.gov

U.S. Food and Drug Administration (FDA)
5600 Fishers Ln.
Rockville, MD 20857
USA
(888) INFO-FDA (888-463-6332)
http://www.fda.gov

World Anti-Doping Agency (WADA)
Stock Exchange Tower, 800 Place Victoria, Suite 1700
P.O. Box 120
Montreal, PQ H4Z 1B7
Canada
(514) 904-9232
(514) 904-8650 (fax)
info@wada-ama.org
www.wada-ama.org/

Index

Volume numbers are in *italic.*

Boldface indicates main entries and their page numbers.

Illustrations are marked by (ill.).

E

X